COMMENTARIES ON THE CIVIL WAR (Illustrated)

TRANSLATED BY W. A. MACDEVITT

WITH AN INTRODUCTION BY THOMAS DE QUINCEY

Commentaries on the Civil War (Illustrated)

Printed in the United States of America
Published by SM&DS through Createspace Independent Publishing Platform
ISBN-13: 978-1495201561
ISBN-10: 1495201562

"THE SAGES OF OLD LIVE AGAIN IN US" - GLANVILL

Table of Contents

INTRODUCTION

BY THOMAS DE QUINCEY

The character of the First Caesar has perhaps never been worse appreciated than by him who in one sense described it best; that is, with most force and eloquence wherever he really did comprehend it. This was Lucan, who has nowhere exhibited more brilliant rhetoric, nor wandered more from the truth, than in the contrasted portraits of Caesar and Pompey. The famous line, "Nil actum reputans si quid superesset agendum," is a fine feature of the real character, finely expressed. But, if it had been Lucan's purpose (as possibly, with a view to Pompey's benefit, in some respects it was) utterly and extravagantly to falsify the character of the great Dictator, by no single trait could he more effectually have fulfilled that purpose, nor in fewer words, than by this expressive passage, "Gaudensque viam fecisse ruina." Such a trait would be almost extravagant applied even to Marius, who (though in many respects a perfect model of Roman grandeur, massy, columnar, imperturbable, and more perhaps than any one man recorded in History capable of justifying the bold illustration of that character in Horace, "Si fractus illabatur orbis, impavidum ferient ruinae") had, however, a ferocity in his character, and a touch of the devil in him, very rarely united with the same tranquil intrepidity. But, for Caesar, the all-accomplished statesman, the splendid orator, the man of elegant habits and polished taste, the patron of the fine arts in a degree transcending all example of his own or the previous age, and as a man of general literature so much beyond his contemporaries, except Cicero, that he looked down even upon the brilliant Sylla as an illiterate person—to class such a man with the race of furious destroyers exulting in the desolations they spread is to err not by an individual trait, but by the whole genus. The Attilas and the Tamerlanes, who rejoice in avowing themselves the scourges of God, and the special instruments of his wrath, have no one feature of affinity to the polished and humane Caesar, and would as little have comprehended his character as he could have respected theirs. Even Cato, the unworthy hero of Lucan, might have suggested to him a little more truth in this instance, by a celebrated remark which he made on the characteristic distinction of Caesar, in comparison with other revolutionary disturbers; for, said he, whereas others had attempted the overthrow of the state in a continued paroxysm of fury, and in a state of mind resembling the lunacy of intoxication, Caesar, on the contrary, among that whole class of civil disturbers, was the only one who had come to the task in a temper of sobriety and moderation(unum accessisse sobrium ad rempublicam delendam)....

Great as Caesar was by the benefit of his original nature, there can be no doubt that he, like others, owed something to circumstances; and perhaps amongst those which were most favourable to the premature development of great self-dependence we must reckon the early death of his father. It is, or it is not, according to the nature of men, an advantage to be orphaned at as early age. Perhaps utter orphanage is rarely or never such: but to lose a father betimes may, under appropriate circumstances, profit a strong mind greatly. To Caesar it was a prodigious benefit that he lost his father when not much more than fifteen. Perhaps it was an advantage also to his father that he died thus early. Had he stayed a year longer, he might have seen himself despised, baffled, and made ridiculous. For where, let us ask, in any age, was the father capable of adequately sustaining that relation to the unique Caius Julius—to him, in the appropriate language of Shakespeare

"The foremost man of all this world?"

And, in this fine and Caesarean line, "this world" is to be understood not of the order of co-existences merely,` but also of the order of successions; he was the foremost man not only of his contemporaries, but also, within his own intellectual class, of men generally—of all that ever should come after him, or should sit on thrones under the denominations of Czars, Kesars, or Caesars of the Bosphorus and the Danube; of all in every age that should inherit his supremacy of mind, or should subject to themselves the generations of ordinary men by qualities analogous to his. Of this infinite superiority some part must be ascribed to his early emancipation from paternal control. There are very many cases in which, simply from considerations of sex, a female cannot stand forward as the head of a family, or as its suitable representative. If they are even ladies paramount, and in situations of command, they are also women. The staff of authority does not annihilate their sex; and scruples of female delicacy interfere for ever to unnerve and emasculate in their hands the sceptre however otherwise potent. Hence we see, in noble families, the merest boys put forward to represent the family dignity, as fitter supporters of that burden than their mature mothers. And of Caesar's mother, though little is recorded, and that little incidentally, this much at least we learn—that, if she looked down upon him with maternal pride and delight, she looked up to him with female ambition as the re-edifier of her husband's honours,— looked with reverence as to a column of the Roman grandeur and with fear and feminine anxieties as to one whose aspiring spirit carried him but too prematurely into the fields of adventurous strife. One slight and evanescent sketch of the relations which subsisted between Caesar and his mother, caught from the wrecks of time, is preserved both by Plutarch and Suetonius. We see in the early dawn the young patrician standing upon the steps of his patrimonial portico, his mother with her arms wreathed about his neck, looking up to his noble countenance, sometimes drawing auguries of hope from features so fitted for command, sometimes boding an early blight to promises so dangerously magnificent. That she had something of her son's aspiring character, or that he presumed so much in a mother of his, we learn from the few words which survive of their conversation. He addressed to her no language that could tranquillise her fears. On the contrary, to any but a Roman mother his valedictory words, taken in connexion with the known determination of his character, were of a nature to consummate her depression, as they tended to confirm the very worst of her fears. He was then going to stand his chance in a popular electioneering contest for an office of the highest dignity, and to launch himself upon the storms of the Campus Martius. At that period, besides other and more ordinary dangers, the bands of gladiators, kept in the pay of the more ambitious or turbulent amongst the Roman nobles, gave a popular tone of ferocity and of personal risk to the course of such contests; and, either to forestall the victory of an antagonist, or to avenge their own defeat, it was not at all impossible that a body of incensed competitors might intercept his final triumph by assassination. For this danger, however, he had no leisure in his thoughts of consolation; the sole danger which he contemplated, or supposed his mother to contemplate, was the danger of defeat, and for that he reserved his consolations. He bade her fear nothing; for that his determination was to return with victory, and with the ensigns of the dignity he sought, or to return a corpse.

Early indeed did Caesar's trials commence; and it is probable, that, had not the death of his father, by throwing him prematurely upon his own resources, prematurely developed the masculine features of his character, forcing him whilst yet a boy under the discipline of civil conflict and the yoke of practical life, even his energies might have been insufficient to sustain them. His age is not exactly ascertained; but it is past a doubt that he had not reached his twentieth year when he had the hardihood to engage in a struggle with Sylla, then Dictator, and exercising the immoderate powers of that office with the licence and the severity which History has made so memorable. He had neither any distinct grounds of hope, nor any eminent example at that time, to countenance him in this struggle—which yet he pushed on in the most uncompromising style, and to the utmost verge of defiance. The subject of the contest gives it a further interest. It was the youthful wife of the youthful Caesar who stood under the shadow of the great Dictator's displeasure; not personally, but politically, on account of her connexions: and her it was, Cornelia, the daughter of a man who had been four times consul, that Caesar was required to divorce: but he spurned the haughty mandate, and carried his determination to a triumphant issue, notwithstanding his life was at stake, and at one time saved only by shifting his place of concealment every night; and this young lady it was who afterwards became the mother of his only daughter. Both mother and daughter, it is remarkable, perished prematurely, and at critical periods of Caesar's life; for it is probable enough that these irreparable wounds to Caesar's domestic affections threw him with more exclusiveness of devotion upon the fascinations of glory and ambition than might have happened under a happier condition of his private life. That Caesar should have escaped destruction in this unequal contest with an enemy then wielding the whole thunders of the state, is somewhat surprising; and historians have sought their solution of the mystery in the powerful intercessions of the vestal virgins, and several others of high rank amongst the connexions of his great house. These may have done something; but it is due to Sylla, who had a sympathy with everything truly noble, to suppose him struck with powerful admiration for the audacity of the young patrician, standing out in such severe solitude among so many examples of timid concession; and that to this magnanimous feeling in the Dictator much of the indulgence which he showed may have been really due. In fact, according to some accounts, it was not Sylla, but the creatures of Sylla (adjutores), who pursued Caesar. We know, at all events, that Sylla formed a right estimate of Caesar's character, and that, from the complexion of his conduct in this one instance, he drew that famous prophecy of his future destiny; bidding his friends beware of that slipshod boy, "for that in him lay couchant many a Marius." A grander testimony to the awe which Caesar inspired, or from one who knew better the qualities of that Cyclopean man by whose scale he measured the patrician boy, cannot be imagined.

It is not our intention, or consistent with our plan, to pursue this great man through the whole circumstances of his romantic career; though it is certain that many parts of his life require investigation much keener than has ever been applied to them, and that many might be placed in a new light. Indeed, the whole of this most momentous section of ancient history ought to be recomposed with the critical scepticism of a Niebuhr, and the same comprehensive collation, resting, if possible, on the felicitous interpretation of authorities. In reality it is the hinge upon which turned the future destiny of the whole earth, and, having therefore a common relation to all modern nations whatsoever, should

naturally have been cultivated with the zeal which belongs to a personal concern. In general, the anecdotes which express most vividly the grandeur of character in the first Caesar are those which illustrate his defiance of danger in extremity: the prodigious energy and rapidity of his decisions and motions in the field (looking to which it was that Cicero called him [Greek: teras] or portentous revelation); the skill with which he penetrated the designs of his enemies, and the electric speed with which he met disasters with remedy and reparation, or, where that was impossible, with relief; the extraordinary presence of mind which he showed in turning adverse omens to his own advantage, as when, upon stumbling in coming on shore (which was esteemed a capital omen of evil), he transfigured as it were in one instant its whole meaning by exclaiming, "Thus, and by this contact with the earth, do I take possession of thee, O Africa!" in that way giving to an accident the semblance of a symbolic purpose. Equally conspicuous was the grandeur of fortitude with which he faced the whole extent of a calamity when palliation could do no good, "non negando, minuendove, sed insuper amplificando, ementiendoque"; as when, upon finding his soldiery alarmed at the approach of Juba, with forces really great, but exaggerated by their terrors, he addressed them in a military harangue to the following effect:—"Know that within a few days the king will come up with us, bringing with him sixty thousand legionaries, thirty thousand cavalry, one hundred thousand light troops, besides three hundred elephants. Such being the case, let me hear no more of conjectures and opinions, for you have now my warrant for the fact, whose information is past doubting. Therefore, be satisfied; otherwise, I will put every man of you on board some crazy old fleet, and whistle you down the tide—no matter under what winds, no matter towards what shore." Finally, we might seek for characteristicanecdotes of Caesar in his unexampled liberalities and contempt of money.
Upon this last topic it is the just remark of Casaubon that some instances of Caesar's munificence have been thought apocryphal, or to rest upon false readings, simply from ignorance of the heroic scale upon which the Roman splendours of that age proceeded. A forum which Caesar built out of the products of his last campaign, by way of a present to the Roman people, cost him—for the ground merely on which it stood— nearly eight hundred thousand pounds. To the citizens of Rome he presented, in one congiary, about two guineas and a half a head. To his army, in one donation, upon the termination of the Civil War, he gave a sum which allowed about two hundred pounds a man to the infantry, and four hundred to the cavalry. It is true that the legionary troops were then much reduced by the sword of the enemy, and by the tremendous hardships of their last campaigns. In this, however, he did

perhaps no more than repay a debt. For it is an instance of military attachment, beyond all that Wallenstein or any commander, the most beloved amongst his troops, has ever experienced, that, on the breaking out of the Civil War, not only did the centurions of every legion severally maintain a horse soldier, but even the privates volunteered to serve without pay, and (what might seem impossible) without their daily rations. This was accomplished by subscriptions amongst themselves, the more opulent undertaking for the maintenance of the needy. Their disinterested love for Caesar appeared in another and more difficult illustration: it was a traditionary anecdote in Rome that the majority of those amongst Caesar's troops who had the misfortune to fall into the enemy's hands refused to accept their lives under the condition of serving against him.

In connexion with this subject of his extraordinary munificence, there is one aspect of Caesar's life which has suffered much from the misrepresentations of historians, and that is—the vast pecuniary embarrassments under which he laboured, until the profits of war had turned the scale even more prodigiously in his favour. At one time of his life, when appointed to a foreign office, so numerous and so clamorous were his creditors that he could not have left Rome on his public duties had not Crassus come forward with assistance in money, or by guarantees, to the amount of nearly two hundred thousand pounds. And at another he was accustomed to amuse himself with computing how much money it would require to make him worth exactly nothing (i.e. simply to clear him of debts); this, by one account, amounted to upwards of two millions sterling. Now, the error of historians has been to represent these debts as the original ground of his ambition and his revolutionary projects, as though the desperate condition of his private affairs had suggested a civil war to his calculations as the best or only mode of redressing it. Such a policy would have resembled the last desperate resource of an unprincipled gambler, who, on seeing his final game at chess, and the accumulated stakes depending upon it, all on the brink of irretrievable sacrifice, dexterously upsets the chess-board, or extinguishes the lights. But Julius, the one sole patriot of Rome, could find no advantage to his plans in darkness or in confusion. Honestly supported, he would have crushed the oligarchies of Rome by crushing in its lairs that venal and hunger-bitten democracy which made oligarchy and its machineries resistless. Caesar's debts, far from being stimulants and exciting causes of his political ambition, stood in an inverse relation to the ambition; they were its results, and represented its natural costs, being contracted from first to last in the service of his political intrigues, for raising and maintaining a powerful body of partisans, both in Rome and elsewhere. Whosoever indeed will take the trouble to investigate the progress of Caesar's ambition, from such materials as even yet remain, may satisfy himself that the scheme of revolutionizing the Republic, and placing himself at its head, was no growth of accident or circumstances; above all, that it did not arise upon any so petty and indirect a suggestion as that of his debts; but that his debts were in their very first origin purely ministerial to his wise, indispensable, and patriotic ambition; and that his revolutionary plans were at all periods of his life a direct and foremost object, but in no case bottomed upon casual impulses. In this there was not only patriotism, but in fact the one sole mode of patriotism which could have prospered, or could have found a field of action.

Chatter not, sublime reader, commonplaces of scoundrel moralists against ambition. In some cases ambition is a hopeful virtue; in others (as in the Rome of our resplendent Julius) ambition was the virtue by which any other could flourish. It had become evident to everybody that Rome, under its present constitution, must fall; and the sole question was—by whom? Even Pompey, not by nature of an aspiring turn, and prompted to his ambitious course undoubtedly by circumstances and, the friends who besieged him, was in the habit of saying, "Sylla potuit: ego non potero?" Sylla found it possible: shall I find it not so? Possible to do what? To overthrow the political system of the Republic. This had silently collapsed into an order of things so vicious, growing also so hopelessly worse, that all honest patriots invoked a purifying revolution, even though bought at the heavy price of a tyranny, rather than face the chaos of murderous distractions to which the tide of feuds and frenzies was violently tending.

Such a revolution at such a price was not less Pompey's object than Caesar's. In a case, therefore, where no benefit of choice was allowed to Rome as respected the thing, but only as respected the person, Caesar had the same right to enter the arena in the character of combatant as could belong to any one of his rivals. And that he did enter that arena constructively, and by secret design, from his very earliest manhood, may be gathered from this—that he suffered no openings towards a revolution, provided they had any hope in them, to escape his participation. It is familiarly known that he was engaged pretty deeply in the conspiracy of Catiline, and that he incurred considerable risk on that occasion; but it is less known that he was a party to at least two other conspiracies. There was even a fourth, meditated by Crassus, which Caesar so far encouraged as to undertake a journey to Rome from a very distant quarter merely with a view to such chances as it might offer to him; but, as it did not, upon examination, seem to him a very promising scheme, he judged it best to look coldly upon it, or not to embark in it by any personal co-operation. Upon these and other facts we build our inference—that the scheme of a revolution was the one great purpose of Caesar from his first entrance upon public life. Nor does it appear that he cared much by whom it was undertaken, provided only there seemed to be any sufficient resources for carrying it through, and for sustaining the first collision with the regular forces of the existing oligarchies, taking or not taking the shape of triumvirates. He relied, it seems, on his own personal superiority for raising him to the head of affairs eventually, let who would take the nominal lead at first.

To the same result, it will be found, tended the vast stream of Caesar's liberalities. From the senator downwards to the lowest faex Romuli, he had a hired body of dependents, both in and out of Rome, equal in numbers to a nation. In the provinces, and in distant kingdoms, he pursued the same schemes. Everywhere he had a body of mercenary partisans; kings even are known to have taken his pay. And it is remarkable that even in his character of commander-in-chief, where the number of legions allowed to him for the accomplishment of his Gaulish mission raised him for a number of years above all fear of coercion or control, he persevered steadily in the same plan of providing for the distant day when he might need assistance, not from the state, but against the state. For, amongst the private anecdotes which came to light under the researches made into his history after his death, was this—that, soon after his first entrance upon his government in Gaul, he had raised, equipped, disciplined, and maintained, from his own private funds, a legion amounting, possibly, to six or seven thousand men, who were bound to no sacrament of military obedience to the state, nor owed fealty to any auspices except those of Caesar. This legion, from the fashion of their crested helmets, which resembled the heads of a small aspiring bird, received the popular name of the Alauda (or Lark) legion. And very singular it was that Cato, or Marcellus, or some amongst those enemies of Caesar who watched his conduct during the period of his Gaulish command with the vigilance of rancorous malice, should not have come to the knowledge of this fact; in which case we may be sure that it would have been denounced to the Senate.

Such, then, for its purpose and its uniform motive, was the sagacious munificence of Caesar. Apart from this motive, and considered in and for itself, and simply with a reference to the splendid forms which it often assumed, this munificence would furnish the materials for a volume. The public entertainments of Caesar, his spectacles and shows, his naumachiae, and the pomps of his unrivalled triumphs (the closing triumphs of the Republic), were severally the finest of their kind which had then been brought forward. Sea-fights were exhibited upon the grandest scale, according to every known variety of nautical equipment and mode of conflict, upon a vast lake formed artificially for that express purpose. Mimic land-fights were conducted, in which all the circumstances of real war were so faithfully rehearsed that even elephants "indorsed with towers," twenty on each side, took part in the combat. Dramas were represented in every known language (per omnium linguarum histriones). And hence (that is, from the conciliatory feeling thus expressed towards the various tribes of foreigners resident in Rome) some have derived an explanation of what is else a mysterious circumstance amongst the ceremonial observances at Caesar's funeral— that all people of foreign nations then residing at Rome distinguished themselves by the conspicuous share which they took in the public mourning; and that, beyond all other foreigners, the Jews for night after night kept watch and ward about the Emperor's grave. Never before, according to traditions which lasted through several generations in Rome, had there been so vast a conflux of the human race congregated to any one centre, on any one attraction of business or of pleasure, as to Rome on occasion of these triumphal spectacles exhibited by Caesar.

In our days, the greatest occasional gatherings of the human race are in India, especially at the great fair of the Hurdwar on the Ganges in northern Hindustan: a confluence of some millions is sometimes seen at that spot, brought together under the mixed influences of devotion and commercial business, but very soon dispersed as rapidly as they had been convoked. Some such spectacle of nations crowding upon nations, and some such Babylonian confusion of dresses, complexions, languages, and jargons, was then witnessed at Rome. Accommodations within doors, and under roofs of houses, or roofs of temples, was altogether impossible. Myriads encamped along the streets, and along the high-roads, fields, or gardens. Myriads lay stretched on the ground, without even the slight protection of tents, in a vast circuit about the city. Multitudes of men, even senators, and others of the highest rank, were trampled to death in the crowds. And the whole family of man might seem at that time to be converged at the bidding of the dead Dictator. But these, or any other themes connected with the public life of Caesar, we notice only in those circumstances which have been overlooked, or partially represented, by historians. Let us now, in conclusion, bring forward, from the obscurity in which they have hitherto lurked, the anecdotes which describe the habits of his private life, his tastes, and personal peculiarities.

In person, he was tall, fair, gracile, and of limbs distinguished for their elegant proportions. His eyes were black and piercing. These circumstances continued to be long remembered, and no doubt were constantly recalled to the eyes of all persons in the imperial palaces by pictures, busts, and statues; for we find the same description of his personal appearance three centuries afterwards in a work of the Emperor Julian's. He was a most accomplished horseman, and a master (peritissimus) in the use of arms. But, notwithstanding his skill and horsemanship, it seems that, when he accompanied his army on marches, he walked oftener than he rode; no doubt, with a view to the benefit of his example, and to express that sympathy with his soldiers which gained him their hearts so entirely. On other occasions, when travelling apart from his army, he seems more frequently to have ridden in a carriage than on horseback. His purpose, in this preference, must have been with a view to the transport of luggage. The carriage which he generally used was a rheda, a sort of gig, or rather curricle; for it was a four-wheeled carriage, and adapted (as we find from the imperial regulations for the public carriages, etc.) to the conveyance of about half a ton. The mere personal baggage which Caesar carried with him was probably considerable; for he was a man of elegant habits, and in

all parts of his life sedulously attentive to elegance of personal appearance. The length of journeys which he accomplished within a given time appears even to us at this day, and might well therefore appear to his contemporaries, truly astonishing. A distance of one hundred miles was no extraordinary day's journey for him in a rheda, such as we have described it. So refined were his habits, and so constant his demand for the luxurious accommodations of polished life as it then existed in Rome, that he is said to have carried with him, as indispensable parts of his personal baggage, the little ivory lozenges, squares and circles or ovals, with other costly materials, wanted for the tessellated flooring of his tent. Habits such as these will easily account for his travelling in a carriage rather than on horseback.
The courtesy and obliging disposition of Caesar were notorious; and both were illustrated in some anecdotes which survived for generations in Rome. Dining on one occasion, as an invited guest, at a table where the servants had inadvertently, for salad-oil, furnished some sort of coarse lamp-oil, Caesar would not allow the rest of the company to point out the mistake to their host, for fear of shocking him too much by exposing what might have been construed into inhospitality. At another time, whilst halting at a little cabaret, when one of his retinue was suddenly taken ill, Caesar resigned to his use the sole bed which the house afforded. Incidents as trifling as these express the urbanity of Caesar's nature; and hence one is the more surprised to find the alienation of the Senate charged, in no trifling degree, upon a gross and most culpable failure in point of courtesy. Caesar, it is alleged— but might we presume to call upon antiquity for its authority?— neglected to rise from his seat, on their approaching him with an address of congratulation. It is said, and we can believe it, that he gave deeper offence by this one defect in a matter of ceremonial observance than by all his substantial attacks upon their privileges. What we find it difficult to believe is not that result from that offence—this is no more than we should all anticipate—not that, but the possibility of the offence itself, from one so little arrogant as Caesar, and so entirely a man of the world. He was told of the disgust which he had given; and we are bound to believe his apology, in which he charged it upon sickness, that would not at the moment allow him to maintain a standing attitude. Certainly the whole tenor of his life was not courteous only, but kind, and to his enemies merciful in a degree which implied so much more magnanimity than men in general could understand that by many it was put down to the account of weakness.
Weakness, however, there was none in Caius Caesar; and, that there might be none, it was fortunate that conspiracy should have cut him off in the full vigour of his faculties, in the very meridian of his glory, and

on the brink of completing a series of gigantic achievements. Amongst these are numbered:—a digest of the entire body of laws, even then become unwieldy and oppressive; the establishment of vast and comprehensive public libraries, Greek as well as Latin; the chastisement of Dacia (that needed a cow-hiding for insolence as much as Affghanistan from us in 1840); the conquest of Parthia; and the cutting a ship canal through the Isthmus of Corinth. The reformation of the Calendar he had already accomplished. And of all his projects it may be said that they were equally patriotic in their purpose and colossal in their proportions.

As an orator, Caesar's merit was so eminent that, according to the general belief, had he found time to cultivate this department of civil exertion, the received supremacy of Cicero would have been made questionable, or the honour would have been divided. Cicero himself was of that opinion, and on different occasions applied the epithet splendidus to Caesar, as though in some exclusive sense, or with some peculiar emphasis, due to him. His taste was much simpler, chaster, and less inclined to the florid and Asiatic, than that of Cicero. So far he would, in that condition of the Roman culture and feeling, have been less acceptable to the public; but, on the other hand, he would have compensated this disadvantage by much more of natural and Demosthenic fervour.

In literature, the merits of Caesar are familiar to most readers. Under the modest title of Commentaries, he meant to offer the records of his Gallic and British campaigns, simply as notes, or memoranda, afterwards to be worked up by regular historians; but, as Cicero observes, their merit was such in the eyes of the discerning that all judicious writers shrank from the attempt to alter them. In another instance of his literary labours he showed a very just sense of true dignity. Rightly conceiving that everything patriotic was dignified, and that to illustrate or polish his native language was a service of real and paramount patriotism, he composed a work on the grammar and orthoepy of the Latin language. Cicero and himself were the only Romans of distinction in that age who applied themselves with true patriotism to the task of purifying and ennobling their mother tongue. Both were aware of a transcendent value in the Grecian literature as it then stood; but that splendour did not depress their hopes of raising their own to something of the same level. As respected the natural wealth of the two languages, it was the private opinion of Cicero that the Latin had the advantage; and, if Caesar did not accompany him to that length—which, perhaps, under some limitations he ought to have done—he yet felt that it was but the more necessary to draw forth any special or exceptional advantage which it really had.

Was Caesar, upon the whole, the greatest of men? We restrict the question, of course, to the classes of men great in action: great by the extent of their influence over their social contemporaries; great by throwing open avenues to extended powers that previously had been closed; great by making obstacles once vast to become trivial, or prizes that once were trivial to be glorified by expansion. I (said Augustus Caesar) found Rome built of brick; but I left it built of marble. Well, my man, we reply, for a wondrously little chap, you did what in Westmoreland they call a good darroch (day's work); and, ifnavvies had been wanted in those days, you should have had our vote to a certainty. But Caius Julius, even under such a limitation of the comparison, did a thing as much transcending this as it was greater to project Rome across the Alps and the Pyrenees,—expanding the grand Republic into crowning provinces of i. France (Gallia), 2. Belgium, 3. Holland (Batavia), 4. England (Britannia), 5. Savoy (Allobroges), 6. Switzerland (Helvetia), 7. Spain (Hispania),—than to decorate a street or to found an amphitheatre. Dr. Beattie once observed that, if that question as to the greatest man in action upon the rolls of History were left to be collected from the suffrages already expressed in books and scattered throughout the literature of all nations, the scale would be found to have turned prodigiously in Caesar's favour as against any single competitor; and there is no doubt whatsoever that even amongst his own countrymen, and his own contemporaries, the same verdict would have been returned, had it been collected upon the famous principle of Themistocles, that he should be reputed the first whom the greatest number of rival voices had pronounced to be the second.

BIBLIOGRAPHY

Works: Latin folio, Rome, 1469; Venice, 1471; Florence, 1514; London, 1585. De Bello Gallico, Esslingen (?), 1473. Translations by John Tiptoft, Earl of Worcester (John Rastell), of Julius Caesar's Commentaries-"newly translated into Englyshe ... as much as concerneth thys realme of England"—1530 folio; by Arthur Goldinge, The Eyght Bookes of C. Julius Caesar, London, 1563, 1565, 1578, 1590; by Chapman, London, 1604 folio; by Clem. Edmonds, London, 1609; the same, with Hirtius, 1655, 1670, 1695 folio with commendatory verses by Camden, Daniel, and Ben Johnson (sic). Works: Translated by W. Duncan, 1753, 1755; by M. Bladen, 8th ed., 1770; MacDevitt, Bohn's Library, 1848. De Bello Gallico, translated by R. Mongan, Dublin, 1850; by J.B. Owgan and C.W. Bateman, 1882. Caesar's Commentaries on the Gallic War, translated by T. Rice

Holmes, London, 1908 (see also Holmes' Caesar's Conquest of Gaul, 1911). Caesar's Gallic War, translated by Rev. F.P. Long, Oxford, 1911; Books IV. and V. translated by C.H. Prichard, Cambridge, 1912. For Latin text of De Bello Gallico see Bell's Illustrated Classical Series; Dent's Temple Series of Classical Texts, 1902; Macmillan and Co., 1905; and Blackie's Latin Texts, 1905-7.

THE CIVIL WAR

BOOK I

I.—When Caesar's letter was delivered to the consuls, they were with great difficulty, and a hard struggle of the tribunes, prevailed on to suffer it to be read in the senate; but the tribunes could not prevail, that any question should be put to the senate on the subject of the letter. The consuls put the question on the regulation of the state. Lucius Lentulus the consul promises that he will not fail the senate and republic, "if they declared their sentiments boldly and resolutely, but if they turned their regard to Caesar, and courted his favour, as they did on former occasions, he would adopt a plan for himself, and not submit to the authority of the senate: that he too had a means of regaining Caesar's favour and friendship." Scipio spoke to the same purport, "that it was Pompey's intention not to abandon the republic, if the senate would support him; but if they should hesitate and act without energy, they would in vain implore his aid, if they should require it hereafter."

II.—This speech of Scipio's, as the senate was convened in the city, and Pompey was near at hand, seemed to have fallen from the lips of Pompey himself. Some delivered their sentiments with more moderation, as Marcellus first, who in the beginning of his speech, said, "that the question ought not to be put to the senate on this matter, till levies were made throughout all Italy, and armies raised under whose protection the senate might freely and safely pass such resolutions as they thought proper": as Marcus Calidius afterwards, who was of opinion, "that Pompey should set out for his province, that there might be no cause for arms: that Caesar was naturally apprehensive as two legions were forced from him, that Pompey was retaining those troops, and keeping them near the city to do him injury": as Marcus Rufus, who followed Calidius almost word for word. They were all harshly rebuked by Lentulus, who peremptorily refused to propose Calidius's motion. Marcellus, overawed by his reproofs, retracted his opinion. Thus most of the senate, intimidated by the expressions of the consul, by the fears of a present army, and the threats of Pompey's friends, unwillingly and reluctantly adopted Scipio's opinion, that Caesar should disband his army by a certain day, and should he not do so, he should be considered as acting against the state. Marcus Antonius, and Quintus Cassius, tribunes of the people, interposed. The question was immediately put on their interposition. Violent opinions were expressed: whoever spoke with the greatest acrimony and cruelty, was most highly commended by Caesar's enemies.

III.—The senate having broken up in the evening, all who belonged to that order were summoned by Pompey. He applauded the forward, and secured their votes for the next day; the more moderate he reproved and excited against Caesar. Many veterans, from all parts, who had served in Pompey's armies, were invited to his standard by the hopes of rewards and promotions. Several officers belonging to the two legions, which had been delivered up by Caesar, were sent for. The city and the Comitium were crowded with tribunes, centurions, and veterans. All the consuls' friends, all Pompey's connections, all those who bore any ancient enmity to Caesar, were forced into the senate house. By their concourse and declarations the timid were awed, the irresolute confirmed, and the greater part deprived of the power of speaking their sentiments with freedom. Lucius Piso, the censor, offered to go to Caesar: as did likewise Lucius Roscius, the praetor, to inform him of these affairs, and require only six days' time to finish the business. Opinions were expressed by some to the effect that commissioners should be sent to Caesar to acquaint him with the senate's pleasure.

IV.—All these proposals were rejected, and opposition made to them all, in the speeches of the consul, Scipio, and Cato. An old grudge against Caesar and chagrin at a defeat actuated Cato. Lentulus was wrought upon by the magnitude of his debts, and the hopes of having the government of an army and provinces, and by the presents which he expected from such princes as should receive the title of friends of the Roman people, and boasted amongst his friends, that he would be a second Sylla, to whom the supreme authority should return. Similar hopes of a province and armies, which he expected to share with Pompey on account of his connection with him, urged on Scipio; and moreover, [he was influenced by] the fear of being called to trial, and the adulation and an ostentatious display of himself and his friends in power, who at that time had great influence in the republic, and courts of judicature. Pompey himself, incited by Caesar's enemies, because he was unwilling that any person should bear an equal degree of dignity, had wholly alienated himself from Caesar's friendship, and procured a reconciliation with their common enemies; the greatest part of whom he had himself brought upon Caesar during his affinity with him. At the same time, chagrined at the disgrace which he had incurred by converting the two legions from their expedition through Asia and Syria, to [augment] his own power and authority, he was anxious to bring matters to a war.

V.—For these reasons everything was done in a hasty and disorderly manner, and neither was time given to Caesar's relations to inform him [of the state of affairs] nor liberty to the tribunes of the people to deprecate their own danger, nor even to retain the last privilege, which Sylla had left them, the interposing their authority; but on the seventh day they were obliged to think of their own safety, which the most turbulent tribunes of the people were not accustomed to attend to, nor to fear being called to an account for their actions, till the eighth month. Recourse is had to that extreme and final decree of the senate (which was never resorted to even by daring proposers except when the city was in danger of being set on fire, or when the public safety was despaired of). "That the consuls, praetors, tribunes of the people, and proconsuls in the city should take care that the state received no injury." These decrees are dated the eighth day before the ides of January; therefore, in the first five days, on which the senate could meet, from the day on which Lentulus entered into his consulate, the two days of election excepted, the severest and most virulent decrees were passed against Caesar's government, and against those most illustrious characters, the tribunes of the people. The latter immediately made their escape from the city, and withdrew to Caesar, who was then at Ravenna, awaiting an answer to his moderate demands; [to see] if matters could be brought to a peaceful termination by any equitable act on the part of the enemies.

VI.—During the succeeding days the senate is convened outside the city. Pompey repeated the same things which he had declared through Scipio. He applauded the courage and firmness of the senate, acquainted them with his force, and told them that he had ten legions ready; that he was moreover informed and assured that Caesar's soldiers were disaffected, and that he could not persuade them to defend or even follow him. Motions were made in the senate concerning other matters; that levies should be made through all Italy; that Faustus Sylla should be sent as propraetor into Mauritania; that money should be granted to Pompey from the public treasury. It was also put to the vote that king Juba should be [honoured with the title of] friend and ally. But Marcellus said that he would not allow this motion for the present. Philip, one of the tribunes, stopped [the appointment of] Sylla; the resolutions respecting the other matters passed. The provinces, two of which were consular, the remainder praetorian, were decreed to private persons; Scipio got Syria, Lucius Domitius Gaul: Philip and Marcellus were omitted, from a private motive, and their lots were not even admitted. To the other provinces praetors were sent, nor was time granted as in former years, to refer to the people on their appointment, nor to make them take the usual oath, and march out of the city in a public manner, robed in the military habit, after offering their vows; a circumstance which had never before happened. Both the consuls leave the city, and private men had lictors in the city and capital, contrary to all precedents of former times. Levies were made throughout Italy, arms demanded, and money exacted from the municipal towns, and violently taken from the temples. All distinctions between things human and divine are confounded.

VII.—These things being made known to Caesar, he harangued his soldiers; he reminded them "of the wrongs done to him at all times by his enemies, and complained that Pompey had been alienated from him and led astray by them through envy and a malicious opposition to his glory, though he had always favoured and promoted Pompey's honour and dignity. He complained that an innovation had been introduced into the republic, that the intercession of the tribunes, which had been restored a few years before by Sylla, was branded as a crime, and suppressed by force of arms; that Sylla, who had stripped the tribunes of every other power, had, nevertheless, left the privilege of intercession unrestrained; that Pompey, who pretended to restore what they had lost, had taken away the privileges which they formerly had; that whenever the senate decreed, "that the magistrates should take care that the republic sustained no injury" (by which words and decree the Roman people were obliged to repair to arms), it was only when pernicious laws were proposed; when the tribunes attempted violent measures; when the people seceded, and possessed themselves of the temples and eminences of the city; (and these instances of former times, he showed them were expiated by the fate of Saturninus and the Gracchi): that nothing of this kind was attempted now, nor even thought of: that no law was promulgated, no intrigue with the people going forward, no secession made; he exhorted them to defend from the malice of his enemies, the reputation and honour of that general, under whose command they had for nine years most successfully supported the state; fought many successful battles, and subdued all Gaul and Germany." The soldiers of the thirteenth legion, which was present (for in the beginning of the disturbances he had called it out, his other legions not having yet arrived), all cry out that they are ready to defend their general, and the tribunes of the commons, from all injuries.

VIII.—Having made himself acquainted with the disposition of his soldiers, Caesar set off with that legion to Ariminum, and there met the tribunes, who had fled to him for protection; he called his other legions from winter quarters, and ordered them to follow him. Thither came Lucius Caesar, a young man, whose father was a lieutenant general under Caesar. He, after concluding the rest of his speech, and stating for what purpose he had come, told Caesar that he had commands of a private nature for him from Pompey; that Pompey wished to clear himself to Caesar, lest he should impute those actions which he did for the republic, to a design of affronting him; that he had ever preferred the interest of the state to his own private connections; that Caesar, too, for his own honour, ought to sacrifice his desires and resentment to the public good, and not vent his anger so violently against his enemies, lest in his hopes of injuring them, he should injure the republic. He spoke a few words to the same purport from himself, in addition to Pompey's apology. Roscius, the praetor, conferred with Caesar almost in the same words, and on the same subject, and declared that Pompey had empowered him to do so.

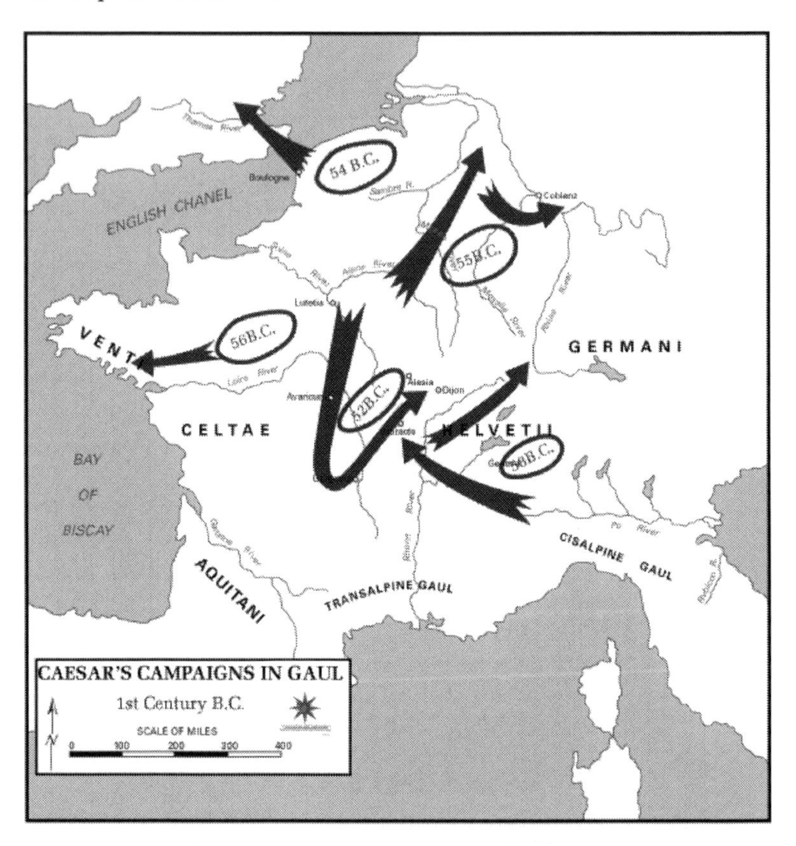

CAESAR'S CAMPAIGNS IN GAUL

IX.—Though these things seemed to have no tendency towards redressing his injuries, yet having got proper persons by whom he could communicate his wishes to Pompey; he required of them both, that as they had conveyed Pompey's demands to him, they should not refuse to convey his demands to Pompey; if by so little trouble they could terminate a great dispute, and liberate all Italy from her fears.

"That the honour of the republic had ever been his first object, and dearer to him than life; that he was chagrined, that the favour of the Roman people was wrested from him by the injurious reports of his enemies; that he was deprived of a half-year's command, and dragged back to the city, though the people had ordered that regard should be paid to his suit for the consulate at the next election, though he was not present; that, however, he had patiently submitted to this loss of honour for the sake of the republic; that when he wrote letters to the senate, requiring that all persons should resign the command of their armies, he did not obtain even that request; that levies were made throughout Italy; that the two legions which had been taken from him, under the pretence of the Parthian war, were kept at home, and that the state was in arms. To what did all these things tend, unless to his ruin? But, nevertheless, he was ready to condescend to any terms, and to endure everything for the sake of the republic. Let Pompey go to his own province; let them both disband their armies; let all persons in Italy lay down their arms; let all fears be removed from the city; let free elections, and the whole republic be resigned to the direction of the senate and Roman people. That these things might be the more easily performed, and conditions secured and confirmed by oath, either let Pompey come to Caesar, or allow Caesar to go to him; it might be that all their disputes would be settled by an interview."

X.—Roscius and Lucius Caesar, having received this message, went to Capua, where they met the consuls and Pompey, and declared to them Caesar's terms. Having deliberated on the matter, they replied, and sent written proposals to him by the same persons, the purport of which was, that Caesar should return into Gaul, leave Ariminum, and disband his army: if he complied with this, that Pompey would go to Spain. In the meantime, until security was given that Caesar would perform his promises, that the consuls and Pompey would not give over their levies.

XI.—It was not an equitable proposal, to require that Caesar should quit Ariminum and return to his province; but that he [Pompey] should himself retain his province and the legions that belonged to another, and desire that Caesar's army should be disbanded, whilst he himself was making new levies: and that he should merely promise to go to his province, without naming the day on which he would set out; so that if he should not set out till after Caesar's consulate expired, yet he would not appear bound by any religious scruples about asserting a falsehood. But his not granting time for a conference, nor promising to set out to meet him, made the expectation of peace appear very hopeless. Caesar, therefore, sent Marcus Antonius, with five cohorts from Ariminum to Arretium; he himself stayed at Ariminum with two legions, with the intention of raising levies there. He secured Pisaurus, Fanum, and Ancona, with a cohort each.

XII.—In the meantime, being informed that Thermus the praetor was in possession of Iguvium, with five cohorts, and was fortifying the town, but that the affections of all the inhabitants were very well inclined towards himself; he detached Curio with three cohorts, which he had at Ariminum and Pisaurus. Upon notice of his approach, Thermus, distrusting the affections of the townsmen, drew his cohorts out of it, and made his escape; his soldiers deserted him on the road, and returned home. Curio recovered Iguvium, with the cheerful concurrence of all the inhabitants. Caesar, having received an account of this, and relying on the affections of the municipal towns, drafted all the cohorts of the thirteenth legion from the garrisons, and set out for Auximum, a town into which Attius had brought his cohorts, and of which he had taken possession, and from which he had sent senators round about the country of Picenum, to raise new levies.

XIII.—Upon news of Caesar's approach, the senate of Auximum went in a body to Attius Varus; and told him that it was not a subject for them to determine upon: yet neither they, nor the rest of the freemen would suffer Caius Caesar, a general, who had merited so well of the republic, after performing such great achievements, to be excluded from their town and walls; wherefore he ought to pay some regard to the opinion of posterity, and his own danger. Alarmed at this declaration, Attius Varus drew out of the town the garrison which he had introduced, and fled. A few of Caesar's front rank having pursued him, obliged him to halt, and when the battle began, Varus is deserted by his troops: some of them disperse to their homes, the rest come over to Caesar; and along with them, Lucius Pupius, the chief centurion, is taken prisoner and brought to Caesar. He had held the same rank before in Cneius Pompey's army. But Caesar applauded the soldiers of Attius, set Pupius at liberty, returned thanks to the people of Auximum, and promised to be grateful for their conduct.

XIV.—Intelligence of this being brought to Rome, so great a panic spread on a sudden that when Lentulus, the consul, came to open the treasury, to deliver money to Pompey by the senate's decree, immediately on opening the hallowed door he fled from the city. For it was falsely rumoured that Caesar was approaching, and that his cavalry were already at the gates. Marcellus, his colleague, followed him, and so did most of the magistrates. Cneius Pompey had left the city the day before, and was on his march to those legions which he had received from Caesar, and had disposed in winter quarters in Apulia. The levies were stopped within the city. No place on this side of Capua was thought secure. At Capua they first began to take courage and to rally, and determined to raise levies in the colonies, which had been sent thither by the Julian law: and Lentulus brought into the public market-place the gladiators which Caesar maintained there for the entertainment of the people, and confirmed them in their liberty, and gave them horses and ordered them to attend him; but afterwards, being warned by his friends that this action was censured by the judgment of all, he distributed them among the slaves of the districts of Campania, to keep guard there.

XV.—Caesar, having moved forward from Auximum, traversed the whole country of Picenum. All the governors in these countries most cheerfully received him, and aided his army with every necessary. Ambassadors came to him even from Cingulum, a town which Labienus had laid out and built at his own expense, and offered most earnestly to comply with his orders. He demanded soldiers: they sent them. In the meantime, the twelfth legion came to join Caesar; with these two he marched to Asculum, the chief town of Picenum. Lentulus Spinther occupied that town with ten cohorts; but, on being informed of Caesar's approach, he fled from the town, and, in attempting to bring off his cohorts with him, was deserted by a great part of his men. Being left on the road with a small number, he fell in with Vibullius Rufus, who was sent by Pompey into Picenum to confirm the people [in their allegiance]. Vibullius, being informed by him of the transactions in Picenum, takes his soldiers from him and dismisses him. He collects, likewise, from the neighbouring countries, as many cohorts as he can from Pompey's new levies. Amongst them he meets with Ulcilles Hirrus fleeing from Camerinum, with six cohorts, which he had in the garrison there; by a junction with which he made up thirteen cohorts. With them he marched by hasty journeys to Corfinium, to Domitius Aenobarbus, and informed him that Caesar was advancing with two legions. Domitius had collected about twenty cohorts from Alba, and the Marsians, Pelignians, and neighbouring states.

XVI.—Caesar, having recovered Asculum and driven out Lentulus, ordered the soldiers that had deserted from him to be sought out and a muster to be made; and, having delayed for one day there to provide corn, he marched to Corfinium. On his approach, five cohorts, sent by Domitius from the town, were breaking down a bridge which was over the river, at three miles' distance from it. An engagement taking place there with Caesar's advanced-guard, Domitius's men were quickly beaten off from the bridge and retreated precipitately into the town. Caesar, having marched his legions over, halted before the town and encamped close by the walls.

XVII.—Domitius, upon observing this, sent messengers well acquainted with the country, encouraged by a promise of being amply rewarded, with despatches to Pompey to Apulia, to beg and entreat him to come to his assistance. That Caesar could be easily enclosed by the two armies, through the narrowness of the country, and prevented from obtaining supplies: unless he did so, that he and upwards of thirty cohorts, and a great number of senators and Roman knights, would be in extreme danger. In the meantime he encouraged his troops, disposed engines on the walls, and assigned to each man a particular part of the city to defend. In a speech to the soldiers he promised them lands out of his own estate; to every private soldier four acres, and a corresponding share to the centurions and veterans.

XVIII.—In the meantime, word was brought to Caesar that the people of Sulmo, a town about seven miles distant from Corfinium, were ready to obey his orders, but were prevented by Quintus Lucretius, a senator, and Attius, a Pelignian, who were in possession of the town with a garrison of seven cohorts. He sent Marcus Antonius thither, with five cohorts of the eighth legion. The inhabitants, as soon as they saw our standards, threw open their gates, and all the people, both citizens and soldiers, went out to meet and welcome Antonius. Lucretius and Attius leaped off the walls. Attius, being brought before Antonius, begged that he might be sent to Caesar. Antonius returned the same day on which he had set out with the cohorts and Attius. Caesar added these cohorts to his own army, and sent Attius away in safety. The three first days Caesar employed in fortifying his camp with strong works, in bringing in corn from the neighbouring free towns, and waiting for the rest of his forces. Within the three days the eighth legion came to him, and twenty-two cohorts of the new levies in Gaul, and about three hundred horse from the king of Noricum. On their arrival he made a second camp on another part of the town, and gave the command of it to Curio. He determined to surround the town with a rampart and turrets during the remainder of the time. Nearly at the time when the greatest part of the work was completed, all the messengers sent to Pompey returned.

XIX.—Having read Pompey's letter, Domitius, concealing the truth, gave out in council that Pompey would speedily come to their assistance; and encouraged them not to despond, but to provide everything necessary for the defence of the town. He held private conferences with a few of his most intimate friends, and determined on the design of fleeing. As Domitius's countenance did not agree with his words, and he did everything with more confusion and fear than he had shown on the preceding days, and as he had several private meetings with his friends, contrary to his usual practice, in order to take their advice, and as he avoided all public councils and assemblies of the people, the truth could be no longer hid nor dissembled; for Pompey had written back in answer, "That he would not put matters to the last

hazard; that Domitius had retreated into the town of Corfinium, without either his advice or consent. Therefore, if any opportunity should offer, he [Domitius] should come to him with the whole force." But the blockade and works round the town prevented his escape.
XX.—Domitius's design being noised abroad, the soldiers in Confinium [**error in original: should be CORFINIUM] early in the evening began to mutiny, and held a conference with each other by their tribunes and centurions, and the most respectable amongst themselves: "that they were besieged by Caesar; that his works and fortifications were almost finished; that their general, Domitius, on whose hopes and expectations they had confided, had thrown them off, and was meditating his own escape; that they ought to provide for their own safety." At first the Marsians differed in opinion, and possessed themselves of that part of the town which they thought the strongest. And so violent a dispute arose between them, that they attempted to fight and decide it by arms. However, in a little time, by messengers sent from one side to the other, they were informed of Domitius's meditated flight, of which they were previously ignorant. Therefore they all with one consent brought Domitius into public view, gathered round him, and guarded him; and sent deputies out of their number to Caesar, to say that they were ready to throw open their gates, to do whatever he should order, and to deliver up Domitius alive into his hands.
XXI.—Upon intelligence of these matters, though Caesar thought it of great consequence to become master of the town as soon as possible, and to transfer the cohorts to his own camp, lest any change should be wrought on their inclinations by bribes, encouragement, or fictitious messages, because in war great events are often brought about by trifling circumstances; yet, dreading lest the town should be plundered by the soldiers entering into it, and taking advantage of the darkness of the night, he commended the persons who came to him, and sent them back to the town, and ordered the gates and walls to be secured. He disposed his soldiers on the works, which he had begun, not at certain intervals, as was his practice before, but in one continued range of sentinels and stations, so that they touched each other, and formed a circle round the whole fortification; he ordered the tribunes and general officers to ride round; and exhorted them not only to be on their guard against sallies from the town, but also to watch that no single person should get out privately. Nor was any man so negligent or drowsy as to sleep that night. To so great height was their expectation raised, that they were carried away, heart and soul, each to different objects, what would become of the Corfinians, what of Domitius, what of Lentulus, what of the rest; what event would be the consequence of another.

XXII.—About the fourth watch, Lentulus Spinther said to our sentinels and guards from the walls, that he desired to have an interview with Caesar, if permission were given him. Having obtained it, he was escorted out of town; nor did the soldiers of Domitius leave him till they brought him into Caesar's presence. He pleaded with Caesar for his life, and entreated him to spare him, and reminded him of their former friendship; and acknowledged that Caesar's favours to him were very great; in that through his interest he had been admitted into the college of priests; in that after his praetorship he had been appointed to the government of Spain; in that he had been assisted by him in his suit for the consulate. Caesar interrupted him in his speech, and told him, "that he had not left his province to do mischief [to any man], but to protect himself from the injuries of his enemies; to restore to their dignity the tribunes of the people who had been driven out of the city on his account, and to assert his own liberty, and that of the Roman people, who were oppressed by a few factious men." Encouraged by this address, Lentulus begged leave to return to the town, that the security which he had obtained for himself might be an encouragement to the rest to hope for theirs; saying that some were so terrified that they were induced to make desperate attempts on their own lives. Leave being granted him, he departed.

XXIII.—When day appeared Caesar ordered all the senators and their children, the tribunes of the soldiers, and the Roman knights, to be brought before him. Among the persons of senatorial rank were Lucius Domitius, Publius Lentulus Spinther, Lucius Vibullius Rufus, Sextus Quintilius Varus, the quaestor, and Lucius Rubrius, besides the son of Domitius, and several other young men, and a great number of Roman knights and burgesses, whom Domitius had summoned from the municipal towns. When they were brought before him he protected them from the insolence and taunts of the soldiers; told them in few words that they had not made him a grateful return, on their part, for his very extraordinary kindness to them, and dismissed them all in safety. Sixty sestertia, which Domitius had brought with him and lodged in the public treasury, being brought to Caesar by the magistrates of Corfinium, he gave them back to Domitius, that he might not appear more moderate with respect to the life of men than in money matters, though he knew that it was public money, and had been given by Pompey to pay his army. He ordered Domitius's soldiers to take the oath to himself, and that day decamped and performed the regular march. He stayed only seven days before Corfinium, and marched into Apulia through the country of the Marrucinians, Frentanians, and Larinates.

XXIV.—Pompey, being informed of what had passed at Corfinium, marches from Luceria to Canusium, and thence to Brundusium. He orders all the forces raised everywhere by the new levies to repair to him. He gives arms to the slaves that attended the flocks, and appoints horses for them. Of these he made up about three hundred horse. Lucius, the praetor, fled from Alba, with six cohorts: Rutilus Lupus, the praetor, from Tarracina, with three. These having descried Caesar's cavalry at a distance, which were commanded by Bivius Curius, and having deserted the praetor, carried their colours to Curius and went over to him. In like manner during the rest of his march, several cohorts fell in with the main body of Caesar's army, others with his horse. Cneius Magius, from Cremona, engineer-general to Pompey, was taken prisoner on the road and brought to Caesar, but sent back by him to Pompey with this message: "As hitherto he had not been allowed an interview, and was now on his march to him at Brundusium, that it deeply concerned the commonwealth and general safety that he should have an interview with Pompey; and that the same advantage could not be gained at a great distance when the proposals were conveyed to them by others, as if terms were argued by them both in person."
XXV.—Having delivered this message he marched to Brundusium with six legions, four of them veterans: the rest those which he had raised in the late levy and completed on his march, for he had sent all Domitius's cohorts immediately from Corfinium to Sicily. He discovered that the consuls were gone to Dyrrachium with a considerable part of the army, and that Pompey remained at Brundusium with twenty cohorts; but could not find out, for a certainty, whether Pompey stayed behind to keep possession of Brundusium, that he might the more easily command the whole Adriatic sea, with the extremities of Italy and the coast of Greece, and be able to conduct the war on either side of it, or whether he remained there for want of shipping; and, being afraid that Pompey would come to the conclusion that he ought not to relinquish Italy, he determined to deprive him of the means of communication afforded by the harbour of Brundusium. The plan of his work was as follows:—Where the mouth of the port was narrowest he threw up a mole of earth on either side, because in these places the sea was shallow. Having gone out so far that the mole could not be continued in the deep water, he fixed double floats, thirty feet on either side, before the mole. These he fastened with four anchors at the four corners, that they might not be carried away by the waves. Having completed and secured them, he then joined to them other floats of equal size. These he covered over with earth and mould, that he might not be prevented from access to them to defend them, and in the front and on both sides he protected them with a parapet of wicker work; and on every fourth

one raised a turret, two stories high, to secure them the better from being attacked by the shipping and set on fire.
XXVI.—To counteract this, Pompey fitted out large merchant ships, which he found in the harbour of Brundusium: on them he erected turrets three stories high, and, having furnished them with several engines and all sorts of weapons, drove them amongst Caesar's works, to break through the floats and interrupt the works; thus there happened skirmishes every day at a distance with slings, arrows, and other weapons. Caesar conducted matters as if he thought that the hopes of peace were not yet to be given up. And though he was very much surprised that Magius, whom he had sent to Pompey with a message, was not sent back to him; and though his attempting a reconciliation often retarded the vigorous prosecution of his plans, yet he thought that he ought by all means to persevere in the same line of conduct. He therefore sent Caninius Rebilus to have an interview with Scribonius Libo, his intimate friend and relation. He charges him to exhort Libo to effect a peace, but, above all things, requires that he should be admitted to an interview with Pompey. He declared that he had great hopes, if that were allowed him, that the consequence would be that both parties would lay down their arms on equal terms; that a great share of the glory and reputation of that event would redound to Libo, if, through his advice and agency, hostilities should be ended. Libo, having parted from the conference with Caninius, went to Pompey, and, shortly after, returns with answer that, as the consuls were absent, no treaty of compositions could be engaged in without them. Caesar therefore thought it time at length to give over the attempt which he had often made in vain, and act with energy in the war.
XXVII.—When Caesar's works were nearly half finished, and after nine days were spent in them, the ships which had conveyed the first division of the army to Dyrrachium being sent back by the consuls, returned to Brundusium. Pompey, either frightened at Caesar's works or determined from the beginning to quit Italy, began to prepare for his departure on the arrival of the ships; and the more effectually to retard Caesar's attack, lest his soldiers should force their way into the town at the moment of his departure, he stopped up the gates, built walls across the streets and avenues, sunk trenches across the ways, and in them fixed palisadoes and sharp stakes, which he made level with the ground by means of hurdles and clay. But he barricaded with large beams fastened in the ground and sharpened at the ends two passages and roads without the walls, which led to the port. After making these arrangements, he ordered his soldiers to go on board without noise, and disposed here and there, on the wall and turrets, some light-armed veterans, archers and slingers. These he designed to call off by a certain

signal, when all the soldiers were embarked, and left row-galleys for them in a secure place.
XXVIII.—The people of Brundusium, irritated by the insolence of Pompey's soldiers, and the insults received from Pompey himself, were in favour of Caesar's party. Therefore, as soon as they were aware of Pompey's departure, whilst his men were running up and down, and busied about their voyage, they made signs from the tops of the houses: Caesar, being apprized of the design by them, ordered scaling ladders to be got ready, and his men to take arms, that he might not lose any opportunity of coming to an action. Pompey weighed anchor at nightfall. The soldiers who had been posted on the wall to guard it, were called off by the signal which had been agreed on, and knowing the roads, ran down to the ships. Caesar's soldiers fixed their ladders and scaled the walls: but being cautioned by the people to beware of the hidden stakes and covered trenches, they halted, and being conducted by the inhabitants by a long circuit, they reached the port, and captured with their long boats and small craft two of Pompey's ships, full of soldiers, which had struck against Caesar's moles.
XXIX.-Though Caesar highly approved of collecting a fleet, and crossing the sea, and pursuing Pompey before he could strengthen himself with his transmarine auxiliaries, with the hope of bringing the war to a conclusion, yet he dreaded the delay and length of time necessary to effect it: because Pompey, by collecting all his ships, had deprived him of the means of pursuing him at present. The only resource left to Caesar, was to wait for a fleet from the distant regions of Gaul, Picenum, and the straits of Gibraltar. But this, on account of the season of the year, appeared tedious and troublesome. He was unwilling that, in the meantime, the veteran army, and the two Spains, one of which was bound to Pompey by the strongest obligations, should be confirmed in his interest; that auxiliaries and cavalry should be provided and Gaul and Italy reduced in his absence.
XXX.—Therefore, for the present, he relinquished all intention of pursuing Pompey, and resolved to march to Spain, and commanded the magistrates of the free towns to procure him ships, and to have them conveyed to Brundusium. He detached Valerius, his lieutenant, with one legion to Sardinia; Curio, the proprietor, to Sicily with three legions; and ordered him, when he had recovered Sicily, to immediately transport his army to Africa. Marcus Cotta was at this time governor of Sardinia: Marcus Cato, of Sicily: and Tubero, by the lots, should have had the government of Africa. The Caralitani, as soon as they heard that Valerius was sent against them, even before he left Italy, of their own accord drove Cotta out of the town; who, terrified because he understood that the whole province was combined [against

him], fled from Sardinia to Africa. Cato was in Sicily, repairing the old ships of war, and demanding new ones from the states, and these things he performed with great zeal. He was raising levies of Roman citizens, among the Lucani and Brutii, by his lieutenants, and exacting a certain quota of horse and foot from the states of Sicily. When these things were nearly completed, being informed of Curio's approach, he made a complaint that he was abandoned and betrayed by Pompey, who had undertaken an unnecessary war, without making any preparation, and when questioned by him and other members in the senate, had assured them that every thing was ready and provided for the war. After having made these complaints in a public assembly, he fled from his province. XXXI.—Valerius found Sardinia, and Curio, Sicily, deserted by their governors when they arrived there with their armies. When Tubero arrived in Africa, he found Attius Varus in the government of the province, who, having lost his cohorts, as already related, at Auximum, had straightway fled to Africa, and finding it without a governor, had seized it of his own accord, and making levies, had raised two legions. From his acquaintance with the people and country, and his knowledge of that province, he found the means of effecting this; because a few years before, at the expiration of his praetorship, he had obtained that province. He, when Tubero came to Utica with his fleet, prevented his entering the port or town, and did not suffer his son, though labouring under sickness, to set foot on shore; but obliged him to weigh anchor and quit the place.

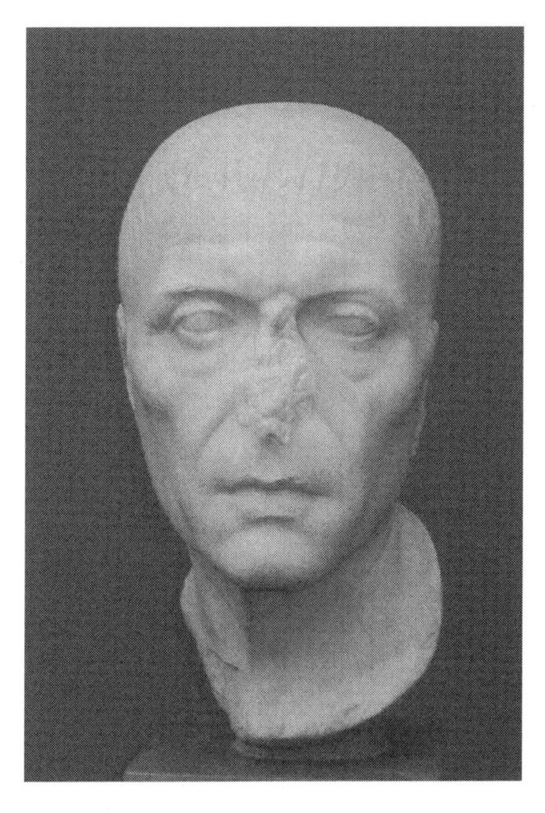

XXXIL.—When these affairs were despatched, Caesar, that there might be an intermission from labour for the rest of the season, drew off his soldiers to the nearest municipal towns, and set off in person for Rome. Having assembled the senate, he reminded them of the injustice of his enemies; and told them, "That he aimed at no extraordinary honour, but had waited for the time appointed by law, for standing candidate for the consulate, being contented with what was allowed to every citizen. That a bill had been carried by the ten tribunes of the people (notwithstanding the resistance of his enemies, and a very violent opposition from Cato, who in his usual manner, consumed the day by a tedious harangue) that he should be allowed to stand candidate, though absent, even in the consulship of Pompey; and if the latter disapproved of the bill, why did he allow it to pass? if he approved of it, why should he debar him [Caesar] from the people's favour? He made mention of his own patience, in that he had freely proposed that all armies should be disbanded, by which he himself would suffer the loss both of dignity and honour. He urged the virulence of his enemies, who refused to comply with what they required from others, and had rather that all things should be thrown into confusion, than that they should lose their power and their armies. He expatiated on their injustice, in taking away his legions: their cruelty and insolence in abridging the privileges of the tribunes; the proposals he had made, and his entreaties of an interview, which had been refused him: For which reasons, he begged and desired that they would undertake the management of the republic, and unite with him in the administration of it. But if through fear they declined it, he would not be a burden to them, but take the management of it on himself. That deputies ought to be sent to Pompey, to propose a reconciliation; as he did not regard what Pompey had lately asserted in the senate, that authority was acknowledged to be vested in those persons to whom ambassadors were sent, and fear implied in those that sent them. That these were the sentiments of low, weak minds: that for his part, as he had made it his study to surpass others in glory, so he was desirous of excelling them in justice and equity."

XXXIII.—The senate approved of sending deputies, but none could be found fit to execute the commission: for every person, from his own private fears, declined the office. For Pompey, on leaving the city, had declared in the open senate, that he would hold in the same degree of estimation, those who stayed in Rome and those in Caesar's camp. Thus three days were wasted in disputes and excuses. Besides, Lucius Metellus, one of the tribunes, was suborned by Caesar's enemies, to prevent this, and to embarrass everything else which Caesar should propose. Caesar having discovered his intention, after spending several days to no purpose, left the city, in order that he might not lose any more time, and went to Transalpine Gaul, without effecting what he had intended.

XXXIV.—On his arrival there, he was informed that, Vibullius Rufus, whom he had taken a few days before at Corfinium, and set at liberty, was sent by Pompey into Spain; and that Domitius also was gone to seize Massilia with seven row-galleys, which were fitted up by some private persons at Igilium and Cosa, and which he had manned with his own slaves, freedmen, and colonists: and that some young noblemen of Massilia had been sent before him; whom Pompey, when leaving Rome had exhorted, that the late services of Caesar should not erase from their minds the memory of his former favours. On receiving this message, the Massilians had shut their gates against Caesar, and invited over to them the Albici, who had formerly been in alliance with them, and who inhabited the mountains that overhung Massilia: they had likewise conveyed the corn from the surrounding country, and from all the forts into the city; had opened armouries in the city: and were repairing the walls, the fleet, and the gates.

XXXV.—Caesar sent for fifteen of the principal persons of Massilia to attend him. To prevent the war commencing among them, he remonstrates [in the following language]; "that they ought to follow the precedent set by all Italy, rather than submit to the will of any one man." He made use of such arguments as he thought would tend to bring them to reason. The deputies reported his speech to their countrymen, and by the authority of the state bring him back this answer: "That they understood that the Roman people was divided into two factions: that they had neither judgment nor abilities to decide which had the juster cause; but that the heads of these factions were Cneius Pompey and Caius Caesar, the two patrons of the state: the former of whom had granted to their state the lands of the Volcae Arecomici, and Helvii; the latter had assigned them a part of his conquests in Gaul, and had augmented their revenue. Wherefore, having received equal favours from both, they ought to show equal affection to both, and assist neither against the other, nor admit either into their city or harbours."

XXXVI.—Whilst this treaty was going forward, Domitius arrived at Massilia with his fleet, and was received into the city, and made governor of it. The chief management of the war was entrusted to him. At his command they send the fleet to all parts; they seize all the merchantmen they could meet with, and carry them into the harbour; they apply the nails, timber, and rigging, with which they were furnished to rig and refit their other vessels. They lay up in the public stores, all the corn that was found in the ships, and reserve the rest of their lading and convoy for the siege of the town, should such an event take place. Provoked at such ill treatment, Caesar led three legions against Massilia, and resolved to provide turrets, and vinae to assault the town, and to build twelve ships at Arelas, which being completed and rigged in thirty days (from the time the timber was cut down), and being brought to Massilia, he put under the command of Decimus Brutus; and left Caius Trebonius his lieutenant, to invest the city.

XXXVII.—Whilst he was preparing and getting these things in readiness, he sent Caius Fabius one of his lieutenants into Spain with three legions, which he had disposed in winter quarters in Narbo, and the neighbouring country; and ordered him immediately to seize the passes of the Pyrenees, which were at that time occupied by detachments from Lucius Afranius, one of Pompey's lieutenants. He desired the other legions, which were passing the winter at a great distance, to follow close after him. Fabius, according to his orders, by using expedition, dislodged the party from the hills, and by hasty marches came up with the army of Afranius.

XXXVIII.—On the arrival of Vibullius Rufus, whom, we have already mentioned, Pompey had sent into Spain, Afranius, Petreius, and Varro, his lieutenants (one of whom had the command of Hither Spain, with three legions; the second of the country from the forest of Castulo to the river Guadiana with two legions; the third from the river Guadiana to the country of the Vettones and Lusitania, with the like number of legions), divided amongst themselves their respective departments. Petreius was to march from Lusitania through the Vettones, and join Afranius with all his forces; Varro was to guard all Further Spain with what legions he had. These matters being settled, reinforcements of horse and foot were demanded from Lusitania, by Petreius; from the Celtiberi, Cantabri, and all the barbarous nations which border on the ocean, by Afranius. When they were raised, Petreius immediately marched through the Vettones to Afranius. They resolved by joint consent to carry on the war in the vicinity of Ilerda, on account of the advantages of its situation.
XXXIX.—Afranius, as above mentioned, had three legions, Petreius two. There were besides about eighty cohorts raised in Hither and Further Spain (of which, the troops belonging to the former province had shields, those of the latter targets), and about five thousand horse raised in both provinces. Caesar had sent his legions into Spain, with about six thousand auxiliary foot, and three thousand horse, which had served under him in all his former wars, and the same number from Gaul, which he himself had provided, having expressly called out all the most noble and valiant men of each state. The bravest of these were from the Aquitani and the mountaineers, who border on the Province in Gaul. He had been informed that Pompey was marching through Mauritania with his legions to Spain, and would shortly arrive. He at the same time borrowed money from the tribunes and centurions, which he distributed amongst his soldiers. By this proceeding he gained two points; he secured the interest of the centurions by this pledge in his hands, and by his liberality he purchased the affections of his army.
XL.—Fabius sounded the inclinations of the neighbouring states by letters and messengers. He had made two bridges over the river Segre, at the distance of four miles from each other. He sent foraging parties over these bridges, because he had already consumed all the forage that was on his side of the river. The generals of Pompey's army did almost the same thing, and for the same reason: and the horse had frequent skirmishes with each other. When two of Fabius's legions had, as was their constant practice, gone forth as the usual protection to the foragers, and had crossed the river, and the baggage, and all the horse were following them, on a sudden, from the weight of the cattle, and the mass of water, the bridge fell, and all the horse were cut off from

the main army, which being known to Petreius and Afranius, from the timber and hurdles that were carried down the river, Afranius immediately crossed his own bridge, which communicated between his camp and the town, with four legions and all the cavalry, and marched against Fabius's two legions. When his approach was announced, Lucius Plancus, who had the command of those legions, compelled by the emergency, took post on a rising ground; and drew up his army with two fronts, that it might not be surrounded by the cavalry. Thus, though engaged with superior numbers, he sustained the furious charge of the legions and the horse. When the battle was begun by the horse, there were observed at a distance by both sides the colours of two legions, which Caius Fabius had sent round by the further bridge to reinforce our men, suspecting, as the event verified, that the enemy's generals would take advantage of the opportunity which fortune had put in their way, to attack our men. Their approach put an end to the battle, and each general led back his legions to their respective camps.
XLI.—In two days after Caesar came to the camp with nine hundred horse, which he had retained for a bodyguard. The bridge which had been broken down by the storm was almost repaired, and he ordered it to be finished in the night. Being acquainted with the nature of the country, he left behind him six cohorts to guard the bridge, the camp, and all his baggage, and the next day set off in person for Ilerda, with all his forces drawn up in three lines, and halted just before the camp of Afranius, and having remained there a short time under arms, he offered him battle on equal terms. When this offer was made, Afranius drew out his forces, and posted them on the middle of a hill, near his camp. When Caesar perceived that Afranius declined coming to an engagement, he resolved to encamp at somewhat less than half a mile's distance from the very foot of the mountain; and that his soldiers whilst engaged in their works, might not be terrified by any sudden attack of the enemy, or disturbed in their work, he ordered them not to fortify it with a wall, which must rise high, and be seen at a distance, but draw, on the front opposite the enemy, a trench fifteen feet broad. The first and second lines continued under arms as was from the first appointed. Behind them the third line was carrying on the work without being seen; so that the whole was completed before Afranius discovered that the camp was being fortified.
XLII.—In the evening Caesar drew his legions within this trench, and rested them under arms the next night. The day following he kept his whole army within it, and as it was necessary to bring materials from a considerable distance, he for the present pursued the same plan in his work; and to each legion, one after the other, he assigned one side of the camp to fortify, and ordered trenches of the same magnitude to be

cut: he kept the rest of the legions under arms without baggage to oppose the enemy. Afranius and Petreius, to frighten us and obstruct the work, drew out their forces at the very foot of the mountain, and challenged us to battle. Caesar, however, did not interrupt his work, relying on the protection of the three legions, and the strength of the fosse. After staying for a short time, and advancing no great distance from the bottom of the hill, they led back their forces to their camp. The third day Caesar fortified his camp with a rampart, and ordered the other cohorts which he had left in the upper camp, and his baggage to be removed to it.
XLIIL-Between the town of Ilerda and the next hill, on which Afranius and Petreius were encamped, there was a plain about three hundred paces broad, and near the middle of it an eminence somewhat raised above the level: Caesar hoped that if he could get possession of this and fortify it, he should be able to cut off the enemy from the town, the bridge, and all the stores which they had laid up in the town. In expectation of this he led three legions out of the camp, and, drawing up his army in an advantageous position, he ordered the advanced men of one legion to hasten forward and seize the eminence. Upon intelligence of this the cohorts which were on guard before Afranius's camp were instantly sent a nearer way to occupy the same post. The two parties engage, and as Afranius's men had reached the eminence first, our men were repulsed, and, on a reinforcement being sent, they were obliged to turn their backs and retreat to the standards of legions.
XLIV.—The manner of fighting of those soldiers was to run forward with great impetuosity and boldly take a post, and not to keep their ranks strictly, but to fight in small scattered parties: if hard pressed they thought it no disgrace to retire and give up the post, being accustomed to this manner of fighting among the Lusitanians and other barbarous nations; for it commonly happens that soldiers are strongly influenced by the customs of those countries in which they have spent much time. This method, however, alarmed our men, who were not used to such a description of warfare. For they imagined that they were about to be surrounded on their exposed flank by the single men who ran forward from their ranks; and they thought it their duty to keep their ranks, and not to quit their colours, nor, without good reason, to give up the post which they had taken. Accordingly, when the advanced guard gave way, the legion which was stationed on that wing did not keep its ground, but retreated to the next hill.
XLV.—Almost the whole army being daunted at this, because it had occurred contrary to their expectations and custom, Caesar encouraged his men and led the ninth legion to their relief, and checked the insolent and eager pursuit of the enemy, and obliged them, in their turn, to show

their backs and retreat to Ilerda, and take post under the walls. But the soldiers of the ninth legion, being over zealous to repair the dishonour which had been sustained, having rashly pursued the fleeing enemy, advanced into disadvantageous ground and went up to the foot of the mountain on which the town Ilerda was built. And when they wished to retire they were again attacked by the enemy from the rising ground. The place was craggy in the front and steep on either side, and was so narrow that even three cohorts, drawn up in order of battle, would fill it; but no relief could be sent on the flanks, and the horse could be of no service to them when hard pressed. From the town, indeed, the precipice inclined with a gentle slope for near four hundred paces. Our men had to retreat this way, as they had, through their eagerness, advanced too inconsiderately. The greatest contest was in this place, which was much to the disadvantage of our troops, both on account of its narrowness, and because they were posted at the foot of the mountain, so that no weapon was thrown at them without effect: yet they exerted their valour and patience, and bore every wound. The enemy's forces were increasing, and cohorts were frequently sent to their aid from the camp through the town, that fresh men might relieve the weary. Caesar was obliged to do the same, and relieve the fatigued by sending cohorts to that post.
XLVI.—After the battle had in this manner continued incessantly for five hours, and our men had suffered much from superior numbers, having spent all their javelins, they drew their swords and charged the enemy up the hill, and, having killed a few, obliged the rest to fly. The cohorts being beaten back to the wall, and some being driven by their fears into the town, an easy retreat was afforded to our men. Our cavalry also, on either flank, though stationed on sloping or low ground, yet bravely struggled up to the top of the hill, and, riding between the two armies, made our retreat more easy and secure. Such were the various turns of fortune in the battle. In the first encounter about seventy of our men fell: amongst them Quintus Fulgenius, first centurion of the second line of the fourteenth legion, who, for his extraordinary valour, had been promoted from the lower ranks to that post. About six hundred were wounded. Of Afranius's party there were killed Titus Caecilius, principal centurion, and four other centurions, and above two hundred men.
XLVII.—But this opinion is spread abroad concerning this day, that each party thought that they came off conquerors. Afranius's soldiers, because, though they were esteemed inferior in the opinion of all, yet they had stood our attack and sustained our charge, and, at first, had kept the post and the hill which had been the occasion of the dispute; and, in the first encounter, had obliged our men to fly: but ours,

because, notwithstanding the disadvantage of the ground and the disparity of numbers, they had maintained the battle for five hours, had advanced up the hill sword in hand, and had forced the enemy to fly from the higher ground and driven them into the town. The enemy fortified the hill, about which the contest had been, with strong works, and posted a garrison on it.

XLVIII.—In two days after this transaction, there happened an unexpected misfortune. For so great a storm arose, that it was agreed that there were never seen higher floods in those countries; it swept down the snow from all the mountains, and broke over the banks of the river, and in one day carried away both the bridges which Fabius had built,—a circumstance which caused great difficulties to Caesar's army. For as our camp, as already mentioned, was pitched between two rivers, the Segre and Cinca, and as neither of these could be forded for the space of thirty miles, they were all of necessity confined within these narrow limits. Neither could the states, which had espoused Caesar's cause, furnish him with corn, nor the troops, which had gone far to forage, return, as they were stopped by the waters: nor could the convoys, coming from Italy and Gaul, make their way to the camp. Besides, it was the most distressing season of the year, when there was no corn in the blade, and it was nearly ripe: and the states were exhausted, because Afranius had conveyed almost all the corn, before Caesar's arrival, into Ilerda, and whatever he had left, had been already consumed by Caesar. The cattle, which might have served as a secondary resource against want, had been removed by the states to a great distance on account of the war. They who had gone out to get forage or corn, were chased by the light troops of the Lusitanians, and the targeteers of Hither Spain, who were well acquainted with the country, and could readily swim across the river, because it is the custom of all those people not to join their armies without bladders.

XLIX.—But Afranius's army had abundance of everything; a great stock of corn had been provided and laid in long before, a large quantity was coming in from the whole province: they had a good store of forage. The bridge of Ilerda afforded an opportunity of getting all these without any danger, and the places beyond the bridge, to which Caesar had no access, were as yet untouched.

L.—Those floods continued several days. Caesar endeavoured to repair the bridges, but the height of the water did not allow him: and the cohorts disposed along the banks did not suffer them to be completed; and it was easy for them to prevent it, both from the nature of the river and the height of the water, but especially because their darts were thrown from the whole course of the bank on one confined spot; and it was no easy matter at one and the same time to execute a work in a very rapid flood, and to avoid the darts.

LI.—Intelligence was brought to Afranius that the great convoys, which were on their march to Caesar, had halted at the river. Archers from the Rutheni, and horse from the Gauls, with a long train of baggage, according to the Gallic custom of travelling, had arrived there; there were besides about six thousand people of all descriptions, with slaves and freed men. But there was no order, or regular discipline, as every one followed his own humour, and all travelled without apprehension, taking the same liberty as on former marches. There were several young noblemen, sons of senators, and of equestrian rank; there were ambassadors from several states; there were lieutenants of Caesar's. The river stopped them all. To attack them by surprise, Afranius set out in the beginning of the night, with all his cavalry and three legions, and sent the horse on before, to fall on them unawares; but the Gallic horse soon got themselves in readiness, and attacked them. Though but few, they withstood the vast number of the enemy, as long as they fought on equal terms: but when the legions began to approach, having lost a few men, they retreated to the next mountains. The delay occasioned by this battle was of great importance to the security of our men; for having gained time, they retired to the higher grounds. There were missing that day about two hundred bow-men, a few horse, and an inconsiderable number of servants and baggage.

LII.—However, by all these things, the price of provisions was raised, which is commonly a disaster attendant, not only on a time of present scarcity, but on the apprehension of future want. Provisions had now reached fifty denarii each bushel; and the want of corn had diminished the strength of the soldiers; and the inconveniences were increasing every day: and so great an alteration was wrought in a few days, and fortune had so changed sides, that our men had to struggle with the want of every necessary; while the enemy had an abundant supply of all things, and were considered to have the advantage. Caesar demanded from those states which had acceded to his alliance, a supply of cattle, as they had but little corn. He sent away the camp followers to the more distant states, and endeavoured to remedy the present scarcity by every resource in his power.

LIII.—Afranius and Petreius, and their friends, sent fuller and more circumstantial accounts of these things to Rome, to their acquaintances. Report exaggerated them so that the war appeared to be almost at an end. When these letters and despatches were received at Rome, a great concourse of people resorted to the house of Afranius, and congratulations ran high: several went out of Italy to Cneius Pompey;

some of them, to be the first to bring him the intelligence; others, that they might not be thought to have waited the issue of the war, and to have come last of all.
LIV.—When Caesar's affairs were in this unfavourable position, and all the passes were guarded by the soldiers and horse of Afranius, and the bridges could not be prepared, Caesar ordered his soldiers to make ships of the kind that his knowledge of Britain a few years before had taught him. First, the keels and ribs were made of light timber, then, the rest of the hulk of the ships was wrought with wicker-work, and covered over with hides. When these were finished, he drew them down to the river in waggons in one night, a distance of twenty-two miles from his camp, and transported in them some soldiers across the river, and on a sudden took possession of a hill adjoining the bank. This he immediately fortified, before he was perceived by the enemy. To this he afterwards transported a legion: and having begun a bridge on both sides, he finished it in two days. By this means, he brought safe to his camp the convoys, and those who had gone out to forage; and began to prepare a conveyance for the provisions.
LV.—The same day he made a great part of his horse pass the river, who, falling on the foragers by surprise as they were dispersed without any suspicions, intercepted an incredible number of cattle and people; and when some Spanish light-armed cohorts were sent to reinforce the enemy, our men judiciously divided themselves into two parts, the one to protect the spoil, the other to resist the advancing foe, and to beat them back, and they cut off from the rest and surrounded one cohort, which had rashly ventured out of the line before the others, and after putting it to the sword, returned safe with considerable booty to the camp over the same bridge.
LVI.—Whilst these affairs are going forward at Ilerda, the Massilians, adopting the advice of Domitius, prepared seventeen ships of war, of which eleven were decked. To these they add several smaller vessels, that our fleet might be terrified by numbers: they man them with a great number of archers and of the Albici, of whom mention has been already made, and these they incited by rewards and promises. Domitius required certain ships for his own use, which he manned with colonists and shepherds, whom he had brought along with him. A fleet being thus furnished with every necessary, he advanced with great confidence against our ships, commanded by Decimus Brutus. It was stationed at an island opposite to Massilia.
LVII.—Brutus was much inferior in number of ships; but Caesar had appointed to that fleet the bravest men selected from all his legions, antesignani and centurions, who had requested to be employed in that service. They had provided iron hooks and harpoons, and had furnished

themselves with a vast number of javelins, darts, and missiles. Thus prepared, and being apprised of the enemy's approach, they put out from the harbour, and engaged the Massilians. Both sides fought with great courage and resolution; nor did the Albici, a hardy people, bred on the highlands and inured to arms, fall much short of our men in valour: and being lately come from the Massilians, they retained in their minds their recent promises: and the wild shepherds, encouraged by the hope of liberty, were eager to prove their zeal in the presence of their masters.

LVIII.—The Massilians themselves, confiding in the quickness of their ships, and the skill of their pilots, eluded ours, and evaded the shock, and as long as they were permitted by clear space, lengthening their line they endeavoured to surround us, or to attack single ships with several of theirs, or to run across our ships, and carry away our oars, if possible; but when necessity obliged them to come nearer, they had recourse, from the skill and art of the pilots, to the valour of the mountaineers. But our men, not having such expert seamen, or skilful pilots, for they had been hastily drafted from the merchant ships, and were not yet acquainted even with the names of the rigging, were moreover impeded by the heaviness and slowness of our vessels, which having been built in a hurry and of green timber, were not so easily manoeuvred. Therefore, when Caesar's men had an opportunity of a close engagement, they cheerfully opposed two of the enemy's ships with one of theirs. And throwing in the grappling irons, and holding both ships fast, they fought on both sides of the deck, and boarded the enemy's; and having killed numbers of the Albici and shepherds, they sank some of their ships, took others with the men on board, and drove the rest into the harbour. That day the Massilians lost nine ships, including those that were taken.

LIX.—When news of this battle was brought to Caesar at Ilerda, the bridge being completed at the same time, fortune soon took a turn. The enemy, daunted by the courage of our horse, did not scour the country as freely or as boldly as before: but sometimes advancing a small distance from the camp, that they might have a ready retreat, they foraged within narrower bounds: at other times, they took a longer circuit to avoid our outposts and parties of horse; or having sustained some loss, or descried our horse at a distance, they fled in the midst of their expedition, leaving their baggage behind them; at length they resolved to leave off foraging for several days, and, contrary to the practice of all nations, to go out at night.

LX.—In the meantime the Oscenses and the Calagurritani, who were under the government of the Oscenses, send ambassadors to Caesar, and offer to submit to his orders. They are followed by the

Tarraconenses, Jacetani, and Ausetani, and in a few days more by the Illurgavonenses, who dwell near the river Ebro. He requires of them all to assist him with corn, to which they agreed, and having collected all the cattle in the country, they convey them into his camp. One entire cohort of the Illurgavonenses, knowing the design of their state, came over to Caesar, from the place where they were stationed, and carried their colours with them. A great change is shortly made in the face of affairs. The bridge being finished, five powerful states being joined to Caesar, a way opened for the receiving of corn, and the rumours of the assistance of legions which were said to be on their march, with Pompey at their head, through Mauritania, having died away, several of the more distant states revolt from Afranius, and enter into league with Caesar.

LXI.—Whilst the spirits of the enemy were dismayed at these things, Caesar, that he might not be always obliged to send his horse a long circuit round by the bridge, having found a convenient place, began to sink several drains, thirty feet deep, by which he might draw off a part of the river Segre, and make a ford over it. When these were almost finished, Afranius and Petreius began to be greatly alarmed, lest they should be altogether cut off from corn and forage, because Caesar was very strong in cavalry. They therefore resolved to quit their posts, and to transfer the war to Celtiberia. There was, moreover, a circumstance that confirmed them in this resolution: for of the two adverse parties, that which had stood by Sertorius in the late war, being conquered by Pompey, still trembled at his name and sway, though absent: the other which had remained firm in Pompey's interest, loved him for the favours which they had received: but Caesar's name was not known to the barbarians. From these they expected considerable aid, both of horse and foot, and hoped to protract the war till winter, in a friendly country. Having come to this resolution, they gave orders to collect all the ships in the river Ebro, and to bring them to Octogesa, a town situated on the river Ebro, about twenty miles distant from their camp. At this part of the river, they ordered a bridge to be made of boats fastened together, and transported two legions over the river Segre, and fortified their camp with a rampart, twelve feet high.

LXII.—Notice of this being given by the scouts, Caesar continued his work day and night, with very great fatigue to the soldiers, to drain the river, and so far effected his purpose, that the horse were both able and bold enough, though with some difficulty and danger, to pass the river; but the foot had only their shoulders and upper part of their breast above the water, so that their fording it was retarded, not only by the depth of the water, but also by the rapidity of the current. However,

almost at the same instant, news was received of the bridge being nearly completed over the Ebro, and a ford was found in the Segre.
LXIII.—Now indeed the enemy began to think that they ought to hasten their march. Accordingly, leaving two auxiliary cohorts in the garrison at Ilerda, they crossed the Segre with their whole force, and formed one camp with the two legions which they had led across a few days before. Caesar had no resource, but to annoy and cut down their rear; since with his cavalry to go by the bridge, required him to take a long circuit; so that they would arrive at the Ebro by a much shorter route. The horse, which he had detached, crossed the ford, and when Afranius and Petreius had broken up their camp about the third watch, they suddenly appeared on their rear, and spreading round them in great numbers, began to retard and impede their march.
LXIV.—At break of day, it was perceived from the rising grounds which joined Caesar's camp, that their rear was vigorously pressed by our horse; that the last line sometimes halted and was broken; at other times, that they joined battle and that our men were beaten back by a general charge of their cohorts, and, in their turn, pursued them when they wheeled about: but through the whole camp the soldiers gathered in parties, and declared their chagrin that the enemy had been suffered to escape from their hands and that the war had been unnecessarily protracted. They applied to their tribunes and centurions, and entreated them to inform Caesar that he need not spare their labour or consider their danger; that they were ready and able, and would venture to ford the river where the horse had crossed. Caesar, encouraged by their zeal and importunity, though he felt reluctant to expose his army to a river so exceedingly large, yet judged it prudent to attempt it and make a trial. Accordingly, he ordered all the weaker soldiers, whose spirit or strength seemed unequal to the fatigue, to be selected from each century, and left them, with one legion besides, to guard the camp: the rest of the legions he drew out without any baggage, and, having disposed a great number of horses in the river, above and below the ford, he led his army over. A few of his soldiers being carried away by the force of the current, were stopped by the horse and taken up, and not a man perished. His army being safe on the opposite bank, he drew out his forces and resolved to lead them forward in three battalions: and so great was the ardour of the soldiers that, notwithstanding the addition of a circuit of six miles and a considerable delay in fording the river, before the ninth hour of the day they came up with those who had set out at the third watch.
LXV.—When Afranius, who was in company with Petreius, saw them at a distance, being affrighted at so unexpected a sight, he halted on a rising ground and drew up his army. Caesar refreshed his army on the

plain that he might not expose them to battle whilst fatigued; and when the enemy attempted to renew their march, he pursued and stopped them. They were obliged to pitch their camp sooner than they had intended, for there were mountains at a small distance; and difficult and narrow roads awaited them about five miles off. They retired behind these mountains that they might avoid Caesar's cavalry, and, placing parties in the narrow roads, stop the progress of his army and lead their own forces across the Ebro without danger or apprehension. This it was their interest to attempt and to effect by any means possible; but, fatigued by the skirmishes all day, and by the labour of their march, they deferred it till the following day: Caesar likewise encamped on the next hill.

LXVI.—About midnight a few of their men who had gone some distance from the camp to fetch water, being taken by our horse, Caesar is informed by them that the generals of the enemy were drawing their troops out of the camp without noise. Upon this information Caesar ordered the signal to be given and the military shout to be raised for packing up the baggage. When they heard the shout, being afraid lest they should be stopped in the night and obliged to engage under their baggage, or lest they should be confined in the narrow roads by Caesar's horse, they put a stop to their march and kept their forces in their camp. The next day Petreius went out privately with a few horse to reconnoitre the country. A similar movement was made from Caesar's camp. Lucius Decidius Saxa was detached with a small party to explore the nature of the country. Each returned with the same account to his camp, that there was a level road for the next five miles, that there then succeeded a rough and mountainous country. Whichever should first obtain possession of the defiles would have no trouble in preventing the other's progress.

LXVII.—There was a debate in the council between Afranius and Petreius, and the time of marching was the subject. The majority were of opinion that they should begin their march at night, "for they might reach the defiles before they should be discovered." Others, because a shout had been raised the night before in Caesar's camp, used this as an argument that they could not leave the camp unnoticed: "that Caesar's cavalry were patrolling the whole night, and that all the ways and roads were beset; that battles at night ought to be avoided, because in civil dissension, a soldier once daunted is more apt to consult his fears than his oath; that the daylight raised a strong sense of shame in the eyes of all, and that the presence of the tribunes and centurions had the same effect: by these things the soldiers would be re strained and awed to their duty. Wherefore they should, by all means, attempt to force their way by day; for, though a trifling loss might be sustained, yet the post which they desired might be secured with safety to the main body of the army." This opinion prevailed in the council, and the next day, at the dawn, they resolved to set forward.

LXVIII.—Caesar, having taken a view of the country, the moment the sky began to grow white, led his forces from the camp and marched at the head of his army by a long circuit, keeping to no regular road; for the road which led to the Ebro and Octogesa was occupied by the enemy's camp, which lay in Caesar's way. His soldiers were obliged to cross extensive and difficult valleys. Craggy cliffs, in several places, interrupted their march, insomuch that their arms had to be handed to one another, and the soldiers were forced to perform a great part of their march unarmed, and were lifted up the rocks by each other. But not a man murmured at the fatigue, because they imagined that there would be a period to all their toils if they could cut off the enemy from the Ebro and intercept their convoys.

LXIX.—At first, Afranius's soldiers ran in high spirits from their camp to look at us, and in contumelious language upbraided us, "that we were forced, for want of necessary subsistence, to run away, and return to Ilerda." For our route was different from what we proposed, and we appeared to be going a contrary way. But their generals applauded their own prudence in keeping within their camp, and it was a strong confirmation of their opinion, that they saw we marched without waggons or baggage, which made them confident that we could not long endure want. But when they saw our army gradually wheel to the right, and observed our van was already passing the line of their camp, there was nobody so stupid, or averse to fatigue, as not to think it necessary to march from the camp immediately, and oppose us. The cry to arms was raised, and all the army, except a few which were left to guard the camp, set out and marched the direct road to the Ebro.

LXX.—The contest depended entirely on despatch, which should first get possession of the defile and the mountain. The difficulty of the roads delayed Caesar's army, but his cavalry pursuing Afranius's forces, retarded their march. However, the affair was necessarily reduced to this point, with respect to Afranius's men, that if they first gained the mountains, which they desired, they would themselves avoid all danger, but could not save the baggage of their whole army, nor the cohorts which they had left behind in the camps, to which, being intercepted by Caesar's army, by no means could assistance be given. Caesar first accomplished the march, and having found a plain behind large rocks, drew up his army there in order of battle and facing the enemy. Afranius, perceiving that his rear was galled by our cavalry, and seeing the enemy before him, having come to a hill, made a halt on it. Thence he detached four cohorts of Spanish light infantry to the highest mountain which was in view: to this he ordered them to hasten with all expedition, and to take possession of it, with the intention of going to the same place with all his forces, then altering his route, and crossing the hills to Octogesa. As the Spaniards were making towards it in an oblique direction, Caesar's horse espied them and attacked them, nor were they able to withstand the charge of the cavalry even for a moment, but were all surrounded and cut to pieces in the sight of the two armies.

LXXI.—There was now an opportunity for managing affairs successfully, nor did it escape Caesar, that an army daunted at suffering such a loss before their eyes, could not stand, especially as they were surrounded by our horse, and the engagement would take place on even and open ground. To this he was importuned on all sides. The lieutenants, centurions, and tribunes, gathered round him, and begged "that he would not hesitate to begin the battle: that the hearts of all the soldiers were very anxious for it: that Afranius's men had by several circumstances betrayed signs of fear; in that they had not assisted their party; in that they had not quitted the hill; in that they did not sustain the charge of our cavalry, but crowding their standards into one place, did not observe either rank or order. But if he had any apprehensions from the disadvantage of the ground, that an opportunity would be given him of coming to battle in some other place: for that Afranius must certainly come down, and would not be able to remain there for want of water."

LXXII.—Caesar had conceived hopes of ending the affair without an engagement, or without striking a blow, because he had cut off the enemy's supplies. Why should he hazard the loss of any of his men, even in a successful battle? Why should he expose soldiers to be wounded; who had deserved so well of him? Why, in short, should he tempt fortune? especially when it was as much a general's duty to conquer by tactics, as by the sword. Besides, he was moved with compassion for those citizens, who, he foresaw, must fall: and he had rather gain his object without any loss or injury to them. This resolution of Caesar was not generally approved of; but the soldiers openly declared to each other, that since such an opportunity of victory was let pass, they would not come to an engagement, even when Caesar should wish it. He persevered however in his resolution, and retired a little from that place to abate the enemy's fears. Petreius and Afranius, having got this opportunity, retired to their camp. Caesar, having disposed parties on the mountains, and cut off all access to the Ebro, fortified his camp as close to the enemy as he could.

LXXIII.—The day following, the generals of his opponents, being alarmed that they had lost all prospect of supplies, and of access to the

Ebro, consulted as to what other course they should take. There were two roads, one to Ilerda, if they chose to return, the other to Tarraco, if they should march to it. Whilst they were deliberating on these matters, intelligence was brought them that their watering parties were attacked by our horse: upon which information, they dispose several parties of horse and auxiliary foot along the road, and intermix some legionary cohorts, and begin to throw up a rampart from the camp to the water, that they might be able to procure water within their lines, both without fear, and without a guard. Petreius and Afranius divided this task between themselves, and went in person to some distance from their camp for the purpose of seeing it accomplished.

LXXIV.—The soldiers having obtained by their absence a free opportunity of conversing with each other, came out in great numbers, and inquired each for whatever acquaintance or fellow citizen he had in our camp, and invited him to him. First they returned them general thanks for sparing them the day before, when they were greatly terrified, and acknowledged that they were alive through their kindness; then they inquired about the honour of our general, and whether they could with safety entrust themselves to him; and declared their sorrow that they had not done so in the beginning, and that they had taken up arms against their relations and kinsmen. Encouraged by these conferences, they desired the general's parole for the lives of Petreius and Afranius, that they might not appear guilty of a crime, in having betrayed their generals. When they were assured of obtaining their demands, they promised that they would immediately remove their standards, and sent centurions of the first rank as deputies to treat with Caesar about a peace. In the meantime some of them invite their acquaintances, and bring them to their camp, others are brought away by their friends, so that the two camps seemed to be united into one, and several of the tribunes and centurions came to Caesar, and paid their respects to him. The same was done by some of the nobility of Spain, whom they summoned to their assistance, and kept in their camp as hostages. They inquired after their acquaintance and friends, by whom each might have the means of being recommended to Caesar. Even Afranius's son, a young man, endeavoured by means of Sulpitius the lieutenant, to make terms for his own and his father's life. Every place was filled with mirth and congratulations; in the one army, because they thought they had escaped so impending danger; in the other, because they thought they had completed so important a matter without blows; and Caesar, in every man's judgment, reaped the advantage of his former lenity, and his conduct was applauded by all.

LXXV.—When these circumstances were announced to Afranius, he left the work which he had begun, and returned to his camp determined,

as it appeared, whatever should be the event to bear it with an even and steady mind. Petreius did not neglect himself; he armed his domestics; with them and the praetorian cohort of Spaniards, and a few foreign horse, his dependants, whom he commonly kept near him to guard his person, he suddenly flew to the rampart, interrupted the conferences of the soldiers, drove our men from the camp, and put to death as many as he caught. The rest formed into a body, and, being alarmed by the unexpected danger, wrapped their left arms in their cloaks, and drew their swords, and in this manner, depending on the nearness of their camp, defended themselves against the Spaniards, and the horse, and made good their retreat to the camp, where they were protected by the cohorts, which were on guard.
LXXVI.—Petreius, after accomplishing this, went round every maniple, calling the soldiers by their names and entreating with tears, that they would not give up him and their absent general Pompey, as a sacrifice to the vengeance of their enemies. Immediately they ran in crowds to the general's pavilion, when he required them all to take an oath that they would not desert nor betray the army nor the generals, nor form any design distinct from the general interest. He himself swore first to the tenor of those words, and obliged Afranius to take the same oath. The tribunes and centurions followed their example; the soldiers were brought out by centuries, and took the same oath. They gave orders, that whoever had any of Caesar's soldiers should produce them; as soon as they were produced, they put them to death publicly in the praetorium, but most of them concealed those that they had entertained, and let them out at night over the rampart. Thus the terror raised by the generals, the cruelty of the punishments, the new obligation of an oath, removed all hopes of surrender for the present, changed the soldiers' minds, and reduced matters to the former state of war.
LXXVII.—Caesar ordered the enemy's soldiers, who had come into his camp to hold a conference, to be searched for with the strictest diligence, and sent back. But of the tribunes and centurions, several voluntarily remained with him, and he afterwards treated them with great respect. The centurions he promoted to higher ranks, and conferred on the Roman knights the honour of tribunes.
LXXVIII.—Afranius's men were distressed in foraging, and procured water with difficulty. The legionary soldiers had a tolerable supply of corn, because they had been ordered to bring from Ilerda sufficient to last twenty-two days; the Spanish and auxiliary forces had none, for they had but few opportunities of procuring any, and their bodies were not accustomed to bear burdens; and therefore a great number of them came over to Caesar every day. Their affairs were under these

difficulties; but of the two schemes proposed, the most expedient seemed to be to return to Ilerda, because they had left some corn there; and there they hoped to decide on a plan for their future conduct. Tarraco lay at a greater distance; and in such a space they knew affairs might admit of many changes. Their design having met with approbation, they set out from their camp. Caesar having sent forward his cavalry, to annoy and retard their rear, followed close after with his legions. Not a moment passed in which their rear was not engaged with our horse.

LXXIX.—Their manner of fighting was this: the light cohorts closed their rear, and frequently made a stand on the level grounds. If they had a mountain to ascend, the very nature of the place readily secured them from any danger; for the advanced guards, from the rising grounds, protected the rest in their ascent. When they approached a valley or declivity, and the advanced men could not impart assistance to the tardy, our horse threw their darts at them from the rising grounds with advantage; then their affairs were in a perilous situation; the only plan left was, that whenever they came near such places, they should give orders to the legions to halt, and by a violent effort repulse our horse; and these being forced to give way, they should suddenly, with the utmost speed, run all together down to the valley, and having passed it, should face about again on the next hill. For so far were they from deriving any assistance from their horse (of which they had a large number), that they were obliged to receive them into the centre of their army, and themselves protect them, as they were daunted by former battles. And on their march no one could quit the line without being taken by Caesar's horse.

LXXX.—Whilst skirmishes were fought in this manner, they advanced but slowly and gradually, and frequently halted to help their rear, as then happened. For having advanced four miles, and being very much harassed by our horse, they took post on a high mountain, and there entrenched themselves on the front only, facing the enemy; and did not take their baggage off their cattle. When they perceived that Caesar's camp was pitched, and the tents fixed up, and his horse sent out to forage, they suddenly rushed out about twelve o'clock the same day, and, having hopes that we should be delayed by the absence of our horse, they began to march, which Caesar perceiving, followed them with the legions that remained. He left a few cohorts to guard his baggage, and ordered the foragers to be called home at the tenth hour, and the horse to follow him. The horse shortly returned to their daily duty on march, and charged the rear so vigorously, that they almost forced them to fly; and several privates and some centurions were

killed. The main body of Caesar's army was at hand, and universal ruin threatened them.
LXXXI.—Then indeed, not having opportunity either to choose a convenient position for their camp, or to march forward, they were obliged to halt, and to encamp at a distance from water, and on ground naturally unfavourable. But for the reasons already given, Caesar did not attack them, nor suffer a tent to be pitched that day, that his men might be the readier to pursue them whether they attempted to run off by night or by day. Observing the defect in their position, they spent the whole night in extending their works, and turn their camp to ours. The next day, at dawn, they do the same, and spend the whole day in that manner, but in proportion as they advanced their works, and extended their camp, they were farther distant from the water; and one evil was remedied by another. The first night, no one went out for water. The next day, they left a guard in the camp, and led out all their forces to water: but not a person was sent to look for forage. Caesar was more desirous that they should be humbled by these means, and forced to come to terms, than decide the contest by battle. Yet he endeavoured to surround them with a wall and trench, that he might be able to check their most sudden sally, to which he imagined that they must have recourse. Hereupon, urged by want of fodder, that they might be the readier for a march, they killed all their baggage cattle.
LXXXII.—In this work, and the deliberations on it, two days were spent. By the third day a considerable part of Caesar's works was finished. To interrupt his progress, they drew out their legions about the eighth hour, by a certain signal, and placed them in order of battle before their camp. Caesar calling his legions off from their work, and ordering the horse to hold themselves in readiness, marshalled his army: for to appear to decline an engagement contrary to the opinion of the soldiers and the general voice, would have been attended with great disadvantage. But for the reasons already known, he was dissuaded from wishing to engage, and the more especially, because the short space between the camps, even if the enemy were put to flight, would not contribute much to a decisive victory; for the two camps were not distant from each other above two thousand feet. Two parts of this were occupied by the armies, and one third left for the soldiers to charge and make their attack. If a battle should be begun, the nearness of the camps would afford a ready retreat to the conquered party in the flight. For this reason Caesar had resolved to make resistance, if they attacked him, but not to be the first to provoke the battle.
LXXXIII.—Afranius's five legions were drawn up in two lines, the auxiliary cohorts formed the third line, and acted as reserves. Caesar had three lines, four cohorts out of each of the five legions formed the

first line. Three more from each legion followed them, as reserves: and three others were behind these. The slingers and archers were stationed in the centre of the line; the cavalry closed the flanks. The hostile armies being arranged in this manner, each seemed determined to adhere to his first intention: Caesar not to hazard a battle, unless forced to it; Afranius to interrupt Caesar's works. However, the matter was deferred, and both armies kept under arms till sunset; when they both returned to their camp. The next day Caesar prepared to finish the works which he had begun. The enemy attempted to pass the river Segre by a ford. Caesar, having perceived this, sent some light-armed Germans and a party of horse across the river, and disposed several parties along the banks to guard them.

LXXXIV.—At length, beset on all sides, their cattle having been four days without fodder, and having no water, wood, or corn, they beg a conference; and that, if possible, in a place remote from the soldiers. When this was refused by Caesar, but a public interview offered if they chose it, Afranius's son was given as a hostage to Caesar. They met in the place appointed by Caesar. In the hearing of both armies, Afranius spoke thus: "That Caesar ought not to be displeased either with him or his soldiers, for wishing to preserve their attachment to their general, Cneius Pompey. That they had now sufficiently discharged their duty to him, and had suffered punishment enough, in having endured the want of every necessary: but now, pent up almost like wild beasts, they were prevented from procuring water, and prevented from walking abroad; and were not able to bear the bodily pain or the mental disgrace: but confessed themselves vanquished: and begged and entreated, if there was any room left for mercy, that they should not be necessitated to suffer the most severe penalties." These sentiments were delivered in the most submissive and humble language.

LXXXV.—Caesar replied, "That either to complain or sue for mercy became no man less than him: for that every other person had done their duty: himself, in having declined to engage on favourable terms, in an advantageous situation and time, that all things tending to a peace might be totally unembarrassed: his army, in having preserved and protected the men whom they had in their power, notwithstanding the injuries which they had received, and the murder of their comrades; and even Afranius's soldiers, who of themselves treated about concluding a peace, by which they thought that they would secure the lives of all. Thus, that the parties on both sides inclined to mercy: that the generals only were averse to peace: that they paid no regard to the laws either of conference or truce; and had most inhumanly put to death ignorant persons, who were deceived by a conference: that therefore, they had met that fate which usually befalls men from excessive obstinacy and arrogance; and were obliged to have recourse, and most earnestly desire that which they had shortly before disdained. That for his part, he would not avail himself of their present humiliation, or his present advantage, to require terms by which his power might be increased, but only that those armies, which they had maintained for so many years to oppose him, should be disbanded: for six legions had been sent into Spain, and a seventh raised there, and many and powerful fleets provided, and generals of great military experience sent to command them, for no other purpose than to oppose him; that none of these measures were adopted to keep the Spains in peace, or for the use of the province, which, from the length of the peace, stood in need of no such aid; that all these things were long since designed against him: that against him a new sort of government was established, that the same person should be at the gates of Rome, to direct the affairs of the city; and though absent, have the government of two most warlike provinces for so many years: that against him the laws of the magistrates had been altered; that the late praetors and consuls should not be sent to govern the provinces as had been the constant custom, but persons approved of and chosen by a faction. That against him the excuse of age was not admitted: but persons of tried experience in former wars were called up to take the command of the armies, that with respect to him only, the routine was not observed which had been allowed to all generals, that, after a successful war, they should return home and disband their armies, if not with some mark of honour, at least without disgrace: that he had submitted to all these things patiently, and would still submit to them: nor did he now desire to take their army from them and keep it to himself (which, however, would not be a difficult matter), but only that they should not have it to employ against him: and therefore, as he said before, let them quit the provinces, and disband their army. If this was complied with, he would injure no person; that these were the last and only conditions of peace."

LXXXVI.—It was very acceptable and agreeable to Afranius's soldiers, as might be easily known from their signs of joy, that they who expected some injury after this defeat, should obtain without solicitation the reward of a dismissal. For when a debate was introduced about the place and time of their dismissal, they all began to express, both by words and signs, from the rampart where they stood, that they should be discharged immediately: for although every security might be given that they would be disbanded, still the matter would be uncertain, if it was deferred to a future day. After a short debate on either side, it was brought to this issue: that those who had any settlement or possession in Spain, should be immediately discharged: the rest at the river Var. Caesar gave security that they should receive no damage, and that no person should be obliged against his inclination to take the military oath under him.

LXXXVII.—Caesar promised to supply them with corn from the present time, till they arrived at the river Var. He further adds, that whatever any of them lost in the war, which was in the possession of his soldiers, should be restored to those that lost them. To his soldiers he made a recompense in money for those things, a just valuation being made. Whatever disputes Afranius's soldiers had afterwards amongst themselves, they voluntarily submitted to Caesar's decision. Afranius and Petreius, when pay was demanded by the legions, a sedition almost breaking out, asserted that the time had not yet come, and required that Caesar should take cognizance of it: and both parties were content with his decision. About a third part of their army being dismissed in two days, Caesar ordered two of his legions to go before, the rest to follow the vanquished enemy: that they should encamp at a small distance from each other. The execution of this business he gave in charge to Quintus Fufius Kalenus, one of his lieutenants. According to his directions, they marched from Spain to the river Var, and there the rest of the army was disbanded.

BOOK II

I.—Whilst these things were going forward in Spain, Caius Trebonius, Caesar's lieutenant, who had been left to conduct the assault of Massilia, began to raise a mound, vineae, and turrets against the town, on two sides: one of which was next the harbour and docks, the other on that part where there is a passage from Gaul and Spain to that sea which forces itself up the mouth of the Rhone. For Massilia is washed almost on three sides by the sea, the remaining fourth part is the only side which has access by land. A part even of this space, which reaches to the fortress, being fortified by the nature of the country, and a very deep valley, required a long and difficult siege. To accomplish these works, Caius Trebonius sends for a great quantity of carriages and men from the whole Province, and orders hurdles and materials to be furnished. These things being provided, he raised a mound eighty feet in height.

II.—But so great a store of everything necessary for a war had been a long time before laid up in the town, and so great a number of engines, that no vineae made of hurdles could withstand their force. For poles twelve feet in length, pointed with iron, and these too shot from very large engines, sank into the ground through four rows of hurdles. Therefore the arches of the vineae were covered over with beams a foot thick, fastened together, and under this the materials of the agger were handed from one to another. Before this was carried a testudo sixty feet long, for levelling the ground, made also of very strong timber, and covered over with every thing that was capable of protecting it against the fire and stones thrown by the enemy. But the greatness of the works, the height of the wall and towers, and the multitude of engines retarded the progress of our works. Besides, frequent sallies were made from the town by the Albici, and fire was thrown on our mound and turrets. These our men easily repulsed, and, doing considerable damage to those who sallied, beat them back into the town.

III.—In the meantime, Lucius Nasidius, being sent by Cneius Pompey with a fleet of sixteen sail, a few of which had beaks of brass, to the assistance of Lucius Domitius and the Massilians, passed the straits of Sicily without the knowledge or expectation of Curio, and, putting with his fleet into Messana, and making the nobles and senate take flight with the sudden terror, carried off one of their ships out of dock. Having joined this to his other ships, he made good his voyage to Massilia, and, having sent in a galley privately, acquaints Domitius and the Massilians of his arrival, and earnestly encourages them to hazard another battle with Brutus's fleet with the addition of his aid.

IV.—The Massilians, since their former loss, had brought the same number of old ships from the docks, and had repaired and fitted them out with great industry: they had a large supply of seamen and pilots. They had got several fishing-smacks, and covered them over, that the seamen might be secure against darts: these they filled with archers and engines. With a fleet thus appointed, encouraged by the entreaties and tears of all the old men, matrons, and virgins to succour the state in this hour of distress, they went on board with no less spirit and confidence than they had fought before. For it happens, from a common infirmity of human nature, that we are more flushed with confidence, or more vehemently alarmed at things unseen, concealed, and unknown, as was the case then. For the arrival of Lucius Nasidius had filled the state with the most sanguine hopes and wishes. Having got a fair wind, they sailed out of port and went to Nasidius to Taurois, which is a fort belonging to the Massilians, and there ranged their fleet and again encouraged each other to engage, and communicated their plan of operation. The command of the right division was given to the Massilians, that of the left to Nasidius.

V.—Brutus sailed to the same place with an augmented fleet: for to those made by Caesar at Arelas were added six ships taken from the Massilians, which he had refitted since the last battle and had furnished with every necessary. Accordingly, having encouraged his men to despise a vanquished people whom they had conquered when yet unbroken, he advanced against them full of confidence and spirit. From Trebonius's camp and all the higher grounds it was easy to see into the town—how all the youth which remained in it, and all persons of more advanced years, with their wives and children, and the public guards, were either extending their hands from the wall to the heavens, or were repairing to the temples of the immortal gods, and, prostrating themselves before their images, were entreating them to grant them victory. Nor was there a single person who did not imagine that his future fortune depended on the issue of that day; for the choice of their youth and the most respectable of every age, being expressly invited and solicited, had gone on board the fleet, that if any adverse fate should befall them they might see that nothing was left for them to attempt, and, if they proved victorious, they might have hopes of preserving the city, either by their internal resources or by foreign assistance.

VI-.-When the battle was begun, no effort of valour was wanting to the Massilians, but, mindful of the instructions which they had a little before received from their friends, they fought with such spirit as if they supposed that they would never have another opportunity to attempt a defence, and as if they believed that those whose lives should be endangered in the battle would not long precede the fate of the rest of the citizens, who, if the city was taken, must undergo the same fortune of war. Our ships being at some distance from each other, room was allowed both for the skill of their pilots and the manoeuvring of their ships; and if at any time ours, gaining an advantage by casting the iron hooks on board their ships, grappled with them, from all parts they assisted those who were distressed. Nor, after being joined by the Albici, did they decline coming to close engagement, nor were they much inferior to our men in valour. At the same time, showers of darts, thrown from a distance from the lesser ships, suddenly inflicted several wounds on our men when off their guard and otherwise engaged; and two of their three-decked galleys, having descried the ship of Decimus Brutus, which could be easily distinguished by its flag, rowed up against him with great violence from opposite sides: but Brutus, seeing into their designs, by the swiftness of his ship extricated himself with such address as to get clear, though only by a moment. From the velocity of their motion they struck against each other with such violence that they were both excessively injured by the shock; the beak, indeed, of one of them being broken off, the whole ship was ready to founder, which circumstance being observed, the ships of Brutus's fleet, which were nearest that station, attack them when in this disorder and sink them both.

VII.—But Nasidius's ships were of no use, and soon left the fight; for the sight of their country, or the entreaties of their relations, did not urge them to run a desperate risk of their lives. Therefore, of the number of the ships not one was lost: of the fleet of the Massilians five were sunk, four taken, and one ran off with Nasidius: all that escaped made the best of their way to Hither Spain, but one of the rest was sent forward to Massilia for the purpose of bearing this intelligence, and when it came near the city, the whole people crowded out to hear the tidings, and on being informed of the event, were so oppressed with grief, that one would have imagined that the city had been taken by an enemy at the same moment. The Massilians, however, began to make the necessary preparations for the defence of their city with unwearied energy.

VIII.—The legionary soldiers who had the management of the works on the right side observed, from the frequent sallies of the enemy, that it might prove a great protection to them to build a turret of brick under the wall for a fort and place of refuge, which they at first built low and small, [to guard them] against sudden attacks. To it they retreated, and from it they made defence if any superior force attacked them; and from it they sallied out either to repel or pursue the enemy. It extended thirty feet on every side, and the thickness of the walls was five feet. But afterwards, as experience is the best master in everything on which the wit of man is employed, it was found that it might be of

considerable service if it was raised to the usual height of turrets, which was effected in the following manner.
IX.-When the turret was raised to the height for flooring, they laid it on the walls in such a manner that the ends of the joists were covered by the outer face of the wall, that nothing should project to which the enemy's fire might adhere. They, moreover, built over the joists with small bricks as high as the protection of the plutei and vineae permitted them; and on that place they laid two beams across, angle-ways, at a small distance from the outer walls, to support the rafters which were to cover the turret, and on the beams they laid joists across in a direct line, and on these they fastened down planks. These joists they made somewhat longer, to project beyond the outside of the wall, that they might serve to hang a curtain on them to defend and repel all blows whilst they were building the walls between that and the next floor, and the floor of this story they faced with bricks and mortar, that the enemy's fire might do them no damage; and on this they spread mattresses, lest the weapons thrown from engines should break through the flooring, or stones from catapults should batter the brickwork. They, moreover, made three mats of cable ropes, each of them the length of the turret walls, and four feet broad, and, hanging them round the turret on the three sides which faced the enemy, fastened them to the projecting joists. For this was the only sort of defence which, they had learned by experience in other places, could not be pierced by darts or engines. But when that part of the turret which was completed was protected and secured against every attempt of the enemy, they removed the plutei to other works. They began to suspend gradually, and raise by screws from the first-floor, the entire roof of the turret, and then they elevated it as high as the length of the mats allowed. Hid and secured within these coverings, they built up the walls with bricks, and again, by another turn of the screw, cleared a place for themselves to proceed with the building; and, when they thought it time to lay another floor, they laid the ends of the beams, covered in by the outer bricks in like manner as in the first story, and from that story they again raised the uppermost floor and the mat-work. In this manner, securely and without a blow or danger, they raised it six stories high, and in laying the materials left loop-holes in such places as they thought proper for working their engines.
X.—When they were confident that they could protect the works which lay around from this turret, they resolved to build a musculus, sixty feet long, of timber, two feet square, and to extend it from the brick tower to the enemy's tower and wall. This was the form of it: two beams of equal length were laid on the ground, at the distance of four feet from each other; and in them were fastened small pillars, five feet high,

which were joined together by braces, with a gentle slope, on which the timber which they must place to support the roof of the musculus should be laid: upon this were laid beams, two feet square, bound with iron plates and nails. To the upper covering of the musculus and the upper beams, they fastened laths, four fingers square, to support the tiles which were to cover the musculus. The roof being thus sloped and laid over in rows in the same manner as the joists were laid on the braces, the musculus was covered with tiles and mortar, to secure it against fire, which might be thrown from the wall. Over the tiles hides are spread, to prevent the water let in on them by spouts from dissolving the cement of the bricks. Again, the hides were covered over with mattresses, that they might not be destroyed by fire or stones. The soldiers under the protection of the vineae, finish this whole work to the very tower, and suddenly, before the enemy were aware of it, moved it forward by naval machinery, by putting rollers under it, close up to the enemy's turret, so that it even touched the building.

XI.—The townsmen, affrighted at this unexpected stroke, bring forward with levers the largest stones they can procure; and pitching them from the wall, roll them down on the musculus. The strength of the timber withstood the shock; and whatever fell on it slid off, on account of the sloping roof. When they perceived this, they altered their plan and set fire to barrels, filled with resin and tar, and rolled them down from the wall on the musculus. As soon as they fell on it, they slid off again, and were removed from its side by long poles and forks. In the meantime, the soldiers, under cover of the musculus, were looting out with crowbars the lowest stones of the enemy's turret, with which the foundation was laid. The musculus was defended by darts, thrown from engines by our men from the brick tower, and the enemy were beaten off from the wall and turrets; nor was a fair opportunity of defending the walls given them. At length several stones being picked away from the foundation of that turret next the musculus, part of it fell down suddenly, and the rest, as if following it, leaned forward.

XII.—Hereupon, the enemy, distressed at the sudden fall of the turret, surprised at the unforeseen calamity, awed by the wrath of the gods, and dreading the pillage of their city, rush all together out of the gate unarmed, with their temples bound with fillets, and suppliantly stretch out their hands to the officers and the army. At this uncommon occurrence, the whole progress of the war was stopped, and the soldiers, turning away from the battle, ran eagerly to hear and listen to them. When the enemy came up to the commanders and the army, they all fell down at their feet, and besought them "to wait till Caesar's arrival; they saw that their city was taken, our works completed, and their tower undermined, therefore they desisted from a defence; that no

obstacle could arise, to prevent their being instantly plundered at a beck, as soon as he arrived, if they refused to submit to his orders." They inform them that, "if the turret had entirely fallen down, the soldiers could not be withheld from forcing into the town and sacking it, in hopes of getting spoil." These and several other arguments to the same effect were delivered, as they were a people of great learning, with great pathos and lamentations.
XIII.—The lieutenants, moved with compassion, draw off the soldiers from the work, desist from the assault, and leave sentinels on the works. A sort of a truce having been made through compassion for the besieged, the arrival of Caesar is anxiously awaited; not a dart was thrown from the walls or by our men, but all remit their care and diligence, as if the business was at an end. For Caesar had given Trebonius strict charge not to suffer the town to be taken by storm, lest the soldiers, too much irritated both by abhorrence of their revolt, by the contempt shown to them, and by their long labour, should put to the sword all the grown-up inhabitants, as they threatened to do. And it was with difficulty that they were then restrained from breaking into the town, and they were much displeased, because they imagined that they were prevented by Trebonius from taking possession of it.
XIV.—But the enemy, destitute of all honour, only waited a time and opportunity for fraud and treachery. And after an interval of some days, when our men were careless and negligent, on a sudden, at noon, when some were dispersed, and others indulging themselves in rest on the very works, after the fatigue of the day, and their arms were all laid by and covered up, they sallied out from the gates, and, the wind being high and favourable to them, they set fire to our works; and the wind spread it in such a manner that, in the same instant, the agger, plutei, testudo, tower, and engines all caught the flames and were consumed before we could conceive how it had occurred. Our men, alarmed at such an unexpected turn of fortune, lay hold on such arms as they could find. Some rush from the camp; an attack is made on the enemy: but they were prevented, by arrows and engines from the walls, from pursuing them when they fled. They retired to their walls, and there, without fear, set the musculus and brick tower on fire. Thus, by the perfidy of the enemy and the violence of the storm, the labour of many months was destroyed in a moment. The Massilians made the same attempt the next day, having got such another storm. They sallied out against the other tower and agger, and fought with more confidence. But as our men had on the former occasion given up all thoughts of a contest, so, warned by the event of the preceding day, they had made every preparation for a defence. Accordingly, they slew several, and forced the rest to retreat into the town without effecting their design.

XV.—Trebonius began to provide and repair what had been destroyed, with much greater zeal on the part of the soldiers; for when they saw that their extraordinary pains and preparations had an unfortunate issue, they were fired with indignation that, in consequence of the impious violation of the truce, their valour should be held in derision. There was no place left them from which the materials for their mound could be fetched, in consequence of all the timber, far and wide, in the territories of the Massilians, having been cut down and carried away; they began therefore to make an agger of a new construction, never heard of before, of two walls of brick, each six feet thick, and to lay floors over them of almost the same breadth with the agger, made of timber. But wherever the space between the walls, or the weakness of the timber, seemed to require it, pillars were placed underneath and traversed beams laid on to strengthen the work, and the space which was floored was covered over with hurdles, and the hurdles plastered over with mortar. The soldiers, covered overhead by the floor, on the right and left by the wall, and in the front by the mantlets, carried whatever materials were necessary for the building without danger: the business was soon finished—the loss of their laborious work was soon repaired by the dexterity and fortitude of the soldiers. Gates for making sallies were left in the wall in such places as they thought proper.
XVI.—But when the enemy perceived that those works, which they had hoped could not be replaced without a great length of time, were put into so thorough repair by a few days' labour and diligence, that there was no room for perfidy or sallies, and that no means were left them by which they could either hurt the men by resistance or the works by fire, and when they found by former examples that their town could be surrounded with a wall and turrets on every part by which it was accessible by land, in such a manner that they could not have room to stand on their own fortifications, because our works were built almost on the top of their walls by our army, and darts could be thrown from our hands, and when they perceived that all advantage arising from their engines, on which they had built great hopes, was totally lost, and that though they had an opportunity of fighting with us on equal terms from walls and turrets, they could perceive that they were not equal to our men in bravery, they had recourse to the same proposals of surrender as before.
XVII.—In Further Spain, Marcus Varro, in the beginning of the disturbances, when he heard of the circumstances which took place in Italy, being diffident of Pompey's success, used to speak in a very friendly manner of Caesar. That though, being pre-engaged to Cneius Pompey in quality of lieutenant, he was bound in honour to him, that, nevertheless, there existed a very intimate tie between him and Caesar;

that he was not ignorant of what was the duty of a lieutenant, who bore an office of trust; nor of his own strength, nor of the disposition of the whole province to Caesar. These sentiments he constantly expressed in his ordinary conversation, and did not attach himself to either party. But afterwards, when he found that Caesar was detained before Massilia, that the forces of Petreius had effected a junction with the army of Afranius, that considerable reinforcements had come to their assistance, that there were great hopes and expectations, and heard that the whole Hither province had entered into a confederacy, and of the difficulties to which Caesar was reduced afterwards at Ilerda for want of provisions, and Afranius wrote to him a fuller and more exaggerated account of these matters, he began to regulate his movements by those of fortune.

XVIII.—He made levies throughout the province; and, having completed his two legions, he added to them about thirty auxiliary cohorts: he collected a large quantity of corn to send partly to the Massilians, partly to Afranius and Petreius. He commanded the inhabitants of Gades to build ten ships of war; besides, he took care that several others should be built in Spain. He removed all the money and ornaments from the temple of Hercules to the town of Gades, and sent six cohorts thither from the province to guard them, and gave the command of the town of Gades to Caius Gallonius, a Roman knight, and friend of Domitius, who had come thither sent by Domitius to recover an estate for him; and he deposited all the arms, both public and private, in Gallonius's house. He himself [Varro] made severe harangues against Caesar. He often pronounced from his tribunal that Caesar had fought several unsuccessful battles, and that a great number of his men had deserted to Afranius. That he had these accounts from undoubted messengers, and authority on which he could rely. By these means he terrified the Roman citizens of that province, and obliged them to promise him for the service of the state one hundred and ninety thousand sesterces, twenty thousand pounds weight of silver, and a hundred and twenty thousand bushels of wheat. He laid heavier burdens on those states which he thought were friendly disposed to Caesar, and billeted troops on them; he passed judgment against some private persons, and condemned to confiscation the properties of those who had spoken or made orations against the republic, and forced the whole province to take an oath of allegiance to him and Pompey. Being informed of all that happened in Hither Spain, he prepared for war. This was his plan of operations. He was to retire with his two legions to Gades, and to lay up all the shipping and provisions there. For he had been informed that the whole province was inclined to favour Caesar's party. He thought that the war might be easily protracted in an island, if he was provided with corn and shipping. Caesar, although called back to Italy by many and important matters, yet had determined to leave no dregs of war behind him in Spain, because he knew that Pompey had many dependants and clients in the Hither province.

XIX.—Having therefore sent two legions into Further Spain under the command of Quintus Cassius, tribune of the people; he himself advances with six hundred horse by forced marches, and issues a proclamation, appointing a day on which the magistrates and nobility of all the states should attend him at Corduba. This proclamation being published through the whole province, there was not a state that did not send a part of their senate to Corduba, at the appointed time; and not a Roman citizen of any note but appeared that day. At the same time the senate at Corduba shut the gates of their own accord against Varro, and posted guards and sentinels on the wall and in the turrets, and detained two cohorts (called Colonicae, which had come there accidentally), for the defence of the town. About the same time the people of Carmona, which is by far the strongest state in the whole province, of themselves drove out of the town the cohorts, and shut the gates against them, although three cohorts had been detached by Varro to garrison the citadel.

XX.—But Varro was in greater haste on this account to reach Gades with his legion as soon as possible, lest he should be stopped either on his march or on crossing over to the island. The affection of the province to Caesar proved so great and so favourable, that he received a letter from Gades, before he was far advanced on his march: that as soon as the nobility of Gades heard of Caesar's proclamation, they had combined with the tribune of the cohorts, which were in garrison there, to drive Gallonius out of the town, and to secure the city and island for Caesar. That having agreed on the design they had sent notice to Gallonius, to quit Gades of his own accord whilst he could do it with safety; if he did not, they would take measures for themselves; that for fear of this Gallonius had been induced to quit the town. When this was known, one of Varro's two legions, which was called Vernacula, carried off the colours from Varro's camp, he himself standing by and looking on, and retired to Hispalis, and took post in the market and public places without doing any injury, and the Roman citizens residing there approved so highly of this act, that every one most earnestly offered to entertain them in their houses. When Varro, terrified at these things, having altered his route, proposed going to Italica, he was informed by his friends that the gates were shut against him. Then indeed, when intercepted from every road, he sends word to Caesar that he was ready to deliver up the legion which he commanded. He sends to him Sextus Caesar, and orders him to deliver it up to him. Varro, having delivered up the legion, went to Caesar to Corduba, and having laid before him the public accounts, handed over to him most faithfully whatever money he had, and told him what quantity of corn and shipping he had, and where.

XXI.—Caesar made a public oration at Corduba, in which he returned thanks to all severally: to the Roman citizens, because they had been zealous to keep the town in their own power; to the Spaniards, for having driven out the garrison; to the Gaditani, for having defeated the attempts of his enemies, and asserted their own liberty; to the Tribunes and Centurions who had gone there as a guard, for having by their valour confirmed them in their purpose. He remitted the tax which the Roman citizens had promised to Varro for the public use: he restored their goods to those who he was informed had incurred that penalty by speaking too freely, having given public and private rewards to some: he filled the rest with flattering hopes of his future intentions; and having stayed two days at Corduba, he set out for Gades: he ordered the money and ornaments which had been carried away from the temple of Hercules, and lodged in the houses of private persons, to be replaced in the temple. He made Quintus Cassius governor of the province, and assigned him four legions. He himself, with those ships which Marcus Varro had built, and others which the Gaditani had built by Varro's orders, arrived in a few days at Tarraco, where ambassadors from the greatest part of the nearer province waited his arrival. Having in the same manner conferred marks of honour both publicly and privately on some states, he left Tarraco, and went thence by land to Narbo, and thence to Massilia. There he was informed that a law was passed for creating a dictator, and that he had been nominated dictator by Marcus Lepidus the praetor.

XXII.—The Massilians, wearied out by misfortunes of every sort, reduced to the lowest ebb for want of corn, conquered in two engagements at sea, defeated in their frequent sallies, and struggling moreover with a fatal pestilence, from their long confinement and change of victuals (for they all subsisted on old millet and damaged barley, which they had formerly provided and laid up in the public stores against an emergency of this kind), their turret being demolished, a great part of their wall having given way, and despairing of any aid, either from the provinces or their armies, for these they had heard had fallen into Caesar's power, resolved to surrender now without dissimulation. But a few days before, Lucius Domitius, having discovered the intention of the Massilians, and having procured three ships, two of which he gave up to his friends, went on board the third himself, having got a brisk wind, put out to sea. Some ships, which by Brutus's orders were constantly cruising near the port, having espied him, weighed anchor, and pursued him. But of these, the ship on board of which he was, persevered itself, and continuing its flight, and by the aid of the wind got out of sight: the other two, affrighted by the approach of our galleys, put back again into the harbour. The Massilians conveyed their arms and engines out of the town, as they were ordered: brought their ships out of the port and docks, and delivered up the money in their treasury. When these affairs were despatched, Caesar, sparing the town more out of regard to their renown and antiquity than to any claim they could lay to his favour, left two legions in garrison there, sent the rest to Italy, and set out himself for Rome.

XXIII.—About the same time Caius Curio, having sailed from Sicily to Africa, and from the first despising the forces of Publius Attius Varus, transported only two of the four legions which he had received from Caesar, and five hundred horse, and having spent two days and three nights on the voyage, arrived at a place called Aquilaria, which is about twenty-two miles distant from Clupea, and in the summer season has a convenient harbour, and is enclosed by two projecting promontories. Lucius Caesar, the son, who was waiting his arrival near Clupea with ten ships which had been taken near Utica in a war with the pirates, and which Publius Attius had had repaired for this war, frightened at the number of our ships, fled the sea, and running his three-decked covered galley on the nearest shore, left her there and made his escape by land to Adrumetum. Caius Considius Longus, with a garrison of one legion, guarded this town. The rest of Caesar's fleet, after his flight, retired to Adrumetum. Marcus Rufus, the quaestor, pursued him with twelve ships, which Curio had brought from Sicily as convoy to the merchantmen, and seeing a ship left on the shore, he brought her off by a towing rope, and returned with his fleet to Curio.

XXIV.—Curio detached Marcus before with the fleet to Utica, and marched thither with his army. Having advanced two days, he came to the river Bagrada, and there left Caius Caninius Rebilus, the lieutenant, with the legions; and went forward himself with the horse to view the Cornelian camp, because that was reckoned a very eligible position for encamping. It is a straight ridge, projecting into the sea, steep and rough on both sides, but the ascent is more gentle on that part which lies opposite Utica. It is not more than a mile distant from Utica in a direct line. But on this road there is a spring, to which the sea comes up, and overflows; an extensive morass is thereby formed; and if a person would avoid it, he must make a circuit of six miles to reach the town.

XXV.—Having examined this place, Curio got a view of Varus's camp, joining the wall and town, at the gate called Bellica, well fortified by its

natural situation, on one side by the town itself, on the other by a theatre which is before the town, the approaches to the town being rendered difficult and narrow by the very extensive out-buildings of that structure. At the same time he observed the roads very full of carriages and cattle which they were conveying from the country into the town on the sudden alarm. He sent his cavalry after them to plunder them and get the spoil. And at the same time Varus had detached as a guard for them six hundred Numidian horse, and four hundred foot, which king Juba had sent to Utica as auxiliaries a few days before. There was a friendship subsisting between his [Juba's] father and Pompey, and a feud between him and Curio, because he, when a tribune of the people, had proposed a law, in which he endeavoured to make public property of the kingdom of Juba. The horse engaged; but the Numidians were not able to stand our first charge; but a hundred and twenty being killed, the rest retreated into their camp near the town. In the meantime, on the arrival of his men-of-war, Curio ordered proclamation to be made to the merchant ships, which lay at anchor before Utica, in number about two hundred, that he would treat as enemies all that did not set sail immediately for the Cornelian camp. As soon as the proclamation was made, in an instant they all weighed anchor and left Utica, and repaired to the place commanded them. This circumstance furnished the army with plenty of everything.
XXVI.—After these transactions, Curio returned to his camp at Bagrada; and by a general shout of the whole army was saluted imperator. The next day he led his army to Utica, and encamped near the town. Before the works of the camp were finished, the horse upon guard brought him word that a large supply of horse and foot sent by king Juba were on their march to Utica, and at the same time a cloud of dust was observed, and in a moment the front of the line was in sight. Curio, surprised at the suddenness of the affair, sent on the horse to receive their first charge, and detain them. He immediately called off his legions from the work, and put them in battle array. The horse began the battle: and before the legions could be completely marshalled and take their ground, the king's entire forces being thrown into disorder and confusion, because they had marched without any order, and were under no apprehensions, betake themselves to flight: almost all the enemy's horse being safe, because they made a speedy retreat into the town along the shore, Caesar's soldiers slay a great number of their infantry.
XXVII.—The next night two Marsian centurions, with twenty-two men belonging to the companies, deserted from Curio's camp to Attius Varus. They, whether they uttered the sentiments which they really entertained, or wished to gratify Varus (for what we wish we readily

give credit to, and what we think ourselves, we hope is the opinion of other men), assured him, that the minds of the whole army were disaffected to Curio, that it was very expedient that the armies should be brought in view of each other, and an opportunity of a conference be given. Induced by their opinion, Varus the next day led his troops out of the camp: Curio did so in like manner, and with only one small valley between them, each drew up his forces.

XXVIII.—In Varus's army there was one Sextus Quintilius Varus who, as we have mentioned before, was at Corfinium. When Caesar gave him his liberty, he went over to Africa; now, Curio had transported to Africa those legions which Caesar had received under his command a short time before at Corfinium: so that the officers and companies were still the same, excepting the change of a few centurions. Quintilius, making this a pretext for addressing them, began to go round Curio's lines, and to entreat the soldiers "not to lose all recollection of the oath which they took first to Domitius and to him their quaestor, nor bear arms against those who had shared the same fortune, and endured the same hardships in a siege, nor fight for those by whom they had been opprobriously called deserters." To this he added a few words by way of encouragement, what they might expect from his own liberality, if they should follow him and Attius. On the delivery of this speech, no intimation of their future conduct is given by Curio's army, and thus both generals led back their troops to their camp.

XXIX.—However, a great and general fear spread through Curio's camp, for it is soon increased by the various discourses of men. For every one formed an opinion of his own; and to what he had heard from others, added his own apprehensions. When this had spread from a single author to several persons, and was handed from one another, there appeared to be many authors for such sentiments as these: ["That it was a civil war; that they were men; and therefore that it was lawful for them to act freely, and follow which party they pleased." These were the legions which a short time before had belonged to the enemy; for the custom of offering free towns to those who joined the opposite party had changed Caesar's kindness. For the harshest expressions of the soldiers in general did not proceed from the Marsi and Peligni, as those which passed in the tents the night before; and some of their fellow soldiers heard them with displeasure. Some additions were also made to them by those who wished to be thought more zealous in their duty.]

XXX.—For these reasons, having called a council, Curio began to deliberate on the general welfare. There were some opinions, which advised by all means an attempt to be made, and an attack on Varus's camp; for when such sentiments prevailed among the soldiers, they thought idleness was improper. In short, they said, "that it was better bravely to try the hazard of war in a battle, than to be deserted and surrounded by their own troops, and forced to submit to the greatest cruelties." There were some who gave their opinion, that they ought to withdraw at the third watch to the Cornelian camp; that by a longer interval of time the soldiers might be brought to a proper way of thinking; and also, that if any misfortune should befall them, they might have a safer and readier retreat to Sicily, from the great number of their ships.

XXXI.—Curio, censuring both measures, said, "that the one was as deficient in spirit, as the other exceeded in it: that the latter advised a shameful flight, and the former recommended us to engage at a great disadvantage. For on what, says he, can we rely that we can storm a camp, fortified both by nature and art? Or, indeed, what advantage do we gain if we give over the assault, after having suffered considerable loss; as if success did not acquire for a general the affection of his army, and misfortune their hatred? But what does a change of camp imply but a shameful flight, and universal despair, and the alienation of the army? For neither ought the obedient to suspect that they are distrusted, nor the insolent to know that we fear them; because our fears augment the licentiousness of the latter, and diminish the zeal of the former. But if, says he, we were convinced of the truth of the reports of the disaffection of the army (which I indeed am confident are either altogether groundless, or at least less than they are supposed to be), how much better to conceal and hide our suspicions of it, than by our conduct confirm it? Ought not the defects of an army to be as carefully concealed as the wounds in our bodies, lest we should increase the enemy's hopes? but they moreover advise us to set out at midnight, in order, I suppose, that those who attempt to do wrong may have a fairer opportunity; for conduct of this kind is restrained either by shame or fear, to the display of which the night is most adverse. Wherefore, I am neither so rash as to give my opinion that we ought to attack their camp without hopes of succeeding; nor so influenced by fear as to despond: and I imagine that every expedient ought first to be tried; and I am in a great degree confident that I shall form the same opinion as yourselves on this matter."

XXXII.—Having broken up the council he called the soldiers together, and reminded them "what advantage Caesar had derived from their zeal at Corfinium; how by their good offices and influence he had brought over a great part of Italy to his interest. For, says he, all the municipal towns afterwards imitated you and your conduct; nor was it without reason that Caesar judged so favourably, and the enemy so harshly of you. For Pompey, though beaten in no engagement, yet was obliged to shift his ground, and leave Italy, from the precedent established by your conduct. Caesar committed me, whom he considered his dearest friend, and the provinces of Sicily and Africa, without which he was not able to protect Rome or Italy, to your protection. There are some here present who encourage you to revolt from us; for what can they wish for more, than at once to ruin us, and to involve you in a heinous crime? or what baser opinions could they in their resentment entertain of you, than that you would betray those who acknowledged themselves indebted to you for everything, and put yourselves in the power of those who think they have been ruined by you? Have you not heard of Caesar's exploits in Spain? that he routed two armies, conquered two generals, recovered two provinces, and effected all this within forty days after he came in sight of the enemy? Can those who were not able to stand against him whilst they were uninjured resist him when they are ruined? Will you, who took part with Caesar whilst victory was uncertain, take part with the conquered enemy when the fortune of the war is decided, and when you ought to reap the reward of your services? For they say that they have been deserted and betrayed by you, and remind you of a former oath. But did you desert Lucius Domitius, or did Lucius Domitius desert you? Did he not, when you were ready to submit to the greatest difficulties, cast you off? Did he not, without your privacy, endeavour to effect his own escape? When you were betrayed by him, were you not preserved by Caesar's generosity? And how could he think you bound by your oath to him, when, after having thrown up the ensigns of power, and abdicated his government, he became a private person, and a captive in another's power? A new obligation is left upon you, that you should disregard the oath, by which you are at present bound; and have respect only to that which was invalidated by the surrender of your general, and his diminution of rank. But I suppose, although you are pleased with Caesar, you are offended with me; however I shall not boast of my services to you, which still are inferior to my own wishes or your expectations. But, however, soldiers have ever looked for the rewards of labour at the conclusion of a war; and what the issue of it is likely to be, not even you can doubt. But why should I omit to mention my own diligence and good fortune, and to what a happy crisis affairs are now arrived? Are you sorry that I transported the army safe and entire, without the loss of a single ship? That on my arrival, in the very first attack, I routed the enemy's fleet? That twice in two days I defeated the enemy's horse? That I carried out of the very harbour and bay, two hundred of the enemy's victuallers, and reduced them to that situation that they can receive no supplies either by land or sea? Will you divorce yourselves from this fortune and these generals; and prefer the disgrace of Corfinium, the defeat of Italy, the surrender of both Spains, and the prestige of the African war? I, for my part, wished to be called a soldier of Caesar's; you honoured me with the title of Imperator. If you repent your bounty, I give it back to you; restore to me my former name that you may not appear to have conferred the honour on me as a reproach."

XXXIII.—The soldiers, being affected by this oration, frequently attempted to interrupt him whilst he was speaking, so that they appeared to bear with excessive anguish the suspicion of treachery, and when he was leaving the assembly they unanimously besought him to be of good spirits, and not hesitate to engage the enemy and put their fidelity and courage to a trial. As the wishes and opinions of all were changed by this act, Curio, with the general consent, determined, whenever opportunity offered, to hazard a battle. The next day he led out his forces and ranged them in order of battle on the same ground where they had been posted the preceding day; nor did Attius Varus hesitate to draw out his men, that, if any occasion should offer, either to tamper with our men or to engage on equal terms, he might not miss the opportunity.

XXXIV.-There lay between the two armies a valley, as already mentioned, not very deep, but of a difficult and steep ascent. Each was waiting till the enemy's forces should to attempt to pass it, that they might engage with the advantage of the ground. At the same time, on the left wing, the entire cavalry of Publius Attius, and several light-armed infantry intermixed with them, were perceived descending into the valley. Against them Curio detached his cavalry and two cohorts of the Marrucini, whose first charge the enemy's horse were unable to stand, but, setting spurs to their horses, fled back to their friends: the light-infantry being deserted by those who had come out along with them, were surrounded and cut to pieces by our men. Varus's whole army, facing that way, saw their men flee and cut down. Upon which Rebilus, one of Caesar's lieutenants, whom Curio had brought with him from Sicily knowing that he had great experience in military matters, cried out, "You see the enemy are daunted, Curio! why do you hesitate to take advantage of the opportunity?" Curio, having merely "expressed this, that the soldiers should keep in mind the professions which they had made to him the day before," then ordered them to follow him, and ran far before them all. The valley was so difficult of ascent that the foremost men could not struggle up it unless assisted by those behind. But the minds of Attius's soldiers being prepossessed with fear and the flight and slaughter of their men, never thought of opposing us; and they all imagined that they were already surrounded by our horse, and,

therefore, before a dart could be thrown or our men come near them, Varus's whole army turned their backs and retreated to their camp.
XXXV.-In this flight one Fabius, a Pelignian and common soldier in Curio's army, pursuing the enemy's rear, with a loud voice shouted to Varus by his name, and often called him, so that he seemed to be one of his soldiers, who wished to speak to him and give him advice. When Varus, after being repeatedly called, stopped and looked at him, and inquired who he was and what he wanted, he made a blow with his sword at his naked shoulder and was very near killing Varus, but he escaped the danger by raising his shield to ward off the blow. Fabius was surrounded by the soldiers near him and cut to pieces; and by the multitude and crowds of those that fled, the gates of the camps were thronged and the passage stopped, and a greater number perished in that place without a stroke than in the battle and flight. Nor were we far from driving them from this camp; and some of them ran straightway to the town without halting. But both the nature of the ground and the strength of the fortifications prevented our access to the camp; for Curio's soldiers, marching out to battle, were without those things which were requisite for storming a camp. Curio, therefore, led his army back to the camp, with all his troops safe except Fabius. Of the enemy about six hundred were killed and a thousand wounded, all of whom, after Curio's return, and several more under pretext of their wounds, but in fact through fear, withdrew from the camp into the town, which Varus perceiving and knowing the terror of his army, leaving a trumpeter in his camp and a few tents for show, at the third watch led back his army quietly into the town.
XXXVI.—The next day Curio resolved to besiege Utica, and to draw lines about it. In the town there was a multitude of people, ignorant of war, owing to the length of the peace; some of them Uticans, very well inclined to Caesar, for his favours to them; the Roman population was composed of persons differing widely in their sentiments. The terror occasioned by former battles was very great; and therefore they openly talked of surrendering, and argued with Attius that he should not suffer the fortune of them all to be ruined by his obstinacy. Whilst these things were in agitation, couriers, who had been sent forward, arrived from king Juba, with the intelligence that he was on his march, with considerable forces, and encouraged them to protect and defend their city, a circumstance which greatly comforted their desponding hearts.
XXXVII.—The same intelligence was brought to Curio; but for some time he could not give credit to it, because he had so great confidence in his own good fortune. And at this time Caesar's success in Spain was announced in Africa by messages and letters. Being elated by all these things, he imagined that the king would not dare to attempt anything

against him. But when he found out, from undoubted authority, that his forces were less than twenty miles distant from Utica, abandoning his works, he retired to the Cornelian camp. Here he began to lay in corn and wood, and to fortify his camp, and immediately despatched orders to Sicily, that his two legions and the remainder of his cavalry should be sent to him. His camp was well adapted for protracting a war, from the nature and strength of the situation, from its proximity to the sea, and the abundance of water and salt, of which a great quantity had been stored up from the neighbouring salt-pits. Timber could not fail him from the number of trees, nor corn, with which the lands abounded. Wherefore, with the general consent, Curio determined to wait for the rest of his forces, and protract the war.

XXXVIII.—This plan being settled, and his conduct approved of, he is informed by some deserters from the town that Juba had stayed behind in his own kingdom, being called home by a neighbouring war, and a dispute with the people of Leptis; and that Sabura, his commander-in-chief, who had been sent with a small force, was drawing near to Utica. Curio rashly believing this information, altered his design, and resolved to hazard a battle. His youth, his spirits, his former good fortune and confidence of success, contributed much to confirm this resolution. Induced by these motives, early in the night he sent all his cavalry to the enemy's camp near the river Bagrada, of which Sabura, of whom we have already spoken, was the commander. But the king was coming after them with all his forces, and was posted at a distance of six miles behind Sabura. The horse that were sent perform their march that night, and attack the enemy unawares and unexpectedly; for the Numidians, after the usual barbarous custom, encamped here and there without any regularity. The cavalry having attacked them, when sunk in sleep and dispersed, killed a great number of them; many were frightened and ran away. After which the horse returned to Curio, and brought some prisoners with them.

XXXIX.—Curio had set out at the fourth watch with all his forces, except five cohorts which he left to guard the camp. Having advanced six miles, he met the horse, heard what had happened, and inquired from the captives who commanded the camp at Bagrada. They replied Sabura. Through eagerness to perform his journey, he neglected to make further inquiries, but looking back to the company next him, "Don't you see, soldiers," says he, "that the answer of the prisoners corresponds with the account of the deserters, that the king is not with him, and that he sent only a small force which was not able to withstand a few horse? Hasten then to spoil, to glory; that we may now begin to think of rewarding you, and returning you thanks." The achievements of the horse were great in themselves, especially if their small number be compared with the vast host of Numidians. However, the account was enlarged by themselves, as men are naturally inclined to boast of their own merit. Besides, many spoils were produced; the men and horses that were taken were brought into their sight, that they might imagine that every moment of time which intervened was a delay to their conquest. By this means the hopes of Curio were seconded by the ardour of the soldiers. He ordered the horse to follow him, and hastened his march, that he might attack them as soon as possible, while in consternation after their flight. But the horse, fatigued by the expedition of the preceding night, were not able to keep up with him, but fell behind in different places. Even this did not abate Curio's hopes.

XL.—Juba, being informed by Sabura of the battle in the night, sent to his relief two thousand Spanish and Gallic horse, which he was accustomed to keep near him to guard his person, and that part of his infantry on which he had the greatest dependence, and he himself followed slowly after with the rest of his forces and forty elephants, suspecting that as Curio had sent his horse before, he himself would follow them. Sabura drew up his army, both horse and foot, and commanded them to give way gradually and retreat through the pretence of fear; that when it was necessary he would give them the signal for battle, and such orders as he found circumstances required. Curio, as his idea of their present behaviour was calculated to confirm his former hopes, imagined that the enemy were running away, and led his army from the rising grounds down to the plain.

XLI.—And when he had advanced from this place about sixteen miles, his army being exhausted with the fatigue, he halted. Sabura gave his men the signal, marshalled his army, and began to go around his ranks and encourage them. But he made use of the foot only for show; and sent the horse to the charge: Curio was not deficient in skill, and encouraged his men to rest all their hopes in their valour. Neither were the soldiers, though wearied, nor the horse, though few and exhausted with fatigue, deficient in ardour to engage, and courage: but the latter were in number but two hundred: the rest had dropped behind on the march. Wherever they charged they forced the enemy to give ground, but they were not able to pursue them far when they fled, or to press their horses too severely. Besides, the enemy's cavalry began to surround us on both wings and to trample down our rear. When any cohorts ran forward out of the line, the Numidians, being fresh, by their speed avoided our charge, and surrounded ours when they attempted to return to their post, and cut them off from the main body. So that it did not appear safe either to keep their ground and maintain their ranks, or to issue from the line, and run the risk. The enemy's troops were frequently reinforced by assistance sent from Juba; strength began to fail our men through fatigue; and those who had been wounded could neither quit the field nor retire to a place of safety, because the whole field was surrounded by the enemy's cavalry. Therefore, despairing of their own safety, as men usually do in the last moment of their lives, they either lamented their unhappy deaths, or recommended their parents to the survivors, if fortune should save any from the impending danger. All were full of fear and grief.

XLII.—When Curio perceived that in the general consternation neither his exhortations nor entreaties were attended to, imagining that the only hope of escaping in their deplorable situation was to gain the nearest hills, he ordered the colours to be borne that way. But a party of horse, that had been sent by Sabura, had already got possession of them. Now indeed our men were reduced to extreme despair: and some of them were killed by the cavalry in attempting to escape: some fell to the ground unhurt. Cneius Domitius, commander of the cavalry, standing round Curio with a small party of horse, urged Curio to endeavour to escape by flight, and to hasten to his camp; and assured him that he would not forsake him. But Curio declared that he would never more appear in Caesar's sight, after losing the army which had been committed by Caesar to his charge, and accordingly fought till he was killed. Very few of the horse escaped from that battle, but those who had stayed behind to refresh their horses having perceived at a distance the defeat of the whole army, retired in safety to their camp.

XLIII.—The soldiers were all killed to a man. Marcus Rufus, the quaestor, who was left behind in the camp by Curio, having got intelligence of these things, encouraged his men not to be disheartened. They beg and entreat to be transported to Sicily. He consented, and ordered the masters of the ships to have all the boats brought close to the shore early in the evening. But so great was the terror in general that some said that Juba's forces were marching up, others that Varus was hastening with his legions, and that they already saw the dust raised by their coming; of which not one circumstance had happened: others suspected that the enemy's fleet would immediately be upon them. Therefore, in the general consternation, every man consulted his own safety. Those who were on board of the fleet, were in a hurry to set sail, and their flight hastened the masters of the ships of burden. A few small fishing boats attended their duty and his orders. But as the shores were crowded, so great was the struggle to determine who of such a vast number should first get on board, that some of the vessels sank with the weight of the multitude, and the fears of the rest delayed them from coming to the shore.

XLIV.—From which circumstances it happened that a few foot and aged men, that could prevail either through interest or pity, or who were able to swim to the ships, were taken on board, and landed safe in Sicily. The rest of the troops sent their centurions as deputies to Varus at night, and surrendered themselves to him. But Juba, the next day having spied their cohorts before the town, claimed them as his booty, and ordered a great part of them to be put to the sword; a few he selected and sent home to his own realm. Although Varus complained that his honour was insulted by Juba, yet he dare not oppose him: Juba rode on horseback into the town, attended by several senators, amongst whom were Servius Sulpicius and Licinius Damasippus, and in a few days arranged and ordered what he would have done in Utica, and in a few days more returned to his own kingdom, with all his forces.

BOOK III

I.—Julius Caesar, holding the election as dictator, was himself appointed consul with Publius Servilius; for this was the year in which it was permitted by the laws that he should be chosen consul. This business being ended, as credit was beginning to fail in Italy, and the debts could not be paid, he determined that arbitrators should be appointed: and that they should make an estimate of the possessions and properties [of the debtors], how much they were worth before the war, and that they should be handed over in payment to the creditors. This he thought the most likely method to remove and abate the apprehension of an abolition of debt, the usual consequence of civil wars and dissensions, and to support the credit of the debtors. He likewise restored to their former condition (the praetors and tribunes first submitting the question to the people) some persons condemned for bribery at the elections, by virtue of Pompey's law, at the time when Pompey kept his legions quartered in the city (these trials were finished in a single day, one judge hearing the merits, and another pronouncing the sentences), because they had offered their service to him in the beginning of the civil war, if he chose to accept them; setting the same value on them as if he had accepted them, because they had put themselves in his power. For he had determined that they ought to be restored, rather by the judgment of the people, than appear admitted to it by his bounty: that he might neither appear ungrateful in repaying an obligation, nor arrogant in depriving the people of their prerogative of exercising this bounty.

II.—In accomplishing these things, and celebrating the Latin festival, and holding all the elections, he spent eleven days; and having resigned the dictatorship, set out from the city, and went to Brundisium, where he had ordered twelve legions and all his cavalry to meet him. But he scarcely found as many ships as would be sufficient to transport fifteen thousand legionary soldiers and five hundred horse. This [the scarcity of shipping] was the only thing that prevented Caesar from putting a speedy conclusion to the war. And even these troops embarked very short of their number, because several had fallen in so many wars in Gaul, and the long march from Spain had lessened their number very much, and a severe autumn in Apulia and the district about Brundisium, after the very wholesome countries of Spain and Gaul, had impaired the health of the whole army.

III.—Pompey having got a year's respite to provide forces, during which he was not engaged in war, nor employed by an enemy, had collected a numerous fleet from Asia, and the Cyclades, from Corcyra, Athens, Pontus, Bithynia, Syria, Cilicia, Phoenicia, and Egypt, and had given directions that a great number should be built in every other place. He had exacted a large sum of money from Asia, Syria, and all the kings, dynasts, tetrarchs, and free states of Achaia; and had obliged the corporations of those provinces, of which he himself had the government, to count down to him a large sum.

IV.—He had made up nine legions of Roman citizens; five from Italy, which he had brought with him; one veteran legion from Sicily, which being composed of two, he called the Gemella; one from Crete and Macedonia, of veterans who had been discharged by their former generals, and had settled in those provinces; two from Asia, which had been levied by the activity of Lentulus. Besides he had distributed among his legions a considerable number, by way of recruits, from Thessaly, Boeotia, Achaia, and Epirus: with his legions he also intermixed the soldiers taken from Caius Antonius. Besides these, he expected two legions from Syria, with Scipio; from Crete, Lacedaemon, Pontus, Syria, and other states, he got about three thousand archers, six cohorts of slingers, two thousand mercenary soldiers, and seven thousand horse; six hundred of which, Deiotarus had brought from Gaul; Ariobarzanes, five hundred from Cappadocia. Cotus had given him about the same number from Thrace, and had sent his son Sadalis with them. From Macedonia there were two hundred, of extraordinary valour, commanded by Rascipolis; five hundred Gauls and Germans; Gabinius's troops from Alexandria, whom Aulus Gabinius had left with king Ptolemy, to guard his person. Pompey, the son, had brought in his fleet eight hundred, whom he had raised among his own and his shepherds' slaves. Tarcundarius, Castor and Donilaus had given three hundred from Gallograecia: one of these came himself, the other sent his son. Two hundred were sent from Syria by Comagenus Antiochus, whom Pompey rewarded amply. The most of them were archers. To these were added Dardanians, and Bessians, some of them mercenaries; others procured by power and influence: also, Macedonians, Thessalians, and troops from other nations and states, which completed the number which we mentioned before.

V.—He had laid in vast quantities of corn from Thessaly, Asia, Egypt, Crete, Cyrene, and other countries. He had resolved to fix his winter quarters at Dyrrachium, Apollonia, and the other sea-ports, to hinder Caesar from passing the sea: and for this purpose had stationed his fleet along the sea-coast. The Egyptian fleet was commanded by Pompey, the son: the Asiatic, by Decimus Laelius, and Caius Triarius: the Syrian, by Caius Cassius: the Rhodian, by Caius Marcellus, in conjunction with Caius Coponius; and the Liburnian, and Achaian, by Scribonius Libo, and Marcus Octavius. But Marcus Bibulus was appointed commander-in-chief of the whole maritime department, and regulated every matter. The chief direction rested upon him.

VI.—When Caesar came to Brundisium, he made a speech to the soldiers: "That since they were now almost arrived at the termination of their toils and dangers, they should patiently submit to leave their slaves and baggage in Italy, and to embark without luggage, that a greater number of men might be put on board: that they might expect everything from victory and his liberality." They cried out with one voice, "he might give what orders he pleased, that they would cheerfully fulfil them." He accordingly set sail the fourth day of January, with seven legions on board, as already remarked. The next day he reached land, between the Ceraunian rocks and other dangerous places; meeting with a safe road for his shipping to ride in, and dreading all other ports which he imagined were in possession of the enemy, he landed his men at a place called Pharsalus, without the loss of a single vessel.
VII.—Lucretius Vespillo and Minutius Rufus were at Oricum, with eighteen Asiatic ships, which were given into their charge by the orders of Decimus Laelius: Marcus Bibulus at Corcyra, with a hundred and ten ships. But they had not the confidence to dare to move out of the harbour; though Caesar had brought only twelve ships as a convoy, only four of which had decks; nor did Bibulus, his fleet being disordered and his seamen dispersed, come up in time: for Caesar was seen at the continent before any account whatsoever of his approach had reached those regions.

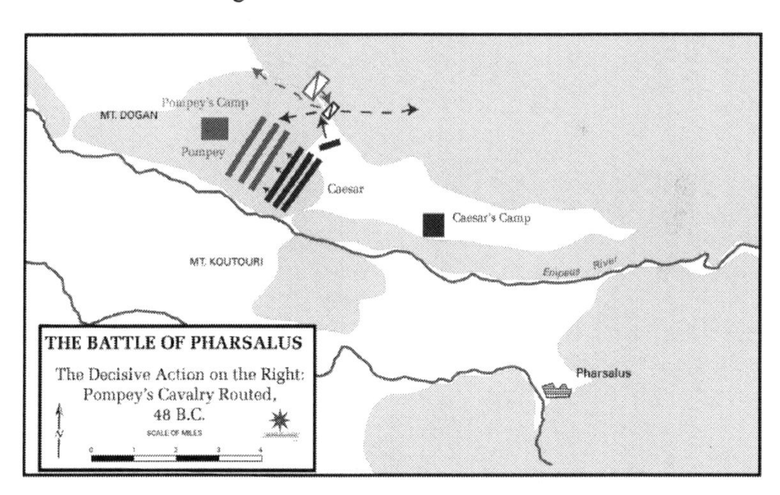

VIII.—Caesar, having landed his soldiers, sent back his ships the same night to Brundisium, to transport the rest of his legions and cavalry. The charge of this business was committed to lieutenant Fufius Kalenus, with orders to be expeditious in transporting the legions. But the ships having put to sea too late, and not having taken advantage of the night breeze, fell a sacrifice on their return. For Bibulus, at Corcyra, being informed of Caesar's approach, hoped to fall in with some part of our ships, with their cargoes, but found them empty; and having taken about thirty, vented on them his rage at his own remissness, and set them all on fire: and, with the same flames, he destroyed the mariners and masters of the vessels, hoping by the severity of the punishment to deter the rest. Having accomplished this affair, he filled all the harbours and shores from Salona to Oricum with his fleets. Having disposed his guard with great care, he lay on board himself in the depth of winter, declining no fatigue or duty, and not waiting for reinforcements, in hopes that he might come within Caesar's reach.

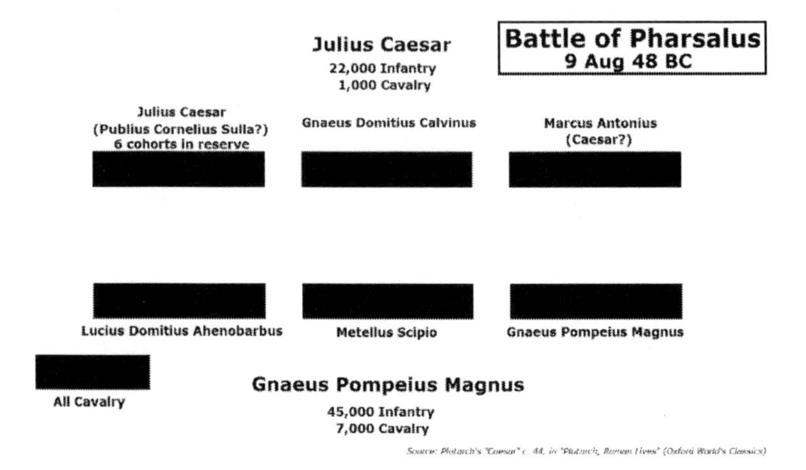

IX.—But after the departure of the Liburnian fleet, Marcus Octavius sailed from Illyricum with what ships he had to Salona; and having spirited up the Dalmatians, and other barbarous nations, he drew Issa off from its connection with Caesar; but not being able to prevail with the council of Salona, either by promises or menaces, he resolved to storm the town. But it was well fortified by its natural situation, and a hill. The Roman citizens built wooden towers, the better to secure it; but when they were unable to resist, on account of the smallness of their numbers, being weakened by several wounds, they stooped to the last resource, and set at liberty all the slaves old enough to bear arms; and cutting the hair off the women's heads, made ropes for their engines. Octavius, being informed of their determination, surrounded the town with five encampments, and began to press them at once with a siege and storm. They were determined to endure every hardship, and their greatest distress was the want of corn. They, therefore, sent deputies to Caesar, and begged a supply from him; all other inconveniences they bore by their own resources, as well as they could: and after a long interval, when the length of the siege had made Octavius's troops more remiss than usual, having got an opportunity at noon, when the enemy were dispersed, they disposed their wives and children on the walls, to keep up the appearance of their usual attention; and forming themselves into one body, with the slaves whom they had lately enfranchised, they made an attack on Octavius's nearest camp, and having forced that, attacked the second with the same fury; and then the third and the fourth, and then the other, and beat them from them all: and having killed a great number, obliged the rest and Octavius himself to fly for refuge to their ships. This put an end to the blockade. Winter was now approaching, and Octavius, despairing of capturing the town, after sustaining such considerable losses, withdrew to Pompey, to Dyrrachium.

X.—We have mentioned that Vibullius Rufus, an officer of Pompey's, had fallen twice into Caesar's power; first at Corfinium, and afterwards in Spain. Caesar thought him a proper person, on account of his favours conferred on him, to send with proposals to Pompey: and he knew that he had an influence over Pompey. This was the substance of his proposals: "That it was the duty of both, to put an end to their obstinacy, and forbear hostilities, and not tempt fortune any further; that sufficient loss had been suffered on both sides, to serve as a lesson and instruction to them, to render them apprehensive of future calamities, by Pompey, in having been driven out of Italy, and having lost Sicily, Sardinia, and the two Spains, and one hundred and thirty cohorts of Roman citizens, in Italy and Spain: by himself, in the death of Curio, and the loss of so great an army in Africa, and the surrender of his soldiers in Corcyra. Wherefore, they should have pity on themselves, and the republic: for, from their own misfortunes, they had sufficient experience of what fortune can effect in war. That this was the only time to treat of peace; when each had confidence in his own strength, and both seemed on an equal footing. Since, if fortune showed ever so little favour to either, he who thought himself superior, would not submit to terms of accommodation; nor would he be content with an equal division, when he might expect to obtain the whole. That, as they could not agree before, the terms of peace ought to be submitted to the senate and people in Rome. That in the meantime, it ought to content the republic and themselves, if they both immediately took oath in a public assembly, that they would disband their forces within the three following days. That having divested themselves of the arms and auxiliaries, on which they placed their present confidence, they must both of necessity acquiesce in the decision of the people and senate. To give Pompey the fuller assurance of his intentions, he would dismiss all his forces on land, even his garrisons.

XI.—Vibullius, having received this commission from Caesar, thought it no less necessary to give Pompey notice of Caesar's sudden approach, that he might adopt such plans as the circumstance required, than to inform him of Caesar's message; and therefore continuing his journey by night as well as by day, and taking fresh horses for despatch, he posted away to Pompey, to inform him that Caesar was marching towards him with all his forces. Pompey was at this time in Candavia, and was on his march from Macedonia to his winter quarters in Apollonia and Dyrrachium; but surprised at the unexpected news, he determined to go to Apollonia by speedy marches, to prevent Caesar from becoming master of all the maritime states. But as soon as Caesar had landed his troops, he set off the same day for Oricum: when he arrived there, Lucius Torquatus, who was governor of the town by Pompey's appointment, and had a garrison of Parthinians in it, endeavoured to shut the gates and defend the town, and ordered the Greeks to man the walls, and to take arms. But as they refused to fight against the power of the Roman people, and as the citizens made a spontaneous attempt to admit Caesar, despairing of any assistance, he threw open the gates, and surrendered himself and the town to Caesar, and was preserved safe from injury by him.

XII.—Having taken Oricum, Caesar marched without making any delay to Apollonia. Staberius the governor, hearing of his approach, began to bring water into the citadel, and to fortify it, and to demand hostages of the town's people. But they refuse to give any, or to shut their gates against the consul, or to take upon them to judge contrary to what all Italy and the Roman people had judged. As soon as he knew their inclinations, he made his escape privately. The inhabitants of Apollonia sent ambassadors to Caesar, and gave him admission into their town. Their example was followed by the inhabitants of Bullis, Amantia, and the other neighbouring states, and all Epirus: and they sent ambassadors to Caesar, and promised to obey his commands.

XIII.—But Pompey having received information of the transactions at Oricum and Apollonia, began to be alarmed for Dyrrachium, and endeavoured to reach it, marching day and night. As soon as it was said that Caesar was approaching, such a panic fell upon Pompey's army, because in his haste he had made no distinction between night and day, and had marched without intermission, that they almost every man deserted their colours in Epirus and the neighbouring countries; several threw down their arms, and their march had the appearance of a flight. But when Pompey had halted near Dyrrachium, and had given orders for measuring out the ground for his camp, his army even yet continuing in their fright, Labienus first stepped forward and swore that he would never desert him, and would share whatever fate fortune should assign to him. The other lieutenants took the same oath, and the tribunes and centurions followed their example: and the whole army swore in like manner. Caesar, finding the road to Dyrrachium already in the possession of Pompey, was in no great haste, but encamped by the river Apsus, in the territory of Apollonia, that the states which had deserved his support might be certain of protection from his out-guards and forts; and there he resolved to wait the arrival of his other legions from Italy, and to winter in tents. Pompey did the same; and pitching his camp on the other side of the river Apsus, collected there all his troops and auxiliaries.

XIV.—Kalenus, having put the legions and cavalry on board at Brundisium, as Caesar had directed him, as far as the number of his ships allowed, weighed anchor: and having sailed a little distance from port, received a letter from Caesar, in which he was informed, that all the ports and the whole shore was occupied by the enemy's fleet: on receiving this information he returned into the harbour, and recalled all the vessels. One of them, which continued the voyage and did not obey Kalenus's command, because it carried no troops, but was private property, bore away for Oricum, and was taken by Bibulus, who spared neither slaves nor free men, nor even children; but put all to the sword. Thus the safety of the whole army depended on a very short space of time and a great casualty.

XV.—Bibulus, as has been observed before, lay with his fleet near Oricum, and as he debarred Caesar of the liberty of the sea and harbours, so he was deprived of all intercourse with the country by land; for the whole shore was occupied by parties disposed in different places by Caesar. And he was not allowed to get either wood or water, or even anchor near the land. He was reduced to great difficulties, and distressed with extreme scarcity of every necessary; insomuch that he was obliged to bring, in transports from Corcyra, not only provisions, but even wood and water; and it once happened that, meeting with violent storms, they were forced to catch the dew by night which fell on the hides that covered their decks; yet all these difficulties they bore patiently and without repining, and thought they ought not to leave the shores and harbours free from blockade. But when they were suffering under the distress which I have mentioned, and Libo had joined Bibulus, they both called from on ship-board to Marcus Acilius and Statius Marcus, the lieutenants, one of whom commanded the town, the other the guards on the coast, that they wished to speak to Caesar on affairs of importance, if permission should be granted them. They add something further to strengthen the impression that they intended to treat about an accommodation. In the meantime they requested a truce, and obtained it from them; for what they proposed seemed to be of importance, and it was well known that Caesar desired it above all things, and it was imagined that some advantage would be derived from Bibulus's proposals.

XVI.—Caesar having set out with one legion to gain possession of the more remote states, and to provide corn, of which he had but a small quantity, was at this time at Buthrotum, opposite to Corcyra. There receiving Acilius and Marcus's letters, informing him of Libo's and Bibulus's demands, he left his legion behind him, and returned himself to Oricum. When he arrived, they were invited to a conference. Libo came and made an apology for Bibulus, "that he was a man of strong passion, and had a private quarrel against Caesar, contracted when he was aedile and praetor; that for this reason he had avoided the conference, lest affairs of the utmost importance and advantage might be impeded by the warmth of his temper. That it now was and ever had been Pompey's most earnest wish, that they should be reconciled, and lay down their arms; but they were not authorized to treat on that subject, because they resigned the whole management of the war, and all other matters, to Pompey, by order of the council. But when they were acquainted with Caesar's demands, they would transmit them to Pompey, who would conclude all of himself by their persuasions. In the meantime, let the truce be continued till the messengers could return from him; and let no injury be done on either side." To this he added a few words of the cause for which they fought, and of his own forces and resources.

XVII.—To this, Caesar did not then think proper to make any reply, nor do we now think it worth recording. But Caesar required "that he should be allowed to send commissioners to Pompey, who should suffer no personal injury; and that either they should grant it, or should take his commissioners in charge, and convey them to Pompey. That as to the truce, the war in its present state was so divided, that they by their fleet deprived him of his shipping and auxiliaries; while he prevented them from the use of the land and fresh water; and if they wished that this restraint should be removed from them, they should relinquish their blockade of the seas, but if they retained the one, he in like manner would retain the other; that nevertheless, the treaty of accommodation might still be carried on, though these points were not conceded, and that they need not be an impediment to it." They would neither receive Caesar's commissioners, nor guarantee their safety, but referred the whole to Pompey. They urged and struggled eagerly to gain the one point respecting a truce. But when Caesar perceived that they had proposed the conference merely to avoid present danger and distress, but that they offered no hopes or terms of peace, he applied his thoughts to the prosecution of the war.

XVIII.—Bibulus, being prevented from landing for several days, and being seized with a violent distemper from the cold and fatigue, as he could neither be cured on board, nor was willing to desert the charge which he had taken upon him, was unable to bear up against the violence of the disease. On his death, the sole command devolved on no single individual, but each admiral managed his own division separately, and at his own discretion. Vibullius, as soon as the alarm, which Caesar's unexpected arrival had raised, was over, began again to deliver Caesar's message in the presence of Libo, Lucius Lucceius, and Theophanes, to whom Pompey used to communicate his most confidential secrets. He had scarcely entered on the subject when Pompey interrupted him, and forbade him to proceed. "What need," says he, "have I of life or Rome, if the world shall think I enjoy them by the bounty of Caesar; an opinion which can never be removed whilst it shall be thought that I have been brought back by him to Italy, from which I set out." After the conclusion of the war, Caesar was informed of these expressions by some persons who were present at the conversation. He attempted, however, by other means to bring about a negotiation of peace.

XIX.—Between Pompey's and Caesar's camp there was only the river Apsus, and the soldiers frequently conversed with each other; and by a private arrangement among themselves, no weapons were thrown during their conferences. Caesar sent Publius Vatinius, one of his lieutenants, to the bank of the river, to make such proposals as should appear most conducive to peace; and to cry out frequently with a loud voice [asking], "Are citizens permitted to send deputies to citizens to treat of peace? a concession which had been made even to fugitives on the Pyrenean mountains, and to robbers, especially when by so doing they would prevent citizens from fighting against citizens." Having spoken much in humble language, as became a man pleading for his own and the general safety, and being listened to with silence by the soldiers of both armies, he received an answer from the enemy's party that Aulus Varro proposed coming the next day to a conference, and that deputies from both sides might come without danger, and explain their wishes, and accordingly a fixed time was appointed for the interview. When the deputies met the next day, a great multitude from both sides assembled, and the expectations of every person concerning this subject were raised very high, and their minds seemed to be eagerly disposed for peace. Titus Labienus walked forward from the crowd, and in submissive terms began to speak of peace, and to argue with Vatinius. But their conversation was suddenly interrupted by darts thrown from all sides, from which Vatinius escaped by being protected by the arms of the soldiers. However, several were wounded; and among them Cornelius Balbus, Marcus Plotius, and Lucius Tiburtius, centurions, and some privates; hereupon Labienus exclaimed, "Forbear, then, to speak any more about an accommodation, for we can have no peace unless we carry Caesar's head back with us."

XX.—At the same time in Rome, Marcus Caelius Rufus, one of the praetors, having undertaken the cause of the debtors, on entering into his office, fixed his tribunal near the bench of Caius Trebonius, the city praetor, and promised if any person appealed to him in regard to the valuation and payment of debts made by arbitration, as appointed by Caesar when in Rome, that he would relieve them. But it happened, from the justice of Trebonius's decrees and his humanity (for he thought that in such dangerous times justice should be administered with moderation and compassion), that not one could be found who would offer himself the first to lodge an appeal. For to plead poverty, to complain of his own private calamities, or the general distresses of the times, or to assert the difficulty of setting the goods to sale, is the behaviour of a man even of a moderate temper; but to retain their possessions entire, and at the same time acknowledge themselves in debt, what sort of spirit, and what impudence would it not have argued! Therefore nobody was found so unreasonable as to make such demands. But Caelius proved more severe to those very persons for whose advantage it had been designed; and starting from this beginning, in order that he might not appear to have engaged in so dishonourable an affair without effecting something, he promulgated a law, that all debts should be discharged in six equal payments, of six months each, without interest.

XXI.—When Servilius, the consul, and the other magistrates opposed him, and he himself effected less than he expected, in order to raise the passions of the people, he dropped it, and promulgated two others; one, by which he remitted the annual rents of the houses to the tenants, the other, an act of insolvency: upon which the mob made an assault on Caius Trebonius, and having wounded several persons, drove him from his tribunal. The consul Servilius informed the senate of his proceedings, who passed a decree that Caelius should be removed from the management of the republic. Upon this decree, the consul forbade him the senate; and when he was attempting to harangue the people, turned him out of the rostrum. Stung with the ignominy and with resentment, he pretended in public that he would go to Caesar, but privately sent messengers to Milo, who had murdered Clodius, and had been condemned for it; and having invited him into Italy, because he had engaged the remains of the gladiators to his interest, by making them supple presents, he joined him, and sent him to Thurinum to tamper with the shepherds. When he himself was on his road to Casilinum, at the same time that his military standards and arms were seized at Capua, his slaves seen at Naples, and the design of betraying the town discovered: his plots being revealed, and Capua shut against him, being apprehensive of danger, because the Roman citizens residing there had armed themselves, and thought he ought to be treated as an enemy to the state, he abandoned his first design, and changed his route.

XXII.—Milo in the meantime despatched letters to the free towns, purporting that he acted as he did by the orders and commands of Pompey, conveyed to him by Bibulus: and he endeavoured to engage in his interest all persons whom he imagined were under difficulties by reason of their debts. But not being able to prevail with them, he set at liberty some slaves from the work-houses, and began to assault Cosa in the district of Thurinum. There having received a blow of a stone thrown from the wall of the town which was commanded by Quintus Pedius with one legion, he died of it; and Caelius having set out, as he pretended for Caesar, went to Thurii, where he was put to death as he was tampering with some of the freemen of the town, and was offering money to Caesar's Gallic and Spanish horse, which he had sent there to strengthen the garrison. And thus these mighty beginnings, which had embroiled Italy, and kept the magistrates employed, found a speedy and happy issue.

XXIII.—Libo having sailed from Oricum, with a fleet of fifty ships, which he commanded, came to Brundisium, and seized an island, which lies opposite to the harbour; judging it better to guard that place, which was our only pass to sea, than to keep all the shores and ports blocked up by a fleet. By his sudden arrival, he fell in with some of our transports, and set them on fire, and carried off one laden with corn; he struck great terror into our men, and having in the night landed a party of soldiers and archers, he beat our guard of horse from their station, and gained so much by the advantage of situation, that he despatched letters to Pompey, that if he pleased he might order the rest of the ships to be hauled upon shore and repaired; for that with his own fleet he could prevent Caesar from receiving his auxiliaries.

XXIV.—Antonius was at this time at Brundisium, and relying on the valour of his troops, covered about sixty of the long-boats belonging to the men-of-war with penthouses and bulwarks of hurdles, and put on board them select soldiers; and disposed them separately along the shore: and under the pretext of keeping the seamen in exercise, he ordered two three-banked galleys, which he had built at Brundisium, to row to the mouth of the port. When Libo saw them advancing boldly towards him, he sent five four-banked galleys against them, in hopes of intercepting them. When these came near our ships, our veteran soldiers retreated within the harbour. The enemy, urged by their eagerness to capture them, pursued them unguardedly; for instantly the boats of Antonius, on a certain signal, rowed with great violence from all parts against the enemy; and at the first charge took one of the four-banked galleys, with the seamen and marines, and forced the rest to flee disgracefully. In addition to this loss, they were prevented from getting water by the horse which Antonius had disposed along the sea-coast. Libo, vexed at the distress and disgrace, departed from Brundisium, and abandoned the blockade.

XXV.—Several months had now elapsed, and winter was almost gone, and Caesar's legions and shipping were not coming to him from Brundisium, and he imagined that some opportunities had been neglected, for the winds had at least been often favourable, and he thought that he must trust to them at last. And the longer it was deferred, the more eager were those who commanded Pompey's fleet to guard the coast, and were more confident of preventing our getting assistance: they receive frequent reproofs from Pompey by letter, that as they had not prevented Caesar's arrival at the first, they should at least stop the remainder of his army: and they were expecting that the season for transporting troops would become more unfavourable every day, as the winds grew calmer. Caesar, feeling some trouble on this account, wrote in severe terms to his officers at Brundisium, [and gave them orders] that as soon as they found the wind to answer, they should not let the opportunity of setting sail pass by, if they were even to steer their course to the shore of Apollonia: because there they might run their ships on ground. That these parts principally were left unguarded by the enemy's fleet, because they dare not venture too far from the harbour.

XXVI.—They [his officers], exerting boldness and courage, aided by the instructions of Marcus Antonius, and Fufius Kalenus, and animated by the soldiers strongly encouraging them, and declining no danger for Caesar's safety, having got a southerly wind, weighed anchor, and the next day were carried past Apollonia and Dyrrachium, and being seen from the continent, Quintus Coponius, who commanded the Rhodian fleet at Dyrrachium, put out of the port with his ships; and when they had almost come up with us, in consequence of the breeze dying away, the south wind sprang up afresh, and rescued us. However, he did not desist from his attempt, but hoped by the labour and perseverance of his seamen to be able to bear up against the violence of the storm; and although we were carried beyond Dyrrachium, by the violence of the wind, he nevertheless continued to chase us. Our men, taking advantage of fortune's kindness, for they were still afraid of being attacked by the enemy's fleet, if the wind abated, having come near a port, called Nymphaeum, about three miles beyond Lissus, put into it (this port is protected from a south-west wind, but is not secure against a south wind); and thought less danger was to be apprehended from the storm than from the enemy. But as soon as they were within the port, the south wind, which had blown for two days, by extraordinary good luck veered round to the south-west.

XXVII.—Here one might observe the sudden turns of fortune. We who, a moment before, were alarmed for ourselves, were safely lodged in a very secure harbour: and they who had threatened ruin to our fleet, were forced to be uneasy on their own account: and thus, by a change of circumstances, the storm protected our ships, and damaged the Rhodian fleet to such a degree, that all their decked ships, sixteen in number, foundered, without exception, and were wrecked: and of the prodigious number of seamen and soldiers, some lost their lives by being dashed against the rocks, others were taken by our men: but Caesar sent them all safe home.

XXVIII.—Two of our ships, that had not kept up with the rest, being overtaken by the night, and not knowing what port the rest had made to, came to an anchor opposite Lissus. Otacilius Crassus, who commanded Pompey's fleet, detached after them several barges and small craft, and attempted to take them. At the same time, he treated with them about capitulating, and promised them their lives if they would surrender. One of them carried two hundred and twenty recruits, the other was manned with somewhat less than two hundred veterans. Here it might be seen what security men derive from a resolute spirit. For the recruits, frightened at the number of vessels, and fatigued with the rolling of the sea; and with sea-sickness, surrendered to Otacilius, after having first received his oath, that the enemy would not injure them; but as soon as they were brought before him, contrary to the obligation of his oath, they were inhumanly put to death in his presence. But the soldiers of the veteran legion, who had also struggled, not only with the inclemency of the weather, but by labouring at the pump, thought it their duty to remit nothing of their former valour: and having protracted the beginning of the night in settling the terms, under pretence of surrendering, they obliged the pilot to run the ship aground: and having got a convenient place on the shore, they spent the rest of the night there, and at daybreak, when Otacilius had sent against them a party of the horse, who guarded that part of the coast, to the number of four hundred, besides some armed men, who had followed them from the garrison, they made a brave defence, and having killed some of them, retreated in safety to our army.

XXIX.—After this action, the Roman citizens, who resided at Lissus, a town which Caesar had before assigned them, and had carefully fortified, received Antony into their town, and gave him every assistance. Otacilius, apprehensive for his own safety, escaped out of the town, and went to Pompey. All his forces, whose number amounted to three veteran legions, and one of recruits, and about eight hundred horse, being landed, Antony sent most of his ships back to Italy, to transport the remainder of the soldiers and horse. The pontons, which are a sort of Gallic ships, he left at Lissus with this object, that if Pompey, imagining Italy defenceless, should transport his army thither (and this notion was spread among the common people), Caesar might have some means of pursuing him; and he sent messengers to him with great despatch, to inform him in what part of the country he had landed his army, and what number of troops he had brought over with him.

XXX.—Caesar and Pompey received this intelligence almost at the same time; for they had seen the ships sail past Apollonia and Dyrrachium. They directed their march after them by land; but at first they were ignorant to what part they had been carried; but when they were informed of it, they each adopted a different plan; Caesar, to form a junction with Antonius as soon as possible, Pompey, to oppose Antonius's forces on their march to Caesar, and, if possible, to fall upon them unexpectedly from ambush. And the same day they both led out their armies from their winter encampment along the river Apsus; Pompey, privately by night; Caesar, openly by day. But Caesar had to march a longer circuit up the river to find a ford. Pompey's route being easy, because he was not obliged to cross the river, he advanced rapidly and by forced marches against Antonius, and being informed of his approach, chose a convenient situation, where he posted his forces; and kept his men close within camp, and forbade fires to be kindled, that his arrival might be the more secret. An account of this was immediately carried to Antonius by the Greeks. He despatched messengers to Caesar, and confined himself in his camp for one day. The next day Caesar came up with him. On learning his arrival, Pompey, to prevent his being hemmed in between two armies, quitted his position, and went with all his forces to Asparagium, in the territory of Dyrrachium, and there encamped in a convenient situation.

XXXI.—During these times, Scipio, though he had sustained some losses near mount Amanus, had assumed to himself the title of imperator, after which he demanded large sums of money from the states and princes. He had also exacted from the tax-gatherers two years' rents that they owed; and enjoined them to lend him the amount of the next year, and demanded a supply of horse from the whole province. When they were collected, leaving behind him his neighbouring enemies, the Parthians (who shortly before had killed Marcus Crassus, the imperator, and had kept Marcus Bibulus besieged), he drew his legions and cavalry out of Syria; and when he came into the province, which was under great anxiety and fear of the Parthian war, and heard some declarations of the soldiers, "That they would march against an enemy, if he would lead them on; but would never bear arms against a countryman and consul"; he drew off his legions to winter quarters to Pergamus, and the most wealthy cities, and made them rich presents: and in order to attach them more firmly to his interest, permitted them to plunder the cities.

XXXII.—In the meantime, the money which had been demanded from the province at large, was most rigorously exacted. Besides, many new imposts of different kinds were devised to gratify his avarice. A tax of so much a head was laid on every slave and child. Columns, doors, corn, soldiers, sailors, arms, engines, and carriages, were made subject to a duty. Wherever a name could be found for anything, it was deemed a sufficient reason for levying money on it. Officers were appointed to collect it, not only in the cities, but in almost every village and fort: and whosoever of them acted with the greatest rigour and inhumanity, was esteemed the best man, and best citizen. The province was overrun with bailiffs and officers, and crowded with overseers and tax-gatherers;

who, besides the duties imposed, exacted a gratuity for themselves; for they asserted, that being expelled from their own homes and countries, they stood in need of every necessary; endeavouring by a plausible pretence to colour the most infamous conduct. To this was added the most exorbitant interest, as usually happens in times of war; the whole sums being called in, on which occasion they alleged that the delay of a single day was a donation. Therefore, in those two years, the debt of the province was doubled: but notwithstanding, taxes were exacted, not only from the Roman citizens, but from every corporation and every state. And they said that these were loans, exacted by the senate's decree. The taxes of the ensuing year were demanded beforehand as a loan from the collectors, as on their first appointment.

XXXIII.—Moreover, Scipio ordered the money formerly lodged in the temple of Diana at Ephesus, to be taken out with the statues of that goddess which remained there. When Scipio came to the temple, letters were delivered to him from Pompey, in the presence of several senators, whom he had called upon to attend him; [informing him] that Caesar had crossed the sea with his legions; that Scipio should hasten to him with his army, and postpone all other business. As soon as he received the letter, he dismissed his attendants, and began to prepare for his journey to Macedonia; and a few days after set out. This circumstance saved the money at Ephesus.

XXXIV.—Caesar, having effected a junction with Antonius's army, and having drawn his legion out of Oricum, which he had left there to guard the coast, thought he ought to sound the inclination of the provinces, and march farther into the country; and when ambassadors came to him from Thessaly and Aetolia, to engage that the states in those countries would obey his orders, if he sent a garrison to protect them, he despatched Lucius Cassius Longinus, with the twenty-seventh, a legion composed of young soldiers, and two hundred horse, to Thessaly: and Caius Calvisius Sabinus, with five cohorts, and a small party of horse, into Aetolia. He recommended them to be especially careful to provide corn, because those regions were nearest to him. He ordered Cneius Domitius Calvinus to march into Macedonia with two legions, the eleventh and twelfth, and five hundred horse; from which province, Menedemus, the principal man of those regions, on that side which is called the Free, having come as ambassador, assured him of the most devoted affection of all his subjects.

XXXV.—Of these Calvisius, on his first arrival in Aetolia, being very kindly received, dislodged the enemy's garrisons in Calydon and Naupactus, and made himself master of the whole country. Cassius went to Thessaly with his legion. As there were two factions there, he found the citizens divided in their inclinations. Hegasaretus, a man of established power, favoured Pompey's interest. Petreius, a young man of a most noble family, warmly supported Caesar with his own and his friends' influence.

XXXVI.—At the same time, Domitius arrived in Macedonia: and when numerous embassies had begun to wait on him from many of the states, news was brought that Scipio was approaching with his legions, which occasioned various opinions and reports; for in strange events, rumour generally goes before. Without making any delay in any part of Macedonia, he marched with great haste against Domitius; and when he was come within about twenty miles of him, wheeled on a sudden towards Cassius Longinus in Thessaly. He effected this with such celerity, that news of his march and arrival came together; for to render his march expeditious, he left the baggage of his legions behind him at the river Haliacmon, which divides Macedonia from Thessaly, under the care of Marcus Favonius, with a guard of eight cohorts, and ordered him to build a strong fort there. At the same time, Cotus's cavalry, which used to infest the neighbourhood of Macedonia, flew to attack Cassius's camp, at which Cassius being alarmed, and having received information of Scipio's approach, and seen the horse, which he imagined to be Scipio's, he betook himself to the mountains that environ Thessaly, and thence began to make his route towards Ambracia. But when Scipio was hastening to pursue him, despatches overtook him from Favonius, that Domitius was marching against him with his legions, and that he could not maintain the garrison over which he was appointed, without Scipio's assistance. On receipt of these despatches, Scipio changed his designs and his route, desisted from his pursuit of Cassius, and hastened to relieve Favonius. Accordingly, continuing his march day and night, he came to him so opportunely, that the dust raised by Domitius's army, and Scipio's advanced guard, were observed at the same instant. Thus, the vigilance of Domitius saved Cassius, and the expedition of Scipio, Favonius.

XXXVII—Scipio, having stayed for two days in his camp, along the river Haliacmon, which ran between him and Domitius's camp, on the third day, at dawn, led his army across a ford, and having made a regular encampment the day following, drew up his forces in front of his camp. Domitius thought he ought not to show any reluctance, but should draw out his forces and hazard a battle. But as there was a plain six miles in breadth between the two camps, he posted his army before Scipio's camp; while the latter persevered in not quitting his entrenchment. However, Domitius with difficulty restrained his men, and prevented their beginning a battle; the more so as a rivulet with steep banks, joining Scipio's camp, retarded the progress of our men. When Scipio perceived the eagerness and alacrity of our troops to

engage, suspecting that he should be obliged the next day, either to fight, against his inclination, or to incur great disgrace by keeping within his camp, though he had come with high expectation, yet by advancing rashly, made a shameful end; and at night crossed the river, without even giving the signal for breaking up the camp, and returned to the ground from which he came, and there encamped near the river, on an elevated situation. After a few days, he placed a party of horse in ambush in the night, where our men had usually gone to forage for several days before. And when Quintus Varus, commander of Domitius's horse, came there as usual, they suddenly rushed from their ambush. But our men bravely supported their charge, and returned quickly every man to his own rank, and in their turn, made a general charge on the enemy: and having killed about eighty of them, and put the rest to flight, retreated to their camp with the loss of only two men.
XXXVIII.—After these transactions, Domitius, hoping to allure Scipio to a battle, pretended to be obliged to change his position through want of corn, and having given the signal for decamping, advanced about three miles, and posted his army and cavalry in a convenient place, concealed from the enemy's view. Scipio being in readiness to pursue him, detached his cavalry and a considerable number of light infantry to explore Domitius's route. When they had marched a short way, and their foremost troops were within reach of our ambush, their suspicions being raised by the neighing of the horses, they began to retreat: and the rest who followed them, observing with what speed they retreated, made a halt. Our men, perceiving that the enemy had discovered their plot, and thinking it in vain to wait for any more, having got two troops in their power, intercepted them. Among them was Marcus Opimius, general of the horse, but he made his escape: they either killed or took prisoners all the rest of these two troops, and brought them to Domitius.
XXXIX.—Caesar, having drawn his garrisons out of the sea-ports, as before mentioned, left three cohorts at Oricum to protect the town, and committed to them the charge of his ships of war, which he had transported from Italy. Acilius, as lieutenant-general, had the charge of this duty and the command of the town; he drew the ships into the inner part of the harbour, behind the town, and fastened them to the shore, and sank a merchant-ship in the mouth of the harbour to block it up; and near it he fixed another at anchor, on which he raised a turret, and faced it to the entrance of the port, and filled it with soldiers, and ordered them to keep guard against any sudden attack.
XL.—Cneius, Pompey's son, who commanded the Egyptian fleet, having got intelligence of these things, came to Oricum, and weighed up the ship, that had been sunk, with a windlass, and by straining at it with several ropes, and attacked the other which had been placed by

Acilius to watch the port with several ships, on which he had raised very high turrets, so that fighting as it were from an eminence, and sending fresh men constantly to relieve the fatigued, and at the same time attempting the town on all sides by land, with ladders and his fleet, in order to divide the force of his enemies, he overpowered our men by fatigue, and the immense number of darts, and took the ship, having beat off the men who were put on board to defend it, who, however, made their escape in small boats; and at the same time he seized a natural mole on the opposite side, which almost formed an island over against the town. He carried over land, into the inner part of the harbour, four galleys, by putting rollers under them, and driving them on with levers. Then attacking on both sides the ships of war which were moored to the shore, and were not manned, he carried off four of them, and set the rest on fire. After despatching this business, he left Decimus Laelius, whom he had taken away from the command of the Asiatic fleet, to hinder provisions from being brought into the town from Biblis and Amantia, and went himself to Lissus, where he attacked thirty merchantmen, left within the port by Antonius, and set them on fire. He attempted to storm Lissus, but being delayed three days by the vigorous defence of the Roman citizens who belonged to that district, and of the soldiers which Caesar had sent to keep garrison there, and having lost a few men in the assault, he returned without effecting his object.

XLI.—As soon as Caesar heard that Pompey was at Asparagium, he set out for that place with his army, and having taken the capital of the Parthinians on his march, where there was a garrison of Pompey's, he reached Pompey in Macedonia, on the third day, and encamped beside him; and the day following, having drawn out all his forces before his camp, he offered Pompey battle. But perceiving that he kept within his trenches, he led his army back to his camp, and thought of pursuing some other plan. Accordingly, the day following, he set out with all his forces by a long circuit, through a difficult and narrow road to Dyrrachium; hoping, either that Pompey would be compelled to follow him to Dyrrachium, or that his communication with it might be cut off, because he had deposited there all his provisions and mat['e]riel of war. And so it happened; for Pompey, at first not knowing his design, because he imagined he had taken a route in a different direction from that country, thought that the scarcity of provisions had obliged him to shift his quarters; but having afterwards got true intelligence from his scouts, he decamped the day following, hoping to prevent him by taking a shorter road; which Caesar suspecting might happen, encouraged his troops to submit cheerfully to the fatigue, and having halted a very small part of the night, he arrived early in the morning at

Dyrrachium, when the van of Pompey's army was visible at a distance, and there he encamped.

XLII.—Pompey, being cut off from Dyrrachium, as he was unable to effect his purpose, took a new resolution, and entrenched himself strongly on a rising ground, which is called Petra, where ships of a small size can come in, and be sheltered from some winds. Here he ordered a part of his men-of-war to attend him, and corn and provisions to be brought from Asia, and from all the countries of which he kept possession. Caesar, imagining that the war would be protracted to too great a length, and despairing of his convoys from Italy, because all the coasts were guarded with great diligence by Pompey's adherents; and because his own fleets, which he had built during the winter, in Sicily, Gaul, and Italy, were detained; sent Lucius Canuleius into Epirus to procure corn; and because these countries were too remote, he fixed granaries in certain places, and regulated the carriage of the corn for the neighbouring states. He likewise gave directions that search should be made for whatever corn was in Lissus, the country of the Parthini, and all the places of strength. The quantity was very small, both from the nature of the land (for the country is rough and mountainous, and the people commonly import what grain they use); and because Pompey had foreseen what would happen, and some days before had plundered the Parthini, and having ravaged and dug up their houses, carried off all the corn, which he collected by means of his horse.

XLIII.—Caesar, on being informed of these transactions, pursued measures suggested by the nature of the country. For round Pompey's camps there were several high and rough hills. These he first of all occupied with guards, and raised strong forts on them. Then drawing a fortification from one fort to another, as the nature of each position allowed, he began to draw a line of circumvallation round Pompey; with these views; as he had but a small quantity of corn, and Pompey was strong in cavalry, that he might furnish his army with corn and other necessaries from all sides with less danger: secondly, to prevent Pompey from foraging, and thereby render his horse ineffectual in the operations of the war; and thirdly, to lessen his reputation, on which he saw he depended greatly, among foreign nations, when a report should have spread throughout the world that he was blockaded by Caesar, and dare not hazard a battle.

XLIV.—Neither was Pompey willing to leave the sea and Dyrrachium, because he had lodged his mat['e]riel there, his weapons, arms, and engines; and supplied his army with corn from it by his ships: nor was he able to put a stop to Caesar's works without hazarding a battle, which at that time he had determined not to do. Nothing was left but to adopt the last resource, namely, to possess himself of as many hills as

he could, and cover as great an extent of country as possible with his troops, and divide Caesar's forces as much as possible; and so it happened: for having raised twenty-four forts, and taken in a compass of fifteen miles, he got forage in this space, and within this circuit there were several fields lately sown, in which the cattle might feed in the meantime. And as our men, who had completed their works by drawing lines of communication from one fort to another, were afraid that Pompey's men would sally out from some part, and attack us in the rear; so the enemy were making a continued fortification in a circuit within ours to prevent us from breaking in on any side, or surrounding them on the rear. But they completed their works first; both because they had a greater number of men, and because they had a smaller compass to enclose. When Caesar attempted to gain any place, though Pompey had resolved not to oppose him with his whole force or to come to a general engagement; yet he detached to particular places slingers and archers, with which his army abounded, and several of our men were wounded, and filled with great dread of the arrows; and almost all the soldiers made coats or coverings for themselves of hair cloths, tarpaulins, or raw hides to defend them against the weapons.
XLV.—In seizing the posts, each exerted his utmost power: Caesar, to confine Pompey within as narrow a compass as possible; Pompey, to occupy as many hills as he could in as large a circuit as possible, and several skirmishes were fought in consequence of it. In one of these, when Caesar's ninth legion had gained a certain post, and had begun to fortify it; Pompey possessed himself of a hill near to and opposite the same place, and endeavoured to annoy the men while at work; and as the approach on one side was almost level, he first surrounded it with archers and slingers, and afterwards by detaching a strong party of light infantry, and using his engines, he stopped our works: and it was no easy matter for our men at once to defend themselves, and to proceed with their fortifications. When Caesar perceived that his troops were wounded from all sides, he determined to retreat and give up the post; his retreat was down a precipice, on which account they pushed on with more spirit, and would not allow us to retire, because they imagined that we resigned the place through fear. It is reported that Pompey said that day in triumph to his friends about him, "That he would consent to be accounted a general of no experience, if Caesar's legions effected a retreat without considerable loss from that ground into which they had rashly advanced."
XLVI.—Caesar, being uneasy about the retreat of his soldiers, ordered hurdles to be carried to the further side of the hill, and to be placed opposite to the enemy, and behind them a trench of a moderate breadth to be sunk by his soldiers under shelter of the hurdles: and the ground

to be made as difficult as possible. He himself disposed slingers in convenient places to cover our men in their retreat. These things being completed, he ordered his legions to file off. Pompey's men insultingly and boldly pursued and chased us, levelling the hurdles that were thrown up in the front of our works, in order to pass over the trench. Which as soon as Caesar perceived, being afraid that his men would appear not to retreat, but to be repulsed, and that greater loss might be sustained, when his men were almost half way down the hill, he encouraged them by Antonius, who commanded that legion, ordered the signal of battle to be sounded, and a charge to be made on the enemy. The soldiers of the ninth legion suddenly closing their files threw their javelins, and advancing impetuously from the low ground up the steep, drove Pompey's men precipitately before them, and obliged them to turn their backs; but their retreat was greatly impeded by the hurdles that lay in a long line before them, and the pallisadoes which were in their way, and the trenches that were sunk. But our men being contented to retreat without injury, having killed several of the enemy, and lost but five of their own, very quietly retired, and having seized some other hills somewhat on this side of that place, completed their fortifications.

XLVII.—This method of conducting a war was new and unusual, as well on account of the number of forts, the extent and greatness of the works, and the manner of attack and defence, as on account of other circumstances. For all who have attempted to besiege any person, have attacked the enemy when they were frightened or weak, or after a defeat; or have been kept in fear of some attack, when they themselves have had a superior force both of foot and horse. Besides, the usual design of a siege is to cut off the enemy's supplies. On the contrary, Caesar, with an inferior force, was enclosing troops sound and unhurt, and who had abundance of all things. For there arrived every day a prodigious number of ships, which brought them provisions: nor could the wind blow from any point that would not be favourable to some of them. Whereas, Caesar, having consumed all the corn far and near, was in very great distress, but his soldiers bore all with uncommon patience. For they remembered that they lay under the same difficulties last year in Spain, and yet by labour and patience had concluded a dangerous war. They recollected too that they had suffered an alarming scarcity at Alesia, and a much greater at Avaricum, and yet had returned victorious over mighty nations. They refused neither barley nor pulse when offered them, and they held in great esteem cattle, of which they got great quantities from Epirus.

XLVIII.—There was a sort of root, called chara, discovered by the troops which served under Valerius. This they mixed up with milk, and it greatly contributed to relieve their want. They made it into a sort of bread. They had great plenty of it: loaves made of this, when Pompey's men upbraided ours with want, they frequently threw among them to damp their hopes.

XLIX.—The corn was now beginning to ripen, and their hope supported their want, as they were confident of having abundance in a short time. And there were frequently heard declarations of the soldiers on guard, in discourse with each other, that they would rather live on the bark of the trees, than let Pompey escape from their hands. For they were often told by deserters, that they could scarcely maintain their horses, and that their other cattle was dead: that they themselves were not in good health from their confinement within so narrow a compass, from the noisome smell, the number of carcasses, and the constant fatigue to them, being men unaccustomed to work, and labouring under a great want of water. For Caesar had either turned the course of all the rivers and streams which ran to the sea, or had dammed them up with strong works. And as the country was mountainous, and the valleys narrow at the bottom, he enclosed them with piles sunk in the ground, and heaped up mould against them to keep in the water. They were therefore obliged to search for low and marshy grounds, and to sink wells, and they had this labour in addition to their daily works. And even these springs were at a considerable distance from some of their posts, and soon dried up with the heat. But Caesar's army enjoyed perfect health and abundance of water, and had plenty of all sorts of provisions except corn; and they had a prospect of better times approaching, and saw greater hopes laid before them by the ripening of the grain.

L.—In this new kind of war, new methods of managing it were invented by both generals. Pompey's men, perceiving by our fires at night, at what part of the works our cohorts were on guard, coming silently upon them discharged their arrows at random among the whole multitude, and instantly retired to their camp: as a remedy against which our men were taught by experience to light their fires in one place, and keep guard in another.

* * * * *

LI.—In the meantime, Publius Sylla, whom Caesar at his departure had left governor of his camp, came up with two legions to assist the cohort; upon whose arrival Pompey's forces were easily repulsed. Nor did they stand the sight and charge of our men, and the foremost falling, the rest turned their backs and quitted the field. But Sylla called our men in from the pursuit, lest their ardour should carry them too far, but most people imagine, that if he had consented to a vigorous pursuit, the war might have been ended that day. His conduct however does not appear to deserve censure; for the duties of a lieutenant-general and of a commander-in-chief are very different; the one is bound to act entirely according to his instructions, the other to regulate his conduct without control, as occasion requires. Sylla, being deputed by Caesar to take care of the camp, and having rescued his men, was satisfied with that, and did not desire to hazard a battle (although this circumstance might probably have had a successful issue), that he might not be thought to have assumed the part of the general. One circumstance laid the Pompeians under great difficulty in making good a retreat: for they had advanced from disadvantageous ground, and were posted on the top of a hill. If they attempted to retire down the steep, they dreaded the pursuit of our men from the rising ground, and there was but a short time till sunset: for in hopes of completing the business, they had protracted the battle almost till night. Taking therefore measures suited to their exigency, and to the shortness of the time, Pompey possessed himself of an eminence, at such a distance from our fort, that no weapon discharged from an engine could reach him. Here he took up a position, and fortified it, and kept all his forces there.

LII.—At the same time, there were engagements in two other places; for Pompey had attacked several forts at once, in order to divide our forces; that no relief might be sent from the neighbouring posts. In one place, Volcatius Tullus sustained the charge of a legion with three cohorts, and beat them off the field. In another, the Germans, having sallied over our fortifications, slew several of the enemy, and retreated safe to our camp.

LIII.—Thus six engagements having happened in one day, three at Dyrrachium, and three at the fortifications, when a computation was made of the number of slain, we found that about two thousand fell on Pompey's side, several of them volunteer veterans and centurions. Among them was Valerius, the son of Lucius Flaccus, who as praetor had formerly had the government of Asia, and six military standards were taken. Of our men, not more than twenty were missing in all the action. But in the fort, not a single soldier escaped without a wound; and in one cohort, four centurions lost their eyes. And being desirous to produce testimony of the fatigue they underwent, and the danger they sustained, they counted to Caesar about thirty thousand arrows which had been thrown into the fort; and in the shield of the centurion Scaeva, which was brought to him, were found two hundred and thirty holes. In reward for this man's services both to himself and the republic, Caesar presented to him two hundred thousand pieces of copper money, and declared him promoted from the eighth to the first centurion. For it appeared that the fort had been in a great measure saved by his exertions; and he afterwards very amply rewarded the cohorts with double pay, corn, clothing, and other military honours.

LIV.—Pompey, having made great additions to his works in the night, the following days built turrets, and having carried his works fifteen feet high, faced that part of his camp with mantlets; and after an interval of five days, taking advantage of a second cloudy night, he barricaded all the gates of his camp to hinder a pursuit, and about midnight quietly marched off his army, and retreated to his old fortifications.

LV.—Aetolia, Acarnania, and Amphilochis, being reduced, as we have related, by Cassius Longinus, and Calvisius Sabinus, Caesar thought he ought to attempt the conquest of Achaia, and to advance farther into the country. Accordingly, he detached Fufius thither, and ordered Quintus Sabinus and Cassius to join him with their cohorts. Upon notice of their approach, Rutilius Lupus, who commanded in Achaia, under Pompey, began to fortify the Isthmus, to prevent Fufius from coming into Achaia. Kalenus recovered Delphi, Thebes, and Orchomenus, by a voluntary submission of those states. Some he subdued by force, the rest he endeavoured to win over to Caesar's interest, by sending deputies round to them. In these things, principally, Fufius was employed.

LVI.—Every day afterwards, Caesar drew up his army on a level ground, and offered Pompey battle, and led his legions almost close to Pompey's camp; and his front line was at no greater distance from the rampart than that no weapons from their engines could reach it. But Pompey, to save his credit and reputation with the world, drew out his legions, but so close to his camp that his rear lines might touch the rampart, and that his whole army, when drawn up, might be protected by the darts discharged from it.

LVII.—Whilst these things were going forward in Achaia and at Dyrrachium, and when it was certainly known that Scipio was arrived in Macedonia, Caesar, never losing sight of his first intention, sends Clodius to him, an intimate friend to both, whom Caesar, on the introduction and recommendation of Pompey, had admitted into the number of his acquaintance. To this man he gave letters and instructions to Pompey, the substance of which was as follows: "That he had made every effort towards peace, and imputed the ill success of those efforts to the fault of those whom he had employed to conduct those negotiations: because they were afraid to carry his proposals to Pompey at an improper time. That Scipio had such authority, that he could not only freely explain what conduct met his approbation, but even in some degree enforce his advice, and govern him [Pompey] if he persisted in error; that he commanded an army independent of Pompey, so that besides his authority, he had strength to compel; and if he did so, all men would be indebted to him for the quiet of Italy, the peace of the provinces, and the preservation of the empire." These proposals Clodius made to him, and for some days at the first appeared to have met with a favourable reception, but afterwards was not admitted to an audience; for Scipio being reprimanded by Favonius, as we found afterwards when the war was ended, and the negotiation having miscarried, Clodius returned to Caesar.

LVIII.—Caesar, that he might the more easily keep Pompey's horse enclosed within Dyrrachium, and prevent them from foraging, fortified the two narrow passes already mentioned with strong works, and erected forts at them. Pompey perceiving that he derived no advantage from his cavalry, after a few days had them conveyed back to his camp by sea. Fodder was so exceedingly scarce that he was obliged to feed his horses upon leaves stripped off the trees, or the tender roots of reeds pounded. For the corn which had been sown within the lines was already consumed, and they would be obliged to supply themselves with fodder from Corcyra and Acarnania, over a long tract of sea; and as the quantity of that fell short, to increase it by mixing barley with it, and by these methods support their cavalry. But when not only the barley and fodder in these parts were consumed, and the herbs cut away, when the leaves too were not to be found on the trees, the horses being almost starved, Pompey thought he ought to make some attempt by a sally.

LIX.—In the number of Caesar's cavalry were two Allobrogians, brothers, named Roscillus and Aegus, the sons of Abducillus, who for several years possessed the chief power in his own state; men of singular valour, whose gallant services Caesar had found very useful in all his wars in Gaul. To them, for these reasons, he had committed the offices of greatest honour in their own country, and took care to have them chosen into the senate at an unusual age, and had bestowed on them lands taken from the enemy, and large pecuniary rewards, and from being needy had made them affluent. Their valour had not only procured them Caesar's esteem, but they were beloved by the whole army. But presuming on Caesar's friendship, and elated with the arrogance natural to a foolish and barbarous people, they despised their countrymen, defrauded their cavalry of their pay, and applied all the plunder to their own use. Displeased at this conduct, their soldiers went in a body to Caesar, and openly complained of their ill usage; and to their other charges added, that false musters were given in to Caesar, and the surcharged pay applied to their own use.

LX.—Caesar, not thinking it a proper time to call them to account, and willing to pardon many faults, on account of their valour, deferred the whole matter, and gave them a private rebuke, for having made a traffic of their troops, and advised them to expect everything from his friendship, and by his past favours to measure their future hopes. This, however, gave them great offence, and made them contemptible in the eyes of the whole army. Of this they became sensible, as well from the reproaches of others, as from the judgment of their own minds, and a consciousness of guilt. Prompted then by shame, and perhaps imagining that they were not liberated from trial, but reserved to a future day, they resolved to break off from us, to put their fortune to a new hazard, and to make trial of new connections. And having conferred with a few of their clients, to whom they could venture to entrust so base an action, they first attempted to assassinate Caius Volusenus, general of the horse (as was discovered at the end of the war), that they might appear to have fled to Pompey after conferring an important service on him. But when that appeared too difficult to put in execution, and no opportunity offered to accomplish it, they borrowed all the money they could, as if they designed to make satisfaction and restitution for what they had defrauded: and having purchased a great number of horses, they deserted to Pompey along with those whom they had engaged in their plot.

LXI.—As they were persons nobly descended and of liberal education, and had come with a great retinue, and several cattle, and were reckoned men of courage, and had been in great esteem with Caesar, and as it was a new and uncommon event, Pompey carried them round all his works, and made an ostentatious show of them, for till that day, not a soldier, either horse or foot, had deserted from Caesar to Pompey, though there were desertions almost every day from Pompey to Caesar: but more commonly among the soldiers levied in Epirus and Aetolia, and in those countries which were in Caesar's possession. But the brothers, having been acquainted with all things, either what was incomplete in our works, or what appeared to the best judges of military matters to be deficient, the particular times, the distance of places, and the various attention of the guards, according to the different temper and character of the officer who commanded the different posts, gave an exact account of all to Pompey.

LXII.—Upon receiving this intelligence, Pompey, who had already formed the design of attempting a sally, as before mentioned, ordered the soldiers to make ozier coverings for their helmets, and to provide fascines. These things being prepared, he embarked on board small boats and row galleys by night, a considerable number of light infantry and archers, with all their fascines, and immediately after midnight, he marched sixty cohorts drafted from the greater camp and the outposts, to that part of our works which extended towards the sea, and were at the farthest distance from Caesar's greater camp. To the same place he sent the ships, which he had freighted with the fascines and light-armed troops; and all the ships of war that lay at Dyrrachium; and to each he gave particular instructions: at this part of the lines Caesar had posted Lentulus Marcellinus, the quaestor, with the ninth legion, and as he was not in a good state of health, Fulvius Costhumus was sent to assist him in the command.

LXIII.—At this place, fronting the enemy, there was a ditch fifteen feet wide, and a rampart ten feet high, and the top of the rampart was ten feet in breadth. At an interval of six hundred feet from that there was another rampart turned the contrary way, with the works lower. For some days before, Caesar, apprehending that our men might be surrounded by sea, had made a double rampart there, that if he should be attacked on both sides, he might have the means in defending himself. But the extent of the lines, and the incessant labour for so many days, because he had enclosed a circuit of seventeen miles with his works, did not allow time to finish them. Therefore the transverse rampart which should make a communication between the other two, was not yet completed. This circumstance was known to Pompey, being told to him by the Allobrogian deserters, and proved of great disadvantage to us. For when our cohorts of the ninth legion were on guard by the sea-side, Pompey's army arrived suddenly by break of day, and their approach was a surprise to our men, and at the same time, the soldiers that came by sea cast their darts on the front rampart; and the ditches were filled with fascines: and the legionary soldiers terrified those that defended the inner rampart, by applying the scaling ladders, and by engines and weapons of all sorts, and a vast multitude of archers poured round upon them from every side. Besides, the coverings of oziers, which they had laid over their helmets, were a great security to them against the blows of stones which were the only weapons that our soldiers had. And therefore, when our men were oppressed in every manner, and were scarcely able to make resistance, the defect in our works was observed, and Pompey's soldiers, landing between the two ramparts, where the work was unfinished, attacked our men in the rear, and having beat them from both sides of the fortification, obliged them to flee.

LXIV.—Marcellinus, being informed of this disorder, detached some cohorts to the relief of our men, who seeing them flee from the camp, were neither able to persuade them to rally at their approach, nor themselves to sustain the enemy's charge. And in like manner, whatever additional assistance was sent, was infected by the fears of the defeated, and increased the terror and danger. For retreat was prevented by the multitude of the fugitives. In that battle, when the eagle-bearer was dangerously wounded, and began to grow weak, having got sight of our horse, he said to them, "This eagle have I defended with the greatest care for many years, at the hazard of my life, and now in my last moments restore it to Caesar with the same fidelity. Do not, I conjure you, suffer a dishonour to be sustained in the field, which never before happened to Caesar's army, but deliver it safe into his hands." By this accident the eagle was preserved, but all the centurions of the first cohorts were killed, except the principal.

LXV.—And now the Pompeians, after great havoc of our troops, were approaching Marcellinus's camp, and had struck no small terror into the rest of the cohorts, when Marcus Antonius, who commanded the nearest fort, being informed of what had happened, was observed descending from the rising ground with twelve cohorts. His arrival checked the Pompeians, and encouraged our men to recover from their extreme affright. And shortly after, Caesar having got notice by the smoke from all the forts, which was the usual signal on such occasions, drafted off some cohorts from the outposts, and went to the scene of action. And having there learnt the loss he had sustained, and perceiving that Pompey had forced our works, and had encamped along the coast, so that he was at liberty to forage, and had a communication with his shipping, he altered his plan for conducting the war, as his design had not succeeded, and ordered a strong encampment to be made near Pompey.

LXVI.—When this work was finished, Caesar's scouts observed that some cohorts, which to them appeared like a legion, were retired behind the wood, and were on their march to the old camp. The situation of the two camps was as follows: a few days before, when Caesar's ninth legion had opposed a party of Pompey's troops, and were endeavouring to enclose them, Caesar's troops formed a camp in that place. This camp joined a certain wood, and was not above four hundred paces distant from the sea. Afterwards, changing his design for certain reasons, Caesar removed his camp to a small distance beyond that place; and after a few days, Pompey took possession of it, and added more extensive works, leaving the inner rampart standing, as he intended to keep several legions there. By this means, the lesser camp included within the greater, answered the purpose of a fort and citadel. He had also carried an entrenchment from the left angle of the camp to the river, about four hundred paces, that his soldiers might have more liberty and less danger in fetching water. But he too, changing his design for reasons not necessary to be mentioned, abandoned the place. In this condition the camp remained for several days, the works being all entire.

LXVII.—Caesar's scouts brought him word that the standard of a legion was carried to this place. That the same thing was seen he was assured by those in the higher forts. This place was half a mile distant from Pompey's new camp. Caesar, hoping to surprise this legion, and anxious to repair the loss sustained that day, left two cohorts employed in the works to make an appearance of entrenching himself, and by a different route, as privately as he could, with his other cohorts amounting to thirty-three, among which was the ninth legion, which had lost so many centurions, and whose privates were greatly reduced in number, he marched in two lines against Pompey's legion and his lesser camp. Nor did this first opinion deceive him. For he reached the place before Pompey could have notice of it; and though the works were strong, yet having made the attack with the left wing, which he commanded in person, he obliged the Pompeians to quit the rampart in disorder. A barricade had been raised before the gates, at which a short contest was maintained, our men endeavouring to force their way in, and the enemy to defend the camp; Titus Pulcio, by whose means we have related that Caius Antonius's army was betrayed, defending them with singular courage. But the valour of our men prevailed, and having cut down the barricade, they first forced the greater camp, and after that the fort which was enclosed within it: and as the legion on its repulse had retired to this, they slew several defending themselves there.
LXVIII.—But Fortune, who exerts a powerful influence as well in other matters, as especially in war, effects great changes from trifling causes, as happened at this time. For the cohorts on Caesar's right wing, through ignorance of the place, followed the direction of that rampart, which ran along from the camp to the river, whilst they were in search of a gate, and imagined that it belonged to the camp. But when they found that it led to the river, and that nobody opposed them, they immediately climbed over the rampart, and were followed by all our cavalry.
LXIX.—In the meantime Pompey, by the great delay which this occasioned, being informed of what had happened, marched with the fifth legion, which he called away from their work to support his party; and at the same time his cavalry were advancing up to ours, and an army in order of battle was seen at a distance by our men who had taken possession of the camp, and the face of affairs was suddenly changed. For Pompey's legion, encouraged by the hope of speedy support, attempted to make a stand at the Decuman gate, and made a bold charge on our men. Caesar's cavalry, who had mounted the rampart by a narrow breach, being apprehensive of their retreat, were the first to flee. The right wing, which had been separated from the left, observing the terror of the cavalry, to prevent their being overpowered

within the lines, were endeavouring to retreat by the same way as they burst in; and most of them, lest they should be engaged in the narrow passes, threw themselves down a rampart ten feet high into the trenches; and the first being trodden to death, the rest procured their safety and escaped over their bodies. The soldiers of the left wing, perceiving from the rampart that Pompey was advancing, and their own friends fleeing, being afraid that they should be enclosed between the two ramparts, as they had an enemy both within and without, strove to secure their retreat the same way they came. All was disorder, consternation, and flight; insomuch that, when Caesar laid hold of the colours of those who were running away, and desired them to stand, some left their horses behind, and continued to run in the same manner; others through fear even threw away their colours, nor did a single man face about.

LXX.—In this calamity, the following favourable circumstance occurred to prevent the ruin of our whole army, viz., that Pompey suspecting an ambuscade (because, as I suppose, the success had far exceeded his hopes, as he had seen his men a moment before fleeing from the camp), durst not for some time approach the fortification; and that his horse were retarded from pursuing, because the passes and gates were in possession of Caesar's soldiers. Thus a trifling circumstance proved of great importance to each party; for the rampart drawn from the camp to the river, interrupted the progress and certainty of Caesar's victory, after he had forced Pompey's camp. The same thing, by retarding the rapidity of the enemy's pursuit, preserved our army.

LXXI.—In the two actions of this day, Caesar lost nine hundred and sixty rank and file, several Roman knights of distinction, Felginas Tuticanus Gallus, a senator's son; Caius Felginas from Placentia; Aulus Gravius from Puteoli; Marcus Sacrativir from Capua; and thirty-two military tribunes and centurions. But the greatest part of all these perished without a wound, being trodden to death in the trenches, on the ramparts and banks of the river by reason of the terror and flight of their own men. Pompey, after this battle, was saluted Imperator; this title he retained, and allowed himself to be addressed by it afterwards. But neither in his letters to the senate, nor in the fasces, did he use the laurel as a mark of honour. But Labienus, having obtained his consent that the prisoners should be delivered up to him, had them all brought out, as it appeared, to make a show of them, and that Pompey might place a greater confidence in him who was a deserter; and calling them fellow soldiers, and asking them in the most insulting manner whether it was usual with veterans to flee, ordered them to be put to death in the sight of the whole army.

LXXII.-Pompey's party were so elated with confidence and spirit at this success, that they thought no more of the method of conducting the war, but thought that they were already conquerors. They did not consider that the smallness of our numbers, and the disadvantage of the place and the confined nature of the ground occasioned by their having first possessed themselves of the camp, and the double danger both from within and without the fortifications, and the separation of the army into two parts, so that the one could not give relief to the other, were the cause of our defeat. They did not consider, in addition, that the contest was not decided by a vigorous attack, nor a regular battle; and that our men had suffered greater loss from their numbers and want of room, than they had sustained from the enemy. In fine, they did not reflect on the common casualties of war; how trifling causes, either from groundless suspicions, sudden affright, or religious scruples, have oftentimes been productive of considerable losses; how often an army has been unsuccessful either by the misconduct of the general, or the oversight of a tribune; but as if they had proved victorious by their valour, and as if no change could ever take place, they published the success of the day throughout the world by reports and letters.
LXXIII.—Caesar, disappointed in his first intentions, resolved to change the whole plan of his operations. Accordingly, he at once called in all out-posts, gave over the siege, and collecting his army into one place, addressed his soldiers and encouraged them "not to be troubled at what had happened, nor to be dismayed at it, but to weigh their many successful engagements against one disappointment, and that, too, a trifling one. That they ought to be grateful to Fortune, through whose favour they had recovered Italy without the effusion of blood; through whose favour they had subdued the two Spains, though protected by a most warlike people under the command of the most skilful and experienced generals: through whose favour they had reduced to submission the neighbouring states that abounded with corn: in fine, that they ought to remember with what success they had been all transported safe through blockading fleets of the enemy, which possessed not only the ports, but even the coasts: that if all their attempts were not crowned with success, the defects of Fortune must be supplied by industry; and whatever loss had been sustained, ought to be attributed rather to her caprices than to any faults in him: that he had chosen a safe ground for the engagement, that he had possessed himself of the enemy's camp; that he had beaten them out, and overcome them when they offered resistance; but whether their own terror or some mistake, or whether Fortune herself had interrupted a victory almost secured and certain, they ought all now to use their utmost efforts to repair by their valour the loss which had been incurred; if they did so,

their misfortunes would turn to their advantage, as it happened at Gergovia, and those who feared to face the enemy would be the first to offer themselves to battle.

LXXIV.—Having concluded his speech, he disgraced some standard-bearers, and reduced them to the ranks; for the whole army was seized with such grief at their loss, and with such an ardent desire of repairing their disgrace, that not a man required the command of his tribune or centurion, but they imposed each on himself severer labours than usual as a punishment, and at the same time were so inflamed with eagerness to meet the enemy, that the officers of the first rank, sensibly affected at their entreaties, were of opinion that they ought to continue in their present posts, and commit their fate to the hazard of a battle. But, on the other hand, Caesar could not place sufficient confidence in men so lately thrown into consternation, and thought he ought to allow them time to recover their dejected spirits; and having abandoned his works, he was apprehensive of being distressed for want of corn.

LXXV.—Accordingly, suffering no time to intervene but what was necessary for a proper attention to be paid to the sick and wounded, he sent on all his baggage privately in the beginning of the night from his camp to Apollonia, and ordered them not to halt till they had performed their journey; and he detached one legion with them as a convoy. This affair being concluded, having retained only two legions in his camp; he marched the rest of his army out at three o'clock in the morning by several gates, and sent them forward by the same route; and in a short space after, that the military practice might be preserved, and his march known as late as possible, he ordered the signal for decamping to be given; and setting out immediately, and following the rear of his own army, he was soon out of sight of the camp. Nor did Pompey, as soon as he had notice of his design, make any delay to pursue him; but with a view to surprise them whilst encumbered with baggage on their march, and not yet recovered from their fright, he led his army out of his camp, and sent his cavalry on to retard our rear; but was not able to come up with them, because Caesar had got far before him, and marched without baggage. But when we reached the river Genusus, the banks being steep, their horse overtook our rear, and detained them by bringing them to action. To oppose whom, Caesar sent his horse, and intermixed with them about four hundred of his advanced light troops, who attacked their horse with such success, that having routed them all, and killed several, they returned without any loss to the main body.

LXXVI.—Having performed the exact march which he had proposed that day, and having led his army over the river Genusus, Caesar posted himself in his old camp opposite Asparagium; and kept his soldiers close within the entrenchments; and ordered the horse, who had been sent out under pretence of foraging, to retire immediately into the camp, through the Decuman gate. Pompey, in like manner, having completed the same day's march, took post in his old camp at Asparagium; and his soldiers, as they had no work (the fortifications being entire), made long excursions, some to collect wood and forage; others, invited by the nearness of the former camp, laid up their arms in their tents, and quitted the entrenchments in order to bring what they had left behind them, because the design of marching being adopted in a hurry, they had left a considerable part of their waggons and luggage behind. Being thus incapable of pursuing, as Caesar had foreseen, about noon he gave the signal for marching, led out his army, and doubling that day's march, he advanced eight miles beyond Pompey's camp; who could not pursue him, because his troops were dispersed.

LXXVII.—The next day Caesar sent his baggage forward early in the night, and marched off himself immediately after the fourth watch: that if he should be under the necessity of risking an engagement, he might meet a sudden attack with an army free from incumbrance. He did so for several days successively, by which means he was enabled to effect his march over the deepest rivers, and through the most intricate roads without any loss. For Pompey, after the first day's delay, and the fatigue which he endured for some days in vain, though he exerted himself by forced marches, and was anxious to overtake us, who had got the start of him, on the fourth day desisted from the pursuit, and determined to follow other measures.

LXXVIII.—Caesar was obliged to go to Apollonia, to lodge his wounded, pay his army, confirm his friends, and leave garrisons in the towns. But for these matters, he allowed no more time than was necessary for a person in haste. And being apprehensive for Domitius, lest he should be surprised by Pompey's arrival, he hastened with all speed and earnestness to join him; for he planned the operations of the whole campaign on these principles: that if Pompey should march after him, he would be drawn off from the sea, and from those forces which he had provided in Dyrrachium, and separated from his corn and magazines, and be obliged to carry on the war on equal terms; but if he crossed over into Italy, Caesar, having effected a junction with Domitius, would march through Illyricum to the relief of Italy; but if he endeavoured to storm Apollonia and Oricum, and exclude him from the whole coast, he hoped, by besieging Scipio, to oblige him, of necessity, to come to his assistance. Accordingly, Caesar despatching couriers, writes to Domitius, and acquaints him with his wishes on the subject: and having stationed a garrison of four cohorts at Apollonia, one at Lissus, and three at Oricum, besides those who were sick of their wounds, he set forward on his march through Epirus and Acarnania.

Pompey, also, guessing at Caesar's design, determined to hasten to Scipio, that if Caesar should march in that direction, he might be ready to relieve him; but that if Caesar should be unwilling to quit the sea-coast and Corcyra, because he expected legions and cavalry from Italy, he himself might fall on Domitius with all his forces.
LXXIX.—For these reasons, each of them studied despatch, that he might succour his friends, and not miss an opportunity of surprising his enemies. But Caesar's engagements at Apolloma had carried him aside from the direct road. Pompey had taken the short road to Macedonia, through Candavia. To this was added another unexpected disadvantage, that Domitius, who for several days had been encamped opposite Scipio, had quitted that post for the sake of provisions, and had marched to Heraclea Sentica, a city subject to Candavia; so that fortune herself seemed to throw him in Pompey's way. Of this, Caesar was ignorant up to this time. Letters likewise being sent by Pompey through all the provinces and states, with an account of the action at Dyrrachium, very much enlarged and exaggerated beyond the real facts, a rumour had been circulated, that Caesar had been defeated and forced to flee, and had lost almost all his forces. These reports had made the roads dangerous, and drawn off some states from his alliance: whence it happened, that the messengers despatched by Caesar, by several different roads to Domitius, and by Domitius to Caesar, were not able by any means to accomplish their journey. But the Allobroges, who were in the retinue of Aegus and Roscillus, and who had deserted to Pompey, having met on the road a scouting party of Domitius; either from old acquaintance, because they had served together in Gaul, or elated with vain glory, gave them an account of all that had happened, and informed them of Caesar's departure, and Pompey's arrival. Domitius, who was scarce four hours' march distant, having got intelligence from these, by the courtesy of the enemy, avoided the danger, and met Caesar coming to join him at Aeginium, a town on the confines of and opposite to Thessaly.
LXXX.—The two armies being united, Caesar marched to Gomphi, which is the first town of Thessaly on the road from Epirus. Now, the Thessalians, a few months before, had of themselves sent ambassadors to Caesar, offering him the free use of everything in their power, and requesting a garrison for their protection. But the report, already spoken of, of the battle at Dyrrachium, which it had exaggerated in many particulars, had arrived before him. In consequence of which, Androsthenes, the praetor of Thessaly, as he preferred to be the companion of Pompey's victory, rather than Caesar's associate in his misfortunes, collected all the people, both slaves and freemen, from the country into the town and shut the gates, and despatched messengers to

Scipio and Pompey "to come to his relief, that he could depend on the strength of the town, if succour was speedily sent; but that it could not withstand a long siege." Scipio, as soon as he received advice of the departure of the armies from Dyrrachium, had marched with his legions to Larissa: Pompey was not yet arrived near Thessaly. Caesar having fortified his camp, ordered scaling ladders and pent-houses to be made for a sudden assault, and hurdles to be provided. As soon as they were ready, he exhorted his soldiers, and told them of what advantage it would be to assist them with all sorts of necessaries if they made themselves masters of a rich and plentiful town: and, at the same time, to strike terror into other states by the example of this, and to effect this with speed, before auxiliaries could arrive. Accordingly, taking advantage of the unusual ardour of the soldiers, he began his assault on the town at a little after three o'clock on the very day on which he arrived, and took it, though defended with very high walls, before sunset, and gave it up to his army to plunder, and immediately decamped from before it, and marched to Metropolis, with such rapidity as to outstrip any messenger or rumour of the taking of Gomphi.

LXXXI.—The inhabitants of Metropolis, at first influenced by the same rumours, followed the same measures, shut the gates and manned their walls. But when they were made acquainted with the fate of the city of Gomphi by some prisoners, whom Caesar had ordered to be brought up to the walls, they threw open their gates. As he preserved them with the greatest care, there was not a state in Thessaly (except Larissa, which was awed by a strong army of Scipio's), but on comparing the fate of the inhabitants of Metropolis with the severe treatment of Gomphi, gave admission to Caesar, and obeyed his orders. Having chosen a position convenient for procuring corn, which was now almost ripe on the ground, he determined there to wait Pompey's arrival, and to make it the centre of all his warlike operations.

LXXXII.—Pompey arrived in Thessaly a few days after, and having harangued the combined army, returned thanks to his own men, and exhorted Scipio's soldiers, that as the victory was now secured, they should endeavour to merit a part of the rewards and booty. And receiving all the legions into one camp, he shared his honours with Scipio, ordered the trumpet to be sounded at his tent, and a pavilion to be erected for him. The forces of Pompey being thus augmented, and two such powerful armies united, their former expectations were confirmed, and their hopes of victory so much increased, that whatever time intervened was considered as so much delay to their return into Italy: and whenever Pompey acted with slowness and caution, they used to exclaim, that it was the business only of a single day, but that

he had a passion for power, and was delighted in having persons of consular and praetorian rank in the number of his slaves. And they now began to dispute openly about rewards and priesthoods, and disposed of the consulate for several years to come. Others put in their claims for the houses and properties of all who were in Caesar's camp, and in that council there was a warm debate, whether Lucius Hirrus, who had been sent by Pompey against the Parthians, should be admitted a candidate for the praetorship in his absence at the next election; his friends imploring Pompey's honour to fulfil the engagements which he had made to him at his departure, that he might not seem deceived through his authority: whilst others, embarked in equal labour and danger, pleaded that no individual ought to have a preference before all the rest.
LXXXIII.—Already Domitius, Scipio, and Lentulus Spinthur, in their daily quarrels about Caesar's priesthood, openly abused each other in the most scurrilous language. Lentulus urging the respect due to his age, Domitius boasting his interest in the city and his dignity, and Scipio presuming on his alliance with Pompey. Attius Rufus charged Lucius Afranius before Pompey with betraying the army in the action that happened in Spain, and Lucius Domitius declared in the council that it was his wish that, when the war should be ended, three billets should be given to all the senators who had taken part with them in the war, and that they should pass sentence on every single person who had stayed behind at Rome, or who had been within Pompey's garrisons and had not contributed their assistance in the military operations; that by the first billet they should-have power to acquit, by the second to pass sentence of death, and by the third to impose a pecuniary fine. In short, Pompey's whole army talked of nothing but the honours or sums of money which were to be their rewards, or of vengeance on their enemies; and never considered how they were to defeat their enemies, but in what manner they should use their victory.
LXXXIV.—Corn being provided, and his soldiers refreshed, and a sufficient time having elapsed since the engagement at Dyrrachium, when Caesar thought he had sufficiently sounded the disposition of his troops, he thought that he ought to try whether Pompey had any intention or inclination to come to a battle. Accordingly he led his troops out of the camp, and ranged them in order of battle, at first on their own ground, and at a small distance from Pompey's camp: but afterwards for several days in succession he advanced from his own camp, and led them up to the hills on which Pompey's troops were posted, which conduct inspired his army every day with fresh courage. However he adhered to his former purpose respecting his cavalry, for as he was by many degrees inferior in number, he selected the youngest and most active of the advanced guard, and desired them to fight

intermixed with the horse, and they by constant practice acquired experience in this kind of battle. By these means it was brought to pass that a thousand of his horse would dare, even on open ground, to stand against seven thousand of Pompey's, if occasion required, and would not be much terrified by their number. For even on one of those days he was successful in a cavalry action, and killed one of the two Allobrogians who had deserted to Pompey, as we before observed, and several others.

LXXXV.—Pompey, because he was encamped on a hill, drew up his army at the very foot of it, ever in expectation, as may be conjectured, that Caesar would expose himself to this disadvantageous situation. Caesar, seeing no likelihood of being able to bring Pompey to an action, judged it the most expedient method of conducting the war, to decamp from that post, and to be always in motion: with this hope, that by shifting his camp and removing from place to place, he might be more conveniently supplied with corn, and also, that by being in motion he might get some opportunity of forcing them to battle, and might by constant marches harass Pompey's army, which was not accustomed to fatigue. These matters being settled, when the signal for marching was given, and the tents struck, it was observed that shortly before, contrary to his daily practice, Pompey's army had advanced farther than usual from his entrenchments, so that it appeared possible to come to an action on equal ground. Then Caesar addressed himself to his soldiers, when they were at the gates of the camp, ready to march out. "We must defer," says he, "our march at present, and set our thoughts on battle, which has been our constant wish; let us then meet the foe with resolute souls. We shall not hereafter easily find such an opportunity." He immediately marched out at the head of his troops.

LXXXVI.—Pompey also, as was afterward known, at the unanimous solicitation of his friends, had determined to try the fate of a battle. For he had even declared in council a few days before that, before the battalions came to battle, Caesar's army would be put to the rout. When most people expressed their surprise at it, "I know," says he, "that I promise a thing almost incredible; but hear the plan on which I proceed, that you may march to battle with more confidence and resolution. I have persuaded our cavalry, and they have engaged to execute it, as soon as the two armies have met, to attack Caesar's right wing on the flank, and enclosing their army on the rear, throw them into disorder, and put them to the rout, before we shall throw a weapon against the enemy. By this means we shall put an end to the war, without endangering the legions, and almost without a blow. Nor is this a difficult matter, as we far outnumber them in cavalry." At the same time he gave them notice to be ready for battle on the day following, and since the opportunity which they had so often wished for was now arrived, not to disappoint the opinion generally entertained of their experience and valour.

LXXXVII.—After him Labienus spoke, as well to express his contempt of Caesar's forces, as to extol Pompey's scheme with the highest encomiums. "Think not, Pompey," says he, "that this is the army which conquered Gaul and Germany; I was present at all those battles and do not speak at random on a subject to which I am a stranger: a very small part of that army now remains, great numbers lost their lives, as must necessarily happen in so many battles, many fell victims to the autumnal pestilence in Italy, many returned home, and many were left behind on the continent. Have you not heard that the cohorts at Brundisium are composed of invalids? The forces which you now behold, have been recruited by levies lately made in Hither Spain, and the greater part from the colonies beyond the Po; moreover, the flower of the forces perished in the two engagements at Dyrrachium." Having so said, he took an oath, never to return to his camp unless victorious; and he encouraged the rest to do the like. Pompey applauded his proposal, and took the same oath; nor did any person present hesitate to take it. After this had passed in the council they broke up full of hopes and joy, and in imagination anticipated victory; because they thought that in a matter of such importance, no groundless assertion could be made by a general of such experience.

LXXXVIII.—When Caesar had approached near Pompey's camp, he observed that his army was drawn up in the following manner:—On the left wing were the two legions delivered over by Caesar at the beginning of the disputes in compliance with the senate's decree, one of which was called the first, the other the third. Here Pompey commanded in person. Scipio with the Syrian legions commanded the centre. The Cilician legion in conjunction with the Spanish cohorts, which we said were brought over by Afranius, were disposed on the right wing. These Pompey considered his steadiest troops. The rest he had interspersed between the centre and the wing, and he had a hundred and ten complete cohorts; these amounted to forty-five thousand men. He had besides two cohorts of volunteers, who having received favours from him in former wars, flocked to his standard: these were dispersed through his whole army. The seven remaining cohorts he had disposed to protect his camp, and the neighbouring forts. His right wing was secured by a river with steep banks; for which reason he placed all his cavalry, archers, and slingers, on his left wing.

LXXXIX.—Caesar, observing his former custom, had placed the tenth legion on the right, the ninth on the left, although it was very much weakened by the battles at Dyrrachium. He placed the eighth legion so

close to the ninth, as to almost make one of the two, and ordered them to support one another. He drew up on the field eighty cohorts, making a total of twenty-two thousand men. He left two cohorts to guard the camp. He gave the command of the left wing to Antonius, of the right to P. Sulla, and of the centre to Cn. Domitius: he himself took his post opposite Pompey. At the same time, fearing, from the disposition of the enemy which we have previously mentioned, lest his right wing might be surrounded by their numerous cavalry, he rapidly drafted a single cohort from each of the legions composing the third line, formed of them a fourth line, and opposed them to Pompey's cavalry, and, acquainting them with his wishes, admonished them that the success of that day depended on their courage. At the same time he ordered the third line, and the entire army not to charge without his command: that he would give the signal whenever he wished them to do so.
XC.—When he was exhorting his army to battle, according to the military custom, and spoke to them of the favours that they had constantly received from him, he took especial care to remind them "that he could call his soldiers to witness the earnestness with which he had sought peace, the efforts that he had made by Vatinius to gain a conference [with Labienus], and likewise by Claudius to treat with Scipio, in what manner he had exerted himself at Oricum, to gain permission from Libo to send ambassadors; that he had been always reluctant to shed the blood of his soldiers, and did not wish to deprive the republic of one or other of her armies." After delivering this speech, he gave by a trumpet the signal to his soldiers, who were eagerly demanding it, and were very impatient for the onset.
XCI.—There was in Caesar's army a volunteer of the name of Crastinus, who the year before had been first centurion of the tenth legion, a man of pre-eminent bravery. He, when the signal was given, says, "Follow me, my old comrades, and display such exertions in behalf of your general as you have determined to do: this is our last battle, and when it shall be won, he will recover his dignity, and we our liberty." At the same time he looked back to Caesar, and said, "General, I will act in such a manner to-day, that you will feel grateful tome living or dead." After uttering these words he charged first on the right wing, and about one hundred and twenty chosen volunteers of the same century followed.
XCII.—There was so much space left between the two lines, as sufficed for the onset of the hostile armies: but Pompey had ordered his soldiers to await Caesar's attack, and not to advance from their position, or suffer their line to be put into disorder. And he is said to have done this by the advice of Caius Triarius, that the impetuosity of the charge of Caesar's soldiers might be checked, and their line broken, and that

Pompey's troops remaining in their ranks, might attack them while in disorder; and he thought that the javelins would fall with less force if the soldiers were kept in their ground, than if they met them in their course; at the same time he trusted that Caesar's soldiers, after running over double the usual ground, would become weary and exhausted by the fatigue. But to me Pompey seems to have acted without sufficient reason: for there is a certain impetuosity of spirit and an alacrity implanted by nature in the hearts of all men, which is inflamed by a desire to meet the foe. This a general should endeavour not to repress, but to increase; nor was it a vain institution of our ancestors, that the trumpets should sound on all sides, and a general shout be raised; by which they imagined that the enemy were struck with terror, and their own army inspired with courage.

XCIII.—But our men, when the signal was given, rushed forward with their javelins ready to be launched, but perceiving that Pompey's men did not run to meet their charge, having acquired experience by custom, and being practised in former battles, they of their own accord repressed their speed, and halted almost midway, that they might not come up with the enemy when their strength was exhausted, and after a short respite they again renewed their course, and threw their javelins, and instantly drew their swords, as Caesar had ordered them. Nor did Pompey's men fail in this crisis, for they received our javelins, stood our charge, and maintained their ranks: and having launched their javelins, had recourse to their swords. At the same time Pompey's horse, according to their orders, rushed out at once from his left wing, and his whole host of archers poured after them. Our cavalry did not withstand their charge: but gave ground a little, upon which Pompey's horse pressed them more vigorously, and began to file off in troops, and flank our army. When Caesar perceived this, he gave the signal to his fourth line, which he had formed of the six cohorts. They instantly rushed forward and charged Pompey's horse with such fury, that not a man of them stood; but all wheeling about, not only quitted their post, but galloped forward to seek a refuge in the highest mountains. By their retreat the archers and slingers, being left destitute and defenceless, were all cut to pieces. The cohorts, pursuing their success, wheeled about upon Pompey's left wing, whilst his infantry still continued to make battle, and attacked them in the rear.

XCIV.—At the same time Caesar ordered his third line to advance, which till then had not been engaged, but had kept their post. Thus, new and fresh troops having come to the assistance of the fatigued, and others having made an attack on their rear, Pompey's men were not able to maintain their ground, but all fled, nor was Caesar deceived in his opinion that the victory, as he had declared in his speech to his soldiers, must have its beginning from those six cohorts which he had placed as a fourth line to oppose the horse. For by them the cavalry were routed; by them the archers and slingers were cut to pieces; by them the left wing of Pompey's army was surrounded, and obliged to be the first to flee. But when Pompey saw his cavalry routed, and that part of his army on which he reposed his greatest hopes thrown into confusion, despairing of the rest, he quitted the field, and retreated straightway on horseback to his camp, and calling to the centurions, whom he had placed to guard the praetorian gate, with a loud voice, that the soldiers might hear: "Secure the camp," says he, "defend it with diligence, if any danger should threaten it; I will visit the other gates, and encourage the guards of the camp." Having thus said, he retired into his tent in utter despair, yet anxiously waiting the issue.

XCV.—Caesar having forced the Pompeians to flee into their entrenchment, and thinking that he ought not to allow them any respite to recover from their fright, exhorted his soldiers to take advantage of fortune's kindness, and to attack the camp. Though they were fatigued by the intense heat, for the battle had continued till mid-day, yet, being prepared to undergo any labour, they cheerfully obeyed his command. The camp was bravely defended by the cohorts which had been left to guard it, but with much more spirit by the Thracians and foreign auxiliaries. For the soldiers who had fled for refuge to it from the field of battle, affrighted and exhausted by fatigue, having thrown away their arms and military standards, had their thoughts more engaged on their further escape than on the defence of the camp. Nor could the troops who were posted on the battlements long withstand the immense number of our darts, but fainting under their wounds, quitted the place, and under the conduct of their centurions and tribunes, fled, without stopping, to the high mountains which joined the camp.

XCVI.—In Pompey's camp you might see arbours in which tables were laid, a large quantity of plate set out, the floors of the tents covered with fresh sods, the tents of Lucius Lentulus and others shaded with ivy, and many other things which were proofs of excessive luxury, and a confidence of victory, so that it might readily be inferred that they had no apprehensions of the issue of the day, as they indulged themselves in unnecessary pleasures, and yet upbraided with luxury Caesar's army, distressed and suffering troops, who had always been in want of common necessaries. Pompey, as soon as our men had forced the trenches, mounting his horse, and stripping off his general's habit, went hastily out of the back gate of the camp, and galloped with all speed to Larissa. Nor did he stop there, but with the same despatch collecting a few of his flying troops, and halting neither day nor night, he arrived at the sea-side, attended by only thirty horse, and went on board a victualling barque, often complaining, as we have been told, that he had been so deceived in his expectation, that he was almost persuaded that he had been betrayed by those from whom he had expected victory, as they began the flight.

XCVII.—Caesar having possessed himself of Pompey's camp, urged his soldiers not to be too intent on plunder, and lose the opportunity of completing their conquest. Having obtained their consent, he began to draw lines round the mountain. The Pompeians distrusting the position, as there was no water on the mountain, abandoned it, and all began to retreat towards Larissa; which Caesar perceiving, divided his troops, and ordering part of his legions to remain in Pompey's camp, sent back a part to his own camp, and taking four legions with him, went by a shorter road to intercept the enemy: and having marched six miles, drew up his army. But the Pompeians observing this, took post on a mountain whose foot was washed by a river. Caesar having encouraged his troops, though they were greatly exhausted by incessant labour the whole day, and night was now approaching, by throwing up works cut off the communication between the river and the mountain, that the enemy might not get water in the night. As soon as the work was finished, they sent ambassadors to treat about a capitulation. A few senators who had espoused that party, made their escape by night.

XCVIII.—At break of day, Caesar ordered all those who had taken post on the mountain, to come down from the higher grounds into the plain, and pile their arms. When they did this without refusal, and with outstretched arms, prostrating themselves on the ground, with tears, implored his mercy: he comforted them and bade them rise, and having spoken a few words of his own clemency to alleviate their fears, he pardoned them all, and gave orders to his soldiers that no injury should be done to them, and nothing taken from them. Having used this diligence, he ordered the legions in his camp to come and meet him, and those which were, with him to take their turn of rest, and go back to the camp; and the same day went to Larissa.

XCIX.—In that battle, no more than two hundred privates were missing, but Caesar lost about thirty centurions, valiant officers. Crastinus, also, of whom mention was made before, fighting most courageously, lost his life by the wound of a sword in the mouth; nor was that false which he declared when marching to battle: for Caesar entertained the highest opinion of his behaviour in that battle, and thought him highly deserving of his approbation. Of Pompey's army, there fell about fifteen thousand; but upwards of twenty-four thousand were made prisoners: for even the cohorts which were stationed in the forts, surrendered to Sylla. Several others took shelter in the neighbouring states. One hundred and eighty stands of colours, and nine eagles, were brought to Caesar. Lucius Domitius, fleeing from the camp to the mountains, his strength being exhausted by fatigue, was killed by the horse.

C.—About this time, Decimus Laelius arrived with his fleet at Brundisium and in the same manner as Libo had done before, possessed himself of an island opposite the harbour of Brundisium. In like manner, Valimus, who was then governor of Brundisium, with a few decked barques, endeavoured to entice Laelius's fleet, and took one five-benched galley and two smaller vessels that had ventured farther than the rest into a narrow part of the harbour: and likewise disposing the horse along the shore, strove to prevent the enemy from procuring fresh water. But Laelius having chosen a more convenient season of the year for his expedition, supplied himself with water brought in transports from Corcyra and Dyrrachium, and was not deterred from his purpose; and till he had received advice of the battle in Thessaly, he could not be forced either by the disgrace of losing his ships, or by the want of necessaries, to quit the port and islands.

CI.—Much about the same time, Cassius arrived in Sicily with a fleet of Syrians, Phoenicians, and Cilicians: and as Caesar's fleet was divided into two parts, Publius Sulpicius the praetor commanding one division at Vibo near the straits, Pomponius the other at Messana, Cassius got into Messana with his fleet before Pomponius had notice of his arrival, and having found him in disorder, without guards or discipline, and the wind being high and favourable, he filled several transports with fir, pitch, and tow, and other combustibles, and sent them against Pomponius's fleet, and set fire to all his ships, thirty-five in number, twenty of which were armed with beaks: and this action struck such terror, that though there was a legion in garrison at Messana, the town with difficulty held out, and had not the news of Caesar's victory been brought at that instant by the horse stationed along the coast, it was generally imagined that it would have been lost, but the town was maintained till the news arrived very opportunely; and Cassius set sail from thence to attack Sulpicius's fleet at Vibo, and our ships being moored to the land, to strike the same terror, he acted in the same manner as before. The wind being favourable, he sent into the port about forty ships provided with combustibles, and the flame catching on both sides, five ships were burnt to ashes. And when the fire began to spread wider by the violence of the wind, the soldiers of the veteran legions, who had been left to guard the fleet, being considered as invalids, could not endure the disgrace, but of themselves went on board the ships and weighed anchor, and having attacked Cassius's fleet, captured two five-banked galleys, in one of which was Cassius himself; but he made his escape by taking to a boat. Two three-banked galleys were taken besides. Intelligence was shortly after received of the action in Thessaly, so well authenticated, that the Pompeians themselves gave credit to it; for they had hitherto believed it a fiction of Caesar's lieutenants and friends. Upon which intelligence Cassius departed with his fleet from that coast.

CII.—Caesar thought he ought to postpone all business and pursue Pompey, whithersoever he should retreat; that he might not be able to provide fresh forces, and renew the war; he therefore marched on every day, as far as his cavalry were able to advance, and ordered one legion to follow him by shorter journeys. A proclamation was issued by Pompey at Amphipolis, that all the young men of that province, Grecians and Roman citizens, should take the military oath; but whether he issued it with an intention of preventing suspicion, and to conceal as long as possible his design of fleeing farther, or to endeavour to keep possession of Macedonia by new levies, if nobody pursued him, it is impossible to judge. He lay at anchor one night, and calling together his friends in Amphipolis, and collecting a sum of money for his necessary expenses, upon advice of Caesar's approach, set sail from that place, and arrived in a few days at Mitylene. Here he was detained two days, and having added a few galleys to his fleet he went to Cilicia, and thence to Cyprus. There he is informed that, by the consent of all the inhabitants of Antioch and Roman citizens who traded there, the castle had been seized to shut him out of the town; and that messengers had been despatched to all those who were reported to have taken refuge in the neighbouring states, that they should not come to Antioch; that if they did that, it would be attended with imminent danger to their lives. The same thing had happened to Lucius Lentulus, who had been consul the year before, and to Publius Lentulus a consular senator, and to several others at Rhodes, who having followed Pompey in his flight, and arrived at the island, were not admitted into the town or port; and having received a message to leave that neighbourhood, set sail much against their will; for the rumour of Caesar's approach had now reached those states.

CIII.—Pompey, being informed of these proceedings, laid aside his design of going to Syria, and having taken the public money from the farmers of the revenue, and borrowed more from some private friends, and having put on board his ships a large quantity of brass for military purposes, and two thousand armed men, whom he partly selected from the slaves of the tax farmers, and partly collected from the merchants, and such persons as each of his friends thought fit on this occasion, he sailed for Pelusium. It happened that king Ptolemy, a minor, was there with a considerable army, engaged in war with his sister Cleopatra, whom a few months before, by the assistance of his relations and friends, he had expelled from the kingdom; and her camp lay at a small distance from his. To him Pompey applied to be permitted to take refuge in Alexandria, and to be protected in his calamity by his powerful assistance, in consideration of the friendship and amity which had subsisted between his father and him. But Pompey's deputies having executed their commission, began to converse with less restraint with the king's troops, and to advise them to act with friendship to Pompey, and not to think meanly of his bad fortune. In Ptolemy's army were several of Pompey's soldiers, of whom Gabinius had received the command in Syria, and had brought them over to Alexandria, and at the conclusion of the war had left with Ptolemy the father of the young king.

CIV.—The king's friends, who were regents of the kingdom during the minority, being informed of these things, either induced by fear, as they afterwards declared, lest Pompey should corrupt the king's army, and seize on Alexandria and Egypt; or despising his bad fortune, as in adversity friends commonly change to enemies, in public gave a favourable answer to his deputies, and desired him to come to the king; but secretly laid a plot against him, and despatched Achillas, captain of the king's guards, a man of singular boldness, and Lucius Septimius a military tribune to assassinate him. Being kindly addressed by them, and deluded by an acquaintance with Septimius, because in the war with the pirates the latter had commanded a company under him, he embarked in a small boat with a few attendants, and was there murdered by Achillas and Septimius. In like manner, Lucius Lentulus was seized by the king's order, and put to death in prison.

CV.—When Caesar arrived in Asia, he found that Titus Ampius had attempted to remove the money from the temple of Diana at Ephesus; and for this purpose had convened all the senators in the province that he might have them to attest the sum, but was interrupted by Caesar's arrival, and had made his escape. Thus, on two occasions, Caesar saved the money of Ephesus. It was also remarked at Elis, in the temple of Minerva, upon calculating and enumerating the days, that on the very day on which Caesar had gained his battle, the image of Victory which was placed before Minerva, and faced her statue, turned about towards the portal and entrance of the temple; and the same day, at Antioch in Syria, such a shout of an army and sound of trumpets was twice heard, that the citizens ran in arms to the walls. The same thing happened at Ptolemais; a sound of drums too was heard at Pergamus, in the private and retired parts of the temple, into which none but the priests are allowed admission, and which the Greeks call Adyta (the inaccessible), and likewise at Tralles, in the temple of Victory, in which there stood a statue consecrated to Caesar; a palm-tree at that time was shown that had sprouted up from the pavement, through the joints of the stones, and shot up above the roof.

CVI.—After a few days' delay in Asia, Caesar, having heard that Pompey had been seen in Cyprus, and conjecturing that he had directed his course into Egypt, on account of his connection with that kingdom, set out for Alexandria with two legions (one of which he ordered to follow him from Thessaly, the other he called in from Achaia, from Fufius, the lieutenant-general) and with eight hundred horse, ten ships of war from Rhodes, and a few from Asia. These legions amounted but to three thousand two hundred men; the rest, disabled by wounds received in various battles, by fatigue and the length of their march, could not follow him. But Caesar, relying on the fame of his exploits; did not hesitate to set forward with a feeble force, and thought that he would be secure in any place. At Alexandria he was informed of the death of Pompey: and at his landing there, heard a cry among the soldiers whom the king had left to garrison the town, and saw a crowd gathering towards him, because the fasces were carried before him; for this the whole multitude thought an infringement of the king's dignity. Though this tumult was appeased, frequent disturbances were raised for several days successively, by crowds of the populace, and a great many of his soldiers were killed in all parts of the city.

CVIL—Having observed this, he ordered other legions to be brought to him from Asia, which he had made up out of Pompey's soldiers; for he was himself detained against his will, by the etesian winds, which are totally unfavourable to persons on a voyage from Alexandria. In the meantime, considering that the disputes of the princes belonged to the jurisdiction of the Roman people, and of him as consul, and that it was a duty more incumbent on him, as in his former consulate a league had been made with Ptolemy the late king, under sanction both of a law, and a decree of the senate, he signified that it was his pleasure, that king Ptolemy, and his sister Cleopatra, should disband their armies, and decide their disputes in his presence by justice, rather than by the sword.

CVIII.—A eunuch named Pothinus, the boy's tutor, was regent of the kingdom on account of his youthfulness. He at first began to complain amongst his friends, and to express his indignation, that the king should be summoned to plead his cause: but afterwards, having prevailed on some of those whom he had made acquainted with his views to join him, he secretly called the army away from Pelusium to Alexandria, and appointed Achillas, already spoken of, commander-in-chief of the forces. Him he encouraged and animated by promises both in his own and the king's name, and instructed him both by letters and messages how he should act. By the will of Ptolemy the father, the elder of his two sons and the more advanced in years of his two daughters were declared his heirs, and for the more effectual performance of his intention, in the same will he conjured the Roman people by all the gods, and by the league which he had entered into at Rome, to see his will executed. One of the copies of his will was conveyed to Rome by his ambassadors to be deposited in the treasury, but the public troubles preventing it, it was lodged with Pompey: another was left sealed up, and kept at Alexandria.

CIX.—Whilst these things were debated before Caesar, and he was very anxious to settle the royal disputes as a common friend and arbitrator; news was brought on a sudden that the king's army and all his cavalry were on their march to Alexandria. Caesar's forces were by no means so strong that he could trust to them, if he had occasion to hazard a battle without the town. His only resource was to keep within the town in the most convenient places, and get information of Achillas's designs. However he ordered his soldiers to repair to their arms; and advised the king to send some of his friends, who had the greatest influence, as deputies to Achillas and to signify his royal pleasure. Dioscorides and Serapion, the persons sent by him, who had both been ambassadors at Rome, and had been in great esteem with Ptolemy the father, went to Achillas. But as soon as they appeared in his presence, without hearing them, or learning the occasion of their coming, he ordered them to be seized and put to death. One of them, after receiving a wound, was taken up and carried off by his attendants as dead: the other was killed on the spot. Upon this, Caesar took care to secure the king's person, both supposing that the king's name would have great influence with his subjects, and to give the war the appearance of the scheme of a few desperate men, rather than of having been begun by the king's consent.

CX.—The forces under Achillas did not seem despicable, either for number, spirit, or military experience; for he had twenty thousand men under arms. They consisted partly of Gabinius's soldiers, who were now become habituated to the licentious mode of living at Alexandria, and had forgotten the name and discipline of the Roman people, and had married wives there, by whom the greatest part of them had children. To these was added a collection of highwaymen and free-booters, from Syria, and the province of Cilicia, and the adjacent countries. Besides several convicts and transports had been collected: for at Alexandria all our runaway slaves were sure of finding protection for their persons on the condition that they should give in their names, and enlist as soldiers: and if any of them was apprehended by his master, he was rescued by a crowd of his fellow soldiers, who being involved in the same guilt, repelled, at the hazard of their lives, every violence offered to any of their body. These by a prescriptive privilege of the Alexandrian army, used to demand the king's favourites to be put to death, pillage the properties of the rich to increase their pay, invest the king's palace, banish some from the kingdom, and recall others from exile. Besides these, there were two thousand horse, who had acquired the skill of veterans by being in several wars in Alexandria. These had restored Ptolemy the father to his kingdom, had killed Bibulus's two sons; and had been engaged in war with the Egyptians; such was their experience in military affairs.

CXI.—Full of confidence in his troops, and despising the small number of Caesar's soldiers, Achillas seized Alexandria, except that part of the town which Caesar occupied with his troops. At first he attempted to force the palace; but Caesar had disposed his cohorts through the streets, and repelled his attack. At the same time there was an action at the port: where the contest was maintained with the greatest obstinacy. For the forces were divided, and the fight maintained in several streets at once, and the enemy endeavoured to seize with a strong party the ships of war; of which fifty had been sent to Pompey's assistance, but after the battle in Thessaly had returned home. They were all of either three or five banks of oars, well equipped and appointed with every necessary for a voyage. Besides these, there were twenty-two vessels with decks, which were usually kept at Alexandria, to guard the port. If they made themselves masters of these, Caesar being deprived of his fleet, they would have the command of the port and whole sea, and could prevent him from procuring provisions and auxiliaries. Accordingly that spirit was displayed, which ought to be displayed when the one party saw that a speedy victory depended on the issue, and the other their safety. But Caesar gained the day, and set fire to all those ships, and to others which were in the docks, because he could not guard so many places with so small a force; and immediately he conveyed some troops to the Pharos by his ships.

CXIL—The Pharos is a tower on an island, of prodigious height, built with amazing works, and takes its name from the island. This island lying over against Alexandria forms a harbour; but on the upper side it is connected with the town by a narrow way eight hundred paces in length, made by piles sunk in the sea, and by a bridge. In this island some of the Egyptians have houses, and a village as large as a town; and whatever ships from any quarter, either through mistaking the channel, or by the storm, have been driven from their course upon the coast, they constantly plunder like pirates. And without the consent of those who are masters of the Pharos, no vessels can enter the harbour, on account of its narrowness. Caesar being greatly alarmed on this account, whilst the enemy were engaged in battle, landed his soldiers, seized the Pharos, and placed a garrison in it. By this means he gained this point, that he could be supplied without danger with corn and auxiliaries: for he sent to all the neighbouring countries, to demand supplies. In other parts of the town, they fought so obstinately, that they quitted the field with equal advantage, and neither were beaten (in consequence of the narrowness of the passes); and a few being killed on both sides, Caesar secured the most necessary posts, and fortified them in the night. In this quarter of the town was a wing of the king's palace, in which Caesar was lodged on his first arrival, and a theatre adjoining the house which served as for citadel, and commanded an avenue to the port and other docks. These fortifications he increased during the succeeding days, that he might have them before him as a rampart, and not be obliged to fight against his will. In the meantime Ptolemy's younger daughter, hoping the throne would become vacant, made her escape from the palace to Achillas, and assisted him in prosecuting the war. But they soon quarrelled about the command, which circumstance enlarged the presents to the soldiers, for each endeavoured by great sacrifices to secure their affection. Whilst the enemy was thus employed, Pothinus, tutor to the young king, and regent of the kingdom, who was in Caesar's part of the town, sent messengers to Achillas, and encouraged him not to desist from his enterprise, nor to despair of success; but his messengers being discovered and apprehended, he was put to death by Caesar. Such was the commencement of the Alexandrian war.

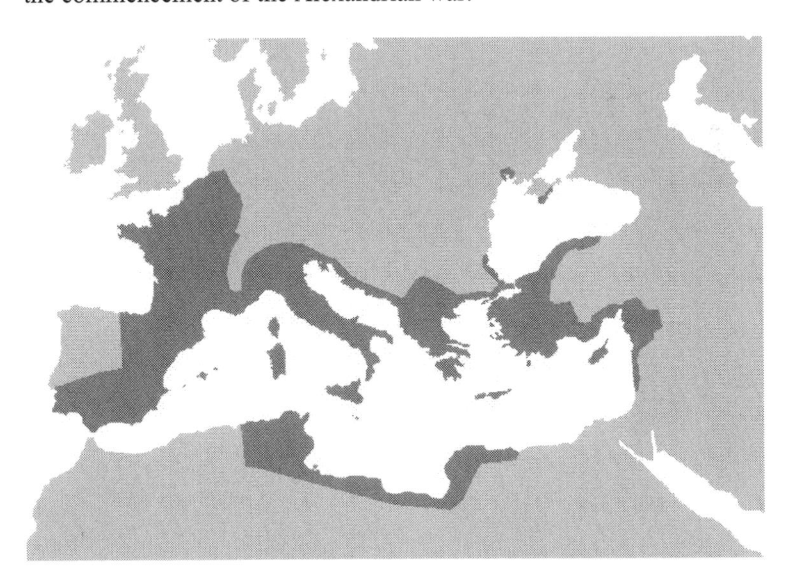

INDEX

N.B. The numerals refer to the book, the figures to the chapter. G. stands for the Gallic War, C. for the Civil.

Acarn[=a]n[)i]a, a region of Greece, Carnia
Acco, prince of the Sen[)o]nes, his conduct on Caesar's approach, G. vi. 4; condemned in a council of the Gauls, vi. 44
Achaia, sometimes taken for all Greece, but most commonly for a part of it only; in Peloponnesus, Romania alta
Achillas, captain of Ptolemy's guards, sent to kill Pompey, C. iii. 104; appointed by Pothinus commander of all the Egyptian forces, ibid. 108; heads an army of twenty thousand veteran troops, ibid. 110
Acilla, or Achilla, or Acholla. There were two cities in Africa of this name, one inland, the other on the coast. The modern name of the latter is Elalia
Acilius, Caesar's lieutenant, C. iii. 15
Act[)i]um, a promontory of Epirus, now called the Cape of Tigalo, famous for a naval victory gained near it, by Augustus, over M. Antony
Act[)i]us, a Pelignian, one of Pompey's followers, taken by Caesar, and dismissed in safety, C. i. 18
Act[)i]us Rufus accuses L. Apanius of treachery, C. iii. 83
Act[)i]us Varus prevents Tubero from landing in Africa, C. i. 31; his forces, C. ii. 23; his camp, ibid. 25; engages Curio, ibid. 34; his danger, defeat, and stratagem, ibid. 35
Adcant[)u]annus sallies upon Crassus at the head of a chosen body of troops, G. iii. 22
Add[)u]a, the Adda, a river that rises in the Alps, and, separating the duchy of Milan from the state of Venice, falls into the Po above Cremona
Adriatic Sea, the Gulf of Venice, at the extremity of which that city is situated
Adrum[=e]tum, a town in Africa, Mahometta; held by Considius Longus with a garrison of one legion, C. ii. 23
Aduat[)u]uci (in some editions Atuatici), descendants of the Teutones and Cimbri, G. ii. 29; they furnish twenty-nine thousand men to the general confederacy of Gaul, ibid. 4; Caesar obliges them to submit,ibid. 29
Aed[)u]i, the Autunois, a people of Gaul, near Autun, in the country now called Lower Burgundy; they complain to Caesar of the ravages committed in their territories by the Helvetii, G. i. 11; join in a petition against Ariovistus, ibid. 33; at the head of one of the two leading factions of Gaul, G. vi. 12; Caesar quiets an intestine commotion among them, C. vii. 33; they revolt from the Romans, G. vii. 54; their law concerning magistrates, ibid. 33; their clients, i. 31; vii. 75

Aeg[=e]an Sea, the Archipelago, a part of the Mediterranean which lies between Greece, Asia Minor, and the Isle of Crete
Aeg[=i]n[)i]um, a town of Thessaly; Domitius joins Caesar near that place, C. iii. 79
Aegus and Roscillus, their perfidious behaviour towards Caesar, C. iii. 59, 60
Aegyptus, Egypt, an extensive country of Africa, bounded on the west by part of Marmarica and the deserts of Lybia, on the north by the Mediterranean, on the east by the Sinus Arabicus, and a line drawn from Arsino[)e] to Rhinocolura, and on the south by Aethiopia. Egypt, properly so called, may be described as consisting of the long and narrow valley which follows the course of the Nile from Syene (Assooan) to Cairo, near the site of the ancient Memphis. The name by which this country is known to Europeans comes from the Greeks, some of whose writers inform us that it received this appellation from Aegyptus, son of Belus, it having been previously called Aeria. In the Hebrew scriptures it is called Mitsraim, and also Matsor and Harets Cham; of these names, however, the first is the one most commonly employed
Aemilia Via, a Roman road in Italy, from Rimini to Aquileia, and from Pisa to Dertona
Aet[=o]lia, a country of Greece, Despotato; recovered from Pompey by the partisans of Caesar, C. iii. 35
Afr[=a]nius, Pompey's lieutenant, his exploits in conjunction with Petreius, C. i. 38; resolves to carry the war into Celtiberia, ibid. 61; surrenders to Caesar, ibid. 84
Afr[)i]ca, one of the four great continents into which the earth is divided; the name seems to have been originally applied by the Romans to the country around Carthage, the first part of the continent with which they became acquainted, and is said to have been derived from a small Carthaginian district on the northern coast, called Frigi. Hence, even when the name had become applied to the whole continent, there still remained in Roman geography the district of Africa Proper, on the Mediterranean coast, corresponding to the modem kingdom of Tunis, with part of that of Tripoli
Agend[)i]cum, a city of the Senones, Sens; Caesar quarters four legions there, G. vi. 44; Labienus leaves his baggage in it under a guard of new levies, and sets out for Lutetia, G. vii. 57
Alba, a town of Latium, in Italy, Albano; Domitius levies troops in that neighbourhood, C. i. 15
Alb[=i]ci, a people of Gaul, unknown; some make them the same with the Vivarois; taken into the service of the Marseillians, C. i. 34

Albis, the Elbe, a large and noble river in Germany, which has its source in the Giant's Mountains in Silesia, on the confines of Bohemia, and passing through Bohemia, Upper and Lower Saxony, falls into the North Sea at Ritzbuttel, about sixty miles below Hamburg
Alces, a species of animals somewhat resembling an elk, to be found in the Hercynian forests, C. vi. 27
Alemanni, or Alamanni, a name assumed by a confederacy of German tribes, situated between the Neckar and the Upper Rhine, who united to resist the encroachments of the Roman power. According to Mannert, they derived their origin from the shattered remains of the army of Ariovistus retired, after the defeat and death of their leader, to the mountainous country of the Upper Rhine. After their overthrow by Clovis, king of the Salian Franks, they ceased to exist as one nation, and were dispersed over Gaul, Switzerland, and Nether Italy. From them L'Allemagne, the French name for Germany, is derived
Alemannia, the country inhabited by the Alemanni
Alesia, or Alexia, a town of the Mandubians, Alise; Caesar shuts up Vercingetorix there, C. vii. 68; surrounds it with lines of circumvallation and contravallation, ibid. 69, 72; obliges it to surrender, ibid. 89
Alexandr[=i]a, a city of Egypt, Scanderia. It was built by Alexander the Great, 330 years before Christ; Caesar pursues Pompey thither, C. iii. 106
Aliso, by some supposed to be the town now called Iselburg; or, according to Junius, Wesel, in the duchy of Cleves, but more probably Elsen
Allier (El[=a]ver), Caesar eludes the vigilance of Vercingetorix, and by an artifice passes that river, G. vii. 35
All[)o]br[)o]ges, an ancient people of Gallia Transalp[=i]na, who inhabited the country which is now called Dauphiny, Savoy, and Piedmont. The name, Allobroges, means highlanders, and is derived from Al, "high," and Broga, "land." They are supposed to be disaffected to the Romans, G. i. 6; complain to Caesar of the ravages of the Helvetians, ibid. 11
Alps, a ridge of high mountains, which separates France and Germany from Italy. That part of them which separates Dauphiny from Piedmont was called the Cottian Alps. Their name is derived from their height, Alp being an old Celtic appellation for "a lofty mountain"; Caesar crosses them with five legions, G. i. 10; sends Galba to open a free passage over them to the Roman merchants, G. iii. 1
Alsati[)a], a province of Germany, in the upper circle of the Rhine, Alsace
Amagetobr[)i]a, a city of Gaul, unknown; famous for a defeat of the

Gauls there by Ariovistus, G. i. 31
Amant[)i]a, a town in Macedonia, Porto Raguseo; it submits to Caesar, and sends ambassadors to know his pleasure, C. iii. 12
Am[=a]nus, a mountain of Syria, Alma Daghy, near which Scipio sustains some losses, C. iii. 31
Am[=a]ni Pylae, or Am[=a]nicae Portae, Straits of Scanderona
Ambarri, a people of Gaul, uncertain; they complain to Caesar of the ravages committed in their territories by the Helvetii, G. i. 11
Ambialites, a people of Gaul, of Lamballe in Bretagne. Others take the word to be only a different name for the Ambiani; they join in a confederacy with the Veneti against Caesar, G. iii. 9
Ambi[=a]ni, or Ambianenses, the people of Amiens; they furnish ten thousand men to the general confederacy of the Belgians against Caesar, G. ii. 4; sue for peace, and submit themselves to Caesar's pleasure, G. ii. 15
Ambi[=a]num, a city of Belgium, Amiens
Amb[)i]b[)a]ri, a people of Gaul, inhabiting Ambie, in Normandy
Amb[)i][)o]rix, his artful speech to Sabinus and Cotta, G. v. 27; Caesar marches against him, G. vi. 249. Ravages and lays waste his territories, ibid. 34; endeavours in vain to get him into his hands, ibid. 43
Ambivar[)e]ti, a people of Gaul, the Vivarais. They are ordered to furnish their contingent for raising the siege of Alesia, G. vii. 75
Ambivar[=i]ti, an ancient people of Brabant, between the Rhine and the Maese; the German cavalry sent to forage among them, G. iv. 9
Ambr[)a]c[)i]a, a city of Epirus, Arta; Cassius directs his march thither, C. iii. 36
Ambrones, an ancient people, who lived in the country which is now called the Canton of Bern, in Switzerland
Amph[)i]l[)o]chia, a region of Epirus, Anfilocha. Its inhabitants reduced by Cassius Longinus, C. iii. 55
Amph[)i]p[)o]lis, a city of Macedonia, Cristopoli, or Emboli. An edict in Pompey's name published there, C. iii. 102
Anartes, a people of Germany, Walachians, Servians, or Bulgarians, bordering upon the Hercynian Forest, G. vi. 25
Anas, a river of Spain, the Guadiana, or Rio Roydera, bounding that part of Spain under the government of Petreius, C. i. 38
Anc[)a]l[=i]tes, a people of Britain, of the hundred of Henley, in Oxfordshire; they send ambassadors to Caesar with an offer of submission, G. v. 21
Anch[)i][)a]los, a city of Thrace, near the Euxine Sea, now called Kenkis
Ancibarii, or Ansivarii, an ancient people of Lower Germany, of and about the town of Ansestaet, or Amslim

Anc[=o]na, Ancona, a city of Italy, on the coast of Pisenum. It is supposed to derive its name from the Greek word [Greek: agkon], an angle or elbow, on account of the angular form of the promontory on which it is built. The foundation of Ancona is ascribed by Strabo to some Syracusans, who were fleeing from the tyranny of Dionysius. Livy speaks of it as a naval station of great importance in the wars of Rome with the Illyrians. We find it occupied by Caesar (C. i. 2) shortly after crossing the Rubicon; Caesar takes possession of it with a garrison of one cohort, C. i. 11

Andes, Angers, in France, the capital of the duchy of Anjou

Andes, a people of Gaul, the ancient inhabitants of the duchy of Anjou; Caesar puts his troops into winter quarters among them, G. ii. 35

Andomad[=u]num Ling[)o]num, a large and ancient city of Champagne, at the source of the river Marne, Langres

Anglesey (Mona), an island situated between Britain and Ireland, where the night, during the winter, is said to be a month long, G. v. 13

Angrivarii, an ancient people of Lower Germany, who dwelt between the
Ems and the Weser, below the Lippe

Ansivarii, see Ancibarii

Antioch[=i]a, Antachia, an ancient and famous city, once the capital of Syria, or rather of the East. It is situate on two rivers, the Orontes and the Phaspar, not far from the Mediterranean; refuses to admit the fugitives after the battle of Pharsalia, C. iii. 102

Ant[=o]nius (Mark Antony), Caesar's lieutenant, G. vii. i i; quaestor, G. viii. 2; governor of Brundusium, C. iii. 24; his standing for that priesthood, G. vii. 50; obliges Libo to raise the siege of Brundusium, C. iii. 24; and in conjunction with Kalenus transports Caesar's troops to Greece, ibid. 26

Apam[=e]a, Apami, a city of Bithynia, built by Nicomedes, the son of Prusias

Apennine Mountains, a large chain of mountains, branching off from the Maritime Alps, in the neighbourhood of Genoa, running diagonally from the Ligurian Gulf to the Adriatic, in the vicinity of Ancona; from which it continues nearly parallel with the latter gulf, as far as the promontory of Garg[=a]nus, and again inclines to Mare Inf[)e]rum, till it finally terminates in the promontory of Leucopetra, near Rhegium. The etymology of the name given to these mountains must be traced to the Celtic, and appears to combine two terms of that language nearly synonymous, Alp, or Ap, "a high mountain," and Penn, "a summit"

Apoll[=o]n[)i]a, a city of Macedonia, Piergo. Pompey resolves to winter there, C. iii. 5; Caesar makes himself master of it, ibid. iii. 12

Appia Via, the Appian road which led from Rome to Campania, and from the sea to Brundusium. It was made, as Livy informs us, by the censor, Appius Caecus, A.U.C. 442, and was, in the first instance, only laid down as far as Capua, a distance of about 125 miles. It was subsequently carried on to Beneventum, and finally to Brundusium. According to Eustace (Classical Tour, vol. iii.), such parts of the Appian Way as have escaped destruction, as at Fondi and Mola, show few traces of wear and decay after a duration of two thousand years
Apsus, a river of Macedonia, the Aspro. Caesar and Pompey encamp over against each other on the banks of that river, C. iii. 13
Apulia, a region of Italy, la Puglia. Pompey quarters there the legions sent by Caesar, C. i. 14
Aquil[=a]ria, a town of Africa, near Clupea. Pompey quarters there the legions sent by Caesar, C. i. 14; Curio arrives there with the troops designed against Africa. C. ii. 23
Aquileia, formerly a famous and considerable city of Italy, not far from the Adriatic, now little more than a heap of ruins, Aquilegia. Caesar draws together the troops quartered there, G. i. 10
Aquitania, a third part of ancient Gaul, now containing Guienne, Gascony, etc.
Aquit[=a]ni, the Aquitanians reduced under the power of the Romans by
Crassus, G. iii. 20-22; very expert in the art of mining, ibid. 21
Arar, or Araris, a river of Gaul, the Sa[^o]ne; the Helvetians receive a considerable check in passing this river, G. i. 12
Arduenna Silva, the forest of Ardenne, in France, reaching from the Rhine to the city of Tournay, in the low countries; Indutiom[)a]rus conceals in it the infirm and aged, G. v. 3; Caesar crosses it in quest of Ambiorix, G. vi. 29
Arecomici Volcae, Caesar plants garrisons among them, G. vii. 7
Arel[=a]te, or Arel[=a]tum, or Arelas, a city of Gaul, Arles. Caesar orders twelve galleys to be built there, C. i. 36
Ar[)i]m[)i]num, a city of Italy, Rimini; Caesar having sounded the disposition of his troops, marches thither, C. i. 8
Ar[)i][)o]vistus, king of the Germans, his tyrannical conduct towards the Gauls, G. i. 31; Caesar sends ambassadors to him demanding an interview, ibid. 34; he is defeated and driven entirely out of Gaul,ibid. 52
Arles, see Arelate
Arm[)e]n[)i]a, a country of Asia, divided into the greater or lesser, and now called Turcomania

Armorici, the ancient people of Armorica, a part of Gallia Celtica, now Bretagne; they assemble in great numbers to attack L. Roscius in his winter quarters, G. v. 53
Arr[=e]t[)i]um, a city of Etruria, in Italy, Arezzo; Antony sent thither with five cohorts, C. i. 10
Arverni, an ancient people of France, on the Loire, whose chief city was Arvernum, now Clermont, the capital of Auvergne; suddenly invaded, and their territories ravaged by Caesar, G. vii. 8
Asculum, a town of Italy, Ascoli; Caesar takes possession of it, C. i. 16
Asparagium, a town in Macedonia, unknown; Pompey encamps near it with all his forces, C. iii. 30
Astigi, or Astingi, a people of Andalusia, in Spain
Athens, one of the most ancient and noble cities of Greece, the capital of Attica. It produced some of the most distinguished statesmen, orators, and poets that the world ever saw, and its sculptors and painters have been rarely rivalled, never surpassed. No city on the earth has ever exercised an equal influence on the educated men of all ages. It contributes to fit out a fleet for Pompey, C. iii. 3
Atreb[)a]tes, an ancient people of Gaul, who lived in that part of the Netherlands which is now called Artois; they furnish fifteen thousand men to the general confederacy of Gaul, G. ii. 4
Attica, a country of Greece, between Achaia and Macedonia, famous on account of its capital, Athens
Attuarii, a people of ancient Germany, who inhabited between the Maese and the Rhine, whose country is now a part of the duchy of Gueldes
Atuatuca, a strong castle, where Caesar deposited all his baggage, on setting out in pursuit of Ambiorix, G. vi. 32; the Germans unexpectedly attack it, ibid. 35
Augustod[=u]num, Autun, a very ancient city of Burgundy, on the river Arroux
Aulerci Eburovices, a people of Gaul, in the country of Evreux, in Normandy
Aulerci Brannovices, a people of Gaul, Morienne
Aulerci Cenomanni, a people of Gaul, the country of Maine
Aulerci Diablintes, a people of Gaul, le Perche
Aulerci reduced by P. Crassus, G, ii. 34; massacre their senate, and join Viridovix, G. iii. 17; Aulerci Brannovices ordered to furnish their contingent to the relief of Alesia, G. vii. 7; Aulerci Cenomanni furnish five thousand, ibid.; Aulerci Eburovices three thousand, ibid.
Ausci, a people of Gaul, those of Auchs or Aux, in Gascony; they submit to Crassus and send hostages, G. iii. 27

Auset[=a]ni, a people of Spain, under the Pyrenean mountains; they send ambassadors to Caesar, with an offer of submission, C. i. 60
Aux[)i]mum, a town in Italy, Osimo, or Osmo; Caesar makes himself master of it, C. i. 15
Av[=a]r[)i]cum, a city of Aquitaine, the capital of the Biturigians, Bourges; besieged by Caesar, G. vii. 13; and at last taken by storm, ibid. 31
Ax[)o]na, the river Aisne, Caesar crosses it in his march against the Belgians, G. ii. 5, 6
Bac[=e]nis, a forest of ancient Germany, which parted the Suevi from the Cherusci; by some supposed to be the Forests of Thuringia, by others the Black Forest; the Suevians encamp at the entrance of that wood, resolving there to await the approach of the Romans, G vi. 10
Bac[)u]lus, P. Sextius, his remarkable bravery, G. vi. 38
Baet[)i]ca, in the ancient geography, about a third part of Spain, containing Andalusia, and a part of Granada
Bagr[)a]das, a river of Africa, near Ut[)i]ca, the Begrada; Curio arrives with his army at that river, C. ii. 38
Bale[=a]res Ins[)u]lae, several islands in the Mediterranean Sea, formerly so called, of which Majorca and Minorca are the chief; the inhabitants famous for their dexterity in the use of the sling, G. ii. 7
Bat[)a]vi, the ancient inhabitants of the island of Batavia
Batavia, or Batavorum Insula, Holland, a part of which still retains the name of Betuwe; formed by the Meuse and the Wal, G. iv. 10
Belgae, the inhabitants of Gallia Belgica. The original Belgae were supposed to be of German extraction; but passing the Rhine, settled themselves in Gaul. The name Belgae belongs to the Cymric language, in which, under the form Belgiaid, the radical of which is Belg, it signifies warlike; they are the most warlike people of Gaul, G. i. 1; withstand the invasion of the Teutones and Cimbri, G. ii. 4; originally of German extraction, ibid.; Caesar obliges them to decamp and return to their several habitations, ibid. 11
Belgia, Belgium, or Gallia Belgica, the Low Countries, or Netherlands
Bellocassi, or Velocasses, a people of Gaul, inhabiting the country of Bayeux, in Normandy; they furnish three thousand men to the relief of Alesia, G. vii. 75
Bell[)o]v[)a]ci, an ancient renowned people among the Belgae, inhabiting the country now called Beauvais in France; they furnish a hundred thousand men to the general confederacy of Belgium, G. ii. 4; join in the general defection under Vercingetorix, G. vii. 59; again take up arms against Caesar, viii. 7; but are compelled to submit and sue for pardon
Bergea, a city of Macedonia, now called Veria

Berones, see Retones
Bessi, a people of Thrace, Bessarabia; they make part of Pompey's army, C. iii. 4
Bethuria, a region of Hispania Lusitanica, Estremadura
Bibracte, a town of Burgundy, now called Autun, the capital of the Aedui; Caesar, distressed for want of corn, marches thither to obtain a supply, G. i. 23
Bibrax, a town of Rheims, Braine, or Bresne; attacked with great fury by the confederate Belgians, G. ii. 6
Bibr[)o]ci, a people of Britain; according to Camden, the hundred of Bray, in Berkshire; they send ambassadors to Caesar to sue for peace, G. v. 21
Bib[)u]lus burns thirty of Caesar's ships, C. iii. 8; his hatred of Caesar, ibid. 8, 16; his cruelty towards the prisoners that fell into his hands, ibid. 14; his death, ibid. 18; death of his two sons, ibid. 110
Bigerriones, a people of Gaul, inhabiting the country now called Bigorre, in Gascony; they surrender and give hostages to Crassus, G. iii. 27
Bithynia, a country of Asia Minor, adjoining to Troas, over against Thrace, Becsangial
Bit[:u]r[)i]ges, a people of Guienne, in France, of the country of Berry; they join with the Arverni in the general defection under Vercingetorix, G. vii. 5
Boeotia, a country in Greece; separated from Attica by Mount Citheron.
It had formerly several other names and was famous for its capital, Thebes; it is now called Stramulipa
Boii, an ancient people of Germany who, passing the Rhine, settled in Gaul, the Bourbonnois; they join with the Helvetians in their expedition against Gaul, G. i. 5; attack the Romans in flank, ibid. 25; Caesar allows them to settle among the Aeduans, ibid. 28
Bor[=a]ni, an ancient people of Germany, supposed by some to be the same as the Burii
Bosphor[=a]ni, a people bordering upon the Euxine Sea, the Tartars
Bosph[)o]rus, two straits of the sea so called, one Bosphorus Thracius, now the Straits of Constantinople; the other Bosphorus Climerius, now the Straits of Caffa
Brannov[=i]ces, the people of Morienne, in France
Brannovii furnished their contingent to the relief of Alesia, C. vii. 75
Bratuspant[)i]um, a city of Gaul, belonging to the Bellov[)a]ci, Beauvais; it submits, and obtains pardon from Caesar, G. ii. 13
Bridge built by Caesar over the Rhine described, G. iv. 7

Br[)i]tannia, Caesar's expedition thither, G. iv. 20; description of the coast, 23; the Romans land in spite of the vigorous opposition of the islanders, 26; the Britons send ambassadors to Caesar to desire a peace, which they obtain on delivery of hostages, 27; they break the peace on hearing that Caesar's fleet was destroyed by a storm, and set upon the Roman foragers, 30; their manner of fighting in chariots; they fall upon the Roman camp, but are repulsed, and petition again for peace, which Caesar grants them, 33-35; Caesar passes over into their island a second time, v. 8; drives them from the woods where they had taken refuge, 9; describes their manners and way of living, 12; defeats them in several encounters, 15-21; grants them a peace, on their giving hostages, and agreeing to pay a yearly tribute, 22
Brundusium, a city of Italy, Brindisi. By the Greeks it was called [Greek: Brentesion], which in the Messapian language signified a stag's head, from the resemblance which its different harbours and creeks bore to that object; Pompey retires thither with his forces, C. i. 24; Caesar lays siege to it, 26; Pompey escapes from it by sea, upon which it immediately surrenders to Caesar, 28; Libo blocks up the port with a fleet, C. iii. 24; but by the valour of Antony is obliged to retire, ibid.
Brutii, a people of Italy, the Calabrians. They were said to be runaway slaves and shepherds of the Lucanians, who, after concealing themselves for a time, became at last numerous enough to attack their masters, and succeeded at length in gaining their independence. Their very name is said to indicate that they were revolted slaves: [Greek: Brettious gar kalousi apostatas], says Strabo, speaking of the Lucanians
Br[=u]tus, appointed to command the fleet in the war against the people of Vannes, G. iii. 11; engages and defeats at sea the Venetians, 14; and also the people of Marseilles, C. i. 58; engages them a second time with the same good fortune, ii. 3
Bullis, a town in Macedonia, unknown; it sends ambassadors to Caesar with an offer of submission, C. iii. 12
Buthr[=o]tum, a city of Epirus, Butrinto, or Botronto
Byzantium, an ancient city of Thrace, called at different times Ligos, Nova Roma, and now Constantinople
Cabill[=o]num, a city of ancient Gaul, Chalons sur Sa[^o]ne
Cad[=e]tes, a people of Gaul, unknown
Cadurci, a people of Gaul, inhabiting the country of Quercy
Caeraesi, a people of Belgic Gaul, inhabiting the country round Namur; they join in the general confederacy of Belgium against Caesar, G. i. 4
Caesar, hastens towards Gaul, C. i. 7; refuses the Helvetians a passage through the Roman province, ibid.; his answer to their ambassadors, 14; defeats and sends them back into their own country, 25-27; sends ambassadors to Ariovistus, 34; calls a council of war: his speech, 40;

ineffectual, 57; joins Domitius, storms and takes the town of Gomphis in Thessaly, in four hours' time, 80; gains a complete victory over Pompey in the battle of Pharsalia, 93; summons Ptolemy and Cleopatra to attend him, 107; burns the Alexandrian fleet, 111
Caesar[=e]a, the chief city of Cappadocia
Caesia Sylva, the Caesian Forest, supposed to be a part of the Hercynian Forest, about the duchy of Cleves and Westphalia
Calagurritani, a people of Hispania Tarraconensis, inhabiting the province of Calahorra; send ambassadors to Caesar with an offer of submission, C. i. 60
Cal[)e]tes, an ancient people of Belgic Gaul, inhabiting the country called Le Pais de Caulx, in Normandy, betwixt the Seine and the sea; they furnish ten thousand men in the general revolt of Belgium, G. ii. 4
Cal[)y]don, a city of Aetolia, Ayton, C. iii. 35
C[)a]m[)e]r[=i]num, a city of Umbria, in Italy, Camarino
Camp[=a]n[)i]a, the most pleasant part of Italy, in the kingdom of Naples, now called Terra di Lavoro
Campi Can[=i]ni, a place in the Milanese, in Italy, not far from Belizona
Campi Catalaunici, supposed to be the large plain which begins about two miles from Chalons sur Marne
Cam[=u]l[)o]g[=e]nus appointed commander-in-chief by the Parisians, G. vii. 57; obliges Labienus to decamp from before Paris, ibid.; is slain, 62
Cadav[)i]a, a country of Macedonia, Canovia
Caninefates, an ancient people of the lower part of Germany, near Batavia, occupying the country in which Gorckum, on the Maese, in South
Holland, now is
Can[=i]nius sets Duracius at liberty, who had been shut up in Limonum by
Dumnacus, G. viii. 26; pursues Drapes, 30; lays siege to Uxellodunum, 33
Cant[)a]bri, the Cantabrians, an ancient warlike people of Spain, properly of the provinces of Guipuscoa and Biscay; they are obliged by Afranius to furnish a supply of troops, C. i. 38
Cantium, a part of England, the county of Kent
C[)a]nus[=i]um, a city of Apulia, in Italy, Canosa. The splendid remains of antiquity discovered among the ruins of Canosa, together with its coins, establish the Grecian origin of the place
Cappadocia, a large country in Asia Minor, upon the Euxine Sea
Capr[)e]a, Capri, an island on the coast of Campania
Cap[)u]a, Capha, a city in the kingdom of Naples, in the Provincia di

Lavoro
C[)a]r[)a]les, a city of Sardinia, Cagliari
C[)a]r[)a]l[)i]t[=a]ni, the people of Cagliari, in Sardinia; they declare against Pompey, and expel Cotta with his garrison, C. i. 30
Carc[)a]so, a city of Gaul, Carcassone
Carm[=o]na, a town of Hispania Baetica, Carmone; declares for Caesar, and expels the enemy's garrison, C. ii. 19
Carni, an ancient people, inhabiting a part of Noricum, whose country is still called Carniola
Carn[=u]tes, an ancient people of France, inhabiting the territory now called Chartres; Caesar quarters some troops among them, G. ii. 35; they openly assassinate Tasgetins, G. v. 25; send ambassadors to Caesar and submit, vi. 4; offer to be the first in taking up alms against the Romans, vii. 2; attack the Biturigians, but are dispersed and put to flight by Caesar. viii. 5
Carpi, an ancient people near the Danube
Cassandr[)e]a, a city of Macedonia, Cassandria
Cassi, a people of ancient Britain, the hundred of Caishow, in Hertfordshire; they send ambassadors and submit to Caesar, G. v. 21
Caesil[=i]num, a town in Italy, Castelluzzo
Cassivellaunus, chosen commander-in-chief of the confederate Britons, G. v. 11; endeavours in vain to stop the course of Caesar's conquests, 18; is obliged to submit, and accept Caesar's terms, 22
Cassius, Pompey's lieutenant, burns Caesar's fleet in Sicily, C. iii. 101
Castellum Menapiorum, Kessel, a town in Brabant, on the river Neerse, not far from the Maese
Cast[)i]cus, the son of Catam['a]ntaledes, solicited by Orgetorix to invade the liberty of his country, G. i. 3
Castra Posthumiana, a town in Hispania Baetica, Castro el Rio
Castra Vetera, an ancient city in Lower Germany, in the duchy of Cleves; some say where Santon, others where Byrthon now is
Castulonensis Saltus, a city of Hispania Tarraconensis, Castona la Vieja
Cativulcus takes up arms against the Romans at the instigation of Indutiomarus, G. v. 24; poisons himself, vi. 31
Cato of Utica, the source of his hatred to Caesar, C. i. 4; made praetor of Sicily, prepares for war, and abdicates his province, 30
Catur[)i]ges, an ancient people of Gaul, inhabiting the country of Embrun, or Ambrun, or Chagres; oppose Caesar's passage over the Alps, G. i. 10
Cavalry, their institution and manner of fighting among the Germans, G. i. 48, iv. 2
Cavarillus taken and brought before Caesar, G. vii. 62

Cavarinus, the Senones attempt to assassinate him, G. v. 54; Caesar orders him to attend him with the cavalry of the Senones, vi. 5
Cebenna Mons, the mountains of the Cevennes, in Gaul, separating the Helvians from Auvergne
Celeja, a city of Noricum Mediterraneum, now Cilley
Celtae, a people of Thrace, about the mountains of Rhodope and Haemus
Celtae, an ancient people of Gaul, in that part called Gallia Comata, between the Garumna (Garonne) and Sequana (Seine), from whom that country was likewise called Gallia Celtica. They were the most powerful of the three great nations that inhabited Gaul, and are supposed to be the original inhabitants of that extensive country. It is generally supposed that they called themselves Gail, or Gael, out of which name the Greeks formed their [Greek: Keltai], and the Romans Galli. Some, however, deduce the name from the Gaelic "Ceilt," an inhabitant of the forest
Celt[)i]b[=e]ri, an ancient people of Spain, descended from the Celtae, who settled about the River Iberus, or Ebro, from whom the country was called Celtiberia, now Arragon; Afranius obliges them to furnish a supply of troops, C. i. 38
Celtillus, the father of Vercingetorix, assassinated by the Arverni, G. vii. 4
Cenimagni, or Iceni, an ancient people of Britain, inhabiting the counties of Suffolk, Norfolk, Cambridgeshire, and Huntingdonshire
Cenis Mons, that part of the Alps which separates Savoy from Piedmont
Cenni, an ancient people of Celtic extraction
Cenom[=a]ni, a people of Gallia Celtica, in the country now called Le Manseau, adjoining to that of the Insubres
Centr[=o]nes, an ancient people of Flanders, about the city of Courtray, dependent on the Nervians
Centr[=o]nes, an ancient people of Gaul, inhabiting the country of Tarantaise
Cerauni Montes, Mountains of Epirus, Monti di Chimera
Cerc[=i]na, an island on the coast of Africa, Chercara, Cercare
Cevennes, mountains of, Caesar passes them in the midst of winter, though covered with snow six feet deep, G. vii. 8
Chara, a root which served to support Caesar's army in extreme necessity, C. iii. 48; manner of preparing it, ibid.
Chariots, manner of fighting with them among the Britons, G. iv. 33; dexterity of the British charioteers, ibid.
Cherron[=e]sus, a peninsula of Africa, near Alexandria

Cherson[=e]sus Cimbr[=i]ca, a peninsula on the Baltic, now Jutland, part of Holstein, Ditmarsh, and Sleswic
Cherusci, a great and warlike people of ancient Germany, between the Elbe and the Weser, about the country now called Mansfield, part of the duchy of Brunswick, and the dioceses of Hildesheim andHalberstadt. The Cherusci, under the command of Arminius (Hermann), lured the unfortunate Varus into the wilds of the Saltus Teutoburgiensis (Tutinger Wold), where they massacred him and his whole army. They were afterwards defeated by Germanicus, who, on his march through the forest so fatal to his countrymen, found the bones of the legions where they had been left to blanch by their barbarian conqueror.—See Tacitus's account of the March of the Roman Legions through the German forests, Annals, b. i. c. 71
Cicero, Quintus, attacked in his winter quarters by Ambi[)o]rix, G. v. 39; informs Caesar of his distress, who marches to relieve him, 46; attacked unexpectedly by the Sigambri, who are nevertheless obliged to retire, vi. 36
Cimbri, the Jutlanders, a very ancient northern people, who inhabited Chersonesus Cimbrica
Cing[)e]t[)o]rix, the leader of one of the factions among the Treviri, and firmly attached to Caesar, G. v. 3; declared a public enemy, and his goods confiscated by Indutiom[)a]rus, 56
Cing[)u]lum, a town of Pic[=e]num, in Italy, Cingoli
Cleopatra, engaged in a war with her brother Ptolemy, C. iii. 103
Clod[)i]us sent by Caesar to Scipio, to treat about a peace, but without effect, C. iii. 90
Cocas[=a]tes, a people of Gaul, according to some the Bazadois
Caelius Rufus raises a sedition in Rome, C. iii. 20; is expelled that city, then joins with Milo, 21; he is killed, 22
C[)o]imbra, an ancient city of Portugal, once destroyed, but now rebuilt, on the river Mendego
Colchis, a country in Asia, near Pontus, including the present Mingrelia and Georgia
Com[=a]na Pont[)i]ca, a city of Asia Minor, Com, or, Tabachzan
Com[=a]na of Cappadocia, Arminacha
Comius sent by Caesar into Britain to dispose the British states to submit, G. iv. 21; persuades the Bellov[)a]ci to furnish their contingent to the relief of Alesia, vii. 76; his distrust of the Romans, occasioned by an attempt to assassinate him, viii. 23; harasses the Romans greatly, and intercepts their convoys, 47; attacks Volusenus Quadratus, and runs him through the thigh, 48; submits to Antony, on condition of not appearing in the presence of any Roman, ibid.
Compsa, a city of Italy, Conza, or Consa

Concordia, an ancient city of the province of Triuli, in Italy, now in ruins
Condr[=u]si, or Condr[=u]s[=o]nes, an ancient people of Belgium, dependent on the Treviri, whose country is now called Condrotz, between Liege and Namur
Conetod[=u]nus heads the Carnutes in their revolt from the Romans, and the massacre at Genabum, G. vii. 3
Confluens Mosae et Rheni, the confluence of the Meuse and Rhine, or the point where the Meuse joins the Vahalis, or Waal, which little river branches out from the Rhine
Convictolit[=a]nis, a division on his account among the Aeduans, C. vii. 32; Caesar confirms his election to the supreme magistracy, 33; he persuades Litavicus and his brothers to rebel, 37
Corc[=y]ra, an island of Epirus, Corfu
Cord[)u]ba, a city of Hispania Baetica, Cordova; Caesar summons the leading men of the several states of Spain to attend him there, C. ii. 19; transactions of that assembly, 21
Corf[=i]n[)i]um, a town belonging to the Peligni, in Italy, St. Pelino, al. Penlina; Caesar lays siege to it, C. i. 16; and obliges it to surrender, 24
Corinth, a famous and rich city of Achaia, in Greece, in the middle of the Isthmus going into Peloponnesus
Corneli[=a]na Castra, a city of Africa, between Carthage and Utica
Correus, general of the Bellov[)a]ci, with six thousand foot, and a thousand horse, lies in ambush for the Roman foragers, and attacks the Roman cavalry with a small party, but is routed and killed, G. viii. 19
Cors[)i]ca, a considerable island in the Mediterranean Sea, near Sardinia, which still retains its name
Cosanum, a city of Calabria, in Italy, Cassano
Cotta, L. Aurunculeius, dissents from Sabinus in relation to the advice given them by Ambiorix, G. v. 28; his behaviour when attacked by the Gauls, 33; is slain, with the great part of his men, after a brave resistance, 37
Cotuatus and Conetodunus massacre all the Roman merchants at Genabum, G. vii. 3
Cotus, a division on his account among the Aeduans, G. vii. 32; obliged to desist from his pretensions to the supreme magistracy, 33
Crassus, P., his expedition into Aquitaine, G. iii. 20; reduces the Sotiates, 22; and other states, obliging them to give hostages, 27
Crast[)i]nus, his character, and courage at the battle of Pharsalia, C. iii. 91; where he is killed, 99
Cr[)e]m[=o]na, an ancient city of Gallia Cisalpina, which retains its name to this day, and is the metropolis of the Cremonese, in Italy

Crete, one of the noblest islands in the Mediterranean Sea, now called Candia
Critognatus, his extraordinary speech and proposal to the garrison of Alesia, G. vii. 77
Curio obliges Cato to abandon the defence of Cicily, C. i. 30; sails for Africa, and successfully attacks Varus, ii. 25; his speech to revive the courage of his men, 32; defeats Varus, 34; giving too easy credit to a piece of false intelligence, is cut off with his whole army, 42
Curiosol[=i]tae, a people of Gaul, inhabiting Cornoualle, in Bretagne
Cycl[)a]des, islands in the Aegean Sea, L'Isole dell' Archipelago
Cyprus, an island in the Mediterranean Sea, between Syria and Cilicia, Cipro
Cyr[=e]ne, an ancient and once a fine city of Africa, situate over against Matapan, the most southern cape of Morea, Cairoan
Cyz[=i]cus, Atraki, formerly one of the largest cities of Asia Minor, in an island of the same name, in the Black Sea
Dacia, an ancient country of Scythia, beyond the Danube, containing part of Hungary, Transylvania, Walachia, and Moldavia
Dalm[=a]tia, a part of Illyricum, now called Sclavonia, lying between Croatia, Bosnia, Servia, and the Adriatic Gulf
D[=a]n[)u]b[)i]us, the largest river in Europe, which rises in the Black Forest, and after flowing through that country, Bavaria, Austria, Hungary, Servia, Bulgaria, Moldavia, and Bessarabia, receiving in its course a great number of noted rivers, some say sixty, and 120 minor streams, falls into the Black or Euxine Sea, in two arms
Dard[=a]nia, the ancient name of a country in Upper Moesia, which became afterwards a part of Dacia; Rascia, and part of Servia
Dec[=e]tia, a town in Gaul,Decise, on the Loire
Delphi, a city of Achaia, Delpho, al. Salona
Delta, a very considerable province of Egypt, at the mouth of the Nile, Errif
Diablintes, an ancient people of Gaul, inhabiting the country called Le Perche; al. Diableres, in Bretagne; al. Lintes of Brabant; al. Lendoul, over against Britain
Divit[)i]i[)a]cus, the Aeduan, his attachment to the Romans and Caesar, G. i. 19; Caesar, for his sake, pardons his brother Dumnorix, ibid.; he complains to Caesar, in behalf of the rest of the Gauls, of the cruelty of Ariovistus, 31; marches against the Bellov[)a]ci create a diversion in favour of Caesar, ii. 10; intercedes for the Bellov[)a]ci, and obtains their pardon from Caesar, 14; goes to Rome to implore aid of the senate, but without effect, vi. 12
Domitius Ahenobarbus, besieged by Caesar in Corfinium, writes to Pompey for assistance, C. i. 15; seized by his own troops, who offer to

deliver him up to Caesar, 20; Caesar's generous behaviour towards him, 23; he enters Marseilles, and is entrusted with the supreme command, 36; is defeated in a sea fight by Decimus Brutus, 58; escapes with great difficulty a little before the surrender of Marseilles, ii. 22
Domitius Calvinus, sent by Caesar into Macedonia, comes very opportunely to the relief of Cassius Longinus, C. iii. 34; gains several advantages over Scipio, 32
Drapes, in conjunction with Luterius, seizes Uxellodunum, G. viii. 30; his camp stormed, and himself made prisoner, 29; he starves himself, 44
Druids, priests so called, greatly esteemed in Gaul, and possessed of many valuable privileges, G. vi. 13
D[=u]bis, a river of Burgundy, Le Doux
Dumn[)a]cus besieges Duracius in Limonum, G. viii. 26; is defeated by Fabius, 27
Dumn[)o]rix, the brother of Divitiacus, his character, G. i. 15; persuades the noblemen of Gaul not to go with Caesar into Britain, v. 5; deserts, and is killed for his obstinacy, 6
Duracius besieged in Limonum by Dumnacus, general of the Andes, G. viii. 26
Durocort[=o]rum, a city of Gaul, Rheims
D[)y]rrh[)a]ch[)i]um, a city of Macedonia, Durazzo, Drazzi; Caesar endeavours to enclose Pompey within his lines near that place, C. iii. 41
Ebur[=o]nes, an ancient people of Germany, inhabiting part of the country, now the bishopric of Liege, and the county of Namur. Caesar takes severe vengeance on them for their perfidy, G. vi. 34, 35
Eb[=u]r[)o]v[=i]ces, a people of Gaul, inhabiting the country of Evreux, in Normandy; they massacre their senate, and join with Viridovix, G. iii. 17
Egypt, see Aegypt
El[=a]ver, a river of Gaul, the Allier
Eleut[=e]ti Cadurci, a branch of the Cadurci, in Aquitania. They are called in many editions Eleutheri Cadurci, but incorrectly, since Eleutheri is a term of Greek origin, and besides could hardly be applied to a Gallic tribe like the Eleuteti, who, in place of being free [Greek: eleutheroi], seem to have been clients of the Arverni; they furnish troops to the relief of Alesia, G. vii. 75
Elis, a city of Peloponnesus, Belvidere
Elus[=a]tes, an ancient people of Gaul, inhabiting the country of Euse, in Gascony
Eph[)e]sus, an ancient and celebrated city of Asia Minor, Efeso; the temple of Diana there in danger of being stripped, G. iii. 32
Epidaurus, a maritime city of Dalmatia, Ragusa

Ep[=i]rus, a country in Greece, between Macedonia, Achaia, and the Ionian Sea, by some now called Albania inferior
Eporedorix, treacherously revolts from Caesar, G. vii. 54
Essui, a people of Gaul; the word seems to be a corruption from Aedui, C. v. 24
Etesian winds detain Caesar at Alexandria, which involves him in a new war, C. iii. 107
Eusubii, corrupted from Unelli, or Lexovii, properly the people of Lisieux, in Normandy
Fabius, C., one of Caesar's lieutenants, sent into Spain, with three legions, C. i. 37; builds two bridges over the Segre for the convenience of foraging, 40
Fanum, a city of Umbria in Italy, Fano, C. i. 11
Fortune, her wonderful power and influence on matters of war, G. vi. 30
Faesulae, Fiesoli, an ancient city of Italy, in the duchy of Florence, anciently one of the twelve considerable cities of Etruria.
Flavum, anciently reckoned the eastern mouth of the Rhine, now called the Ulie, and is a passage out of the Zuyder Sea into the North Sea
Gab[)a]li, an ancient people of Gaul, inhabiting the country of Givaudan. Their chief city was Anduitum, now Mende, G. vii. 64; they join the general confederacy of Vercingetorix, and give hostages to Luterius, G. vii. 7
Gadit[=a]ni, the people of Gades, C. ii. 18
Gal[=a]tia, a country in Asia Minor, lying between Cappadocia, Pontus, and Paphlagonia, now called Chiangare
Galba Sergius, sent against the Nantuates, Veragrians, and Seduni, G. iii. 1; the barbarians attack his camp unexpectedly, but are repulsed with great loss, iii. 6
Galli, the Gauls, the people of ancient Gaul, now France; their country preferable to that of the Germans, G. i. 31; their manner of attacking towns, ii.6; of greater stature than the Romans, 30; quick and hasty in their resolves, iii.8; forward in undertaking wars, but soon fainting under misfortunes, 19; their manners, chiefs, druids, discipline, cavalry, religion, origin, marriages, and funerals, vi.13; their country geographically described, i.1
Gall[=i]a, the ancient and renowned country of Gaul, now France. It was divided by the Romans into—
Gallia Cisalpina, Tonsa, or Togata, now Lombardy, between the Alps and the river Rubicon: and—
Gallia Transalpina, or Com[=a]ta, comprehending France, Holland, the Netherlands: and farther subdivided into—

Gallia Belg[)i]ca, now a part of Lower Germany, and the Netherlands, with Picardy; divided by Augustus into Belgica and Germania__ and the latter into Prima and Secunda
Gallia Celt[)i]ca, now France properly so called, divided by Augustus into Lugdun[=e]nsis, and Rothomagensis
Gallia Aquitan[)i]ca, now Gascony; divided by Augustus into Prima, Secunda, and Tertia: and—
Gallia Narbonensis, or Bracc[=a]ta, now Languedoc, Dauphiny, and Provence
Gallograecia, a country of Asia Minor, the same as Galatia
Gar[=i]tes, a people of Gaul, inhabiting the country now called Gavre, Gavaraan
Garoceli, or Graioc[)e]li, an ancient people of Gaul, about Mount Genis, or Mount Genevre others place them in the Val de Gorienne; they oppose Caesar's passage over the Alps, G. i. 10
Garumna, the Garonne, one of the largest rivers of France, which, rising in the Pyrenees, flows through Guienne, forms the vast Bay of Garonne, and falls, by two mouths, into the British Seas. The Garonne is navigable as far as Toulouse, and communicates with the Mediterranean by means of the great canal, G. i. 1
Garumni, an ancient people of Gaul, in the neighbourhood of the Garonne, G. iii. 27
Geld[=u]ra, a fortress of the Ubii, on the Rhine, not improbably the present village of Gelb, on that river eleven German miles from N[=e]us
Gen[)a]bum, Orleans, an ancient town in Gaul, famous for the massacre of the Roman citizens committed there by the Carn[=u]tes
Gen[=e]va, a city of Savoy, now a free republic, upon the borders of Helvetia, where the Rhone issues from the Lake Lemanus, anciently a city of the Allobr[)o]ges
Gen[=u]sus, a river of Macedonia, uncertain
Gerg[=o]via, the name of two cities in ancient Gaul, the one belonging to the Boii, the other to the Arverni. The latter was the only Gallic city which baffled the attacks of Caesar
Gerg[=o]via of the Averni, Vercingetorix expelled thence by Gobanitio, G. vii. 4; the Romans attacking it eagerly, are repulsed with great slaughter, 50
Gerg[=o]via of the Boii, besieged in vain by Vercingetorix, G. vii. 9
Germania, Germany, one of the largest countries of Europe, and the mother of those nations which, on the fall of the Roman empire, conquered all the rest. The name appears to be derived from wer, war, and man, a man, and signifies the country of warlike men

Germans, habituated from their infancy to arms, G. i. 36; their manner of training their cavalry, 48; their superstition 50; defeated by Caesar, 53; their manners, religion, vi. 23; their huge stature and strength, G. i. 39
G[=e]tae, an ancient people of Scythia, who inhabited betwixt Moesia and Dacia, on each side of the Danube. Some think their country the same with the present Walachia, or Moldavia
Getulia, a province in the kingdom of Morocco, in Barbary
Gomphi, a town in Thessaly, Gonfi, refusing to open its gates to Caesar, is stormed and taken, C. iii. 80
Gord[=u]ni, a people of Belgium, the ancient inhabitants of Ghent, according to others of Courtray; they join with Ambiorix in his attack of Cicero's camp, G. v. 39
Got[=i]ni, an ancient people of Germany, who were driven out of their country by Maroboduus Graecia, Greece, a large part of Europe, called by the Turks Rom[=e]lia, containing many countries, provinces, and islands, once the nursery of arts, learning, and sciences
Graioc[)e]li, see Garoceli
Grudii, the inhabitants about Louvaine, or, according to some, about Bruges; they join with Ambiorix in his attack of Cicero's camp, G. v. 39
Gugerni, a people of ancient Germany, who dwelt on the right banks of the Rhine, between the Ubii and the Batavi
Gutt[=o]nes, or Gyth[=o]nes, an ancient people of Germany, inhabiting about the Vistula
Haemus, a mountain dividing Moesia and Thrace, Argentaro
Haliacmon, a river of Macedonia, uncertain; Scipio leaves Favonius with orders to build a fort on that river, C. iii. 36
Har[=u]des, or Har[=u]di, a people of Gallia Celtica, supposed to have been originally Germans: and by some to have inhabited the country about Constance Helv[=e]tia, Switzerland, now divided into thirteen cantons
Helv[=e]tii, the Helvetians, or Switzers, ancient inhabitants of the country of Switzerland; the most warlike people of Gaul, G. i. 1; their design of abandoning their own country, 2; attacked with considerable loss near the river Sa[^o]ne, 12; vanquished and obliged to return home by Caesar, 26
Helvii, an ancient people of Gaul, inhabiting the country now possessed by the Vivarois; Caesar marches into their territories, G. vii. 7
Heracl[=e]a, a city of Thrace, on the Euxine Sea, Pantiro
Heracl[=e]a Sent[)i]ca, a town in Macedonia, Chesia
Hercynia Silva, the Hercinian Forest, the largest forest of ancient Germany, being reckoned by Caesar to have been sixty days' journey in

length, and nine in breadth. Many parts of it have been since cut down, and many are yet remaining; of which, among others, is that called the Black Forest; its prodigious extent, G. vi. 4
Hermand[=u]ri, an ancient people of Germany, particularly in the country now called Misnia, in Upper Saxony; though they possessed a much larger tract of land, according to some, all Bohemia
Hermin[)i]us Mons, a mountain of Lusitania, Monte Arm[)i]no; according to others, Monte della Strella
Her[)u]li, an ancient northern people, who came first out of Scandavia, but afterwards inhabited the country now called Mecklenburg in Lower Saxony, towards the Baltic
Hibernia, Ireland, a considerable island to the west of Great Britain, G. v. 13
Hisp[=a]n[)i]a, Spain, one of the most considerable kingdoms of Europe, divided by the ancients into Tarraconensis, Baetica, and Lusitania. This name appears to be derived from the Phoenician Saphan, a rabbit, vast numbers of these animals being found there by the Phoenician colonists
Ib[=e]rus, a river of Hispania Tarraconensis, the Ebro, C. i. 60
Iccius, or Itius Portus, a seaport town of ancient Gaul; Boulogne, or, according to others, Calais
Ig[)i]l[)i]um, an island in the Tuscan Sea, il Giglio, l'Isle du Lys
Ig[)u]v[)i]um, a city of Umbria in Italy, Gubio; it forsakes Pompey, and submits to Caesar, C. i. 12
Illurgavonenses, a people of Hispania Tarraconensis, near the Iberus; they submit to Caesar, and supply him with corn, C. i. 60
Illurgis, a town of Hispania Baetica, Illera
Induti[)o]m[)a]rus, at the head of a considerable faction among the Treviri, G. v. 3; endeavouring to make himself master of Labienus's camp, is repulsed and slain, 53
Is[)a]ra, the Is[`e]re, a river of France, which rises in Savoy, and falls into the Rhone above Valance
Isauria, a province anciently of Asia Minor, now a part of Caramania, and subject to the Turks
Issa (an island of the Adriatic Sea, Lissa), revolts from Caesar at the instigation of Octavius, C. iii. 9
Ister, that part of the Danube which passed by Illyricum
Istr[)i]a, a country now in Italy, under the Venetians, bordering on Illyricum, so called from the river Ister
Istr[)o]p[)o]lis, a city of Lower Moesia, near the south entrance of the Danube, Prostraviza

It[)a]l[)i]a, Italy, one of the most famous countries in Europe, once the seat of the Roman empire, now under several princes, and free commonwealths
It[)a]l[)i]ca, a city of Hispania Baetica, Servila la Veja; according to others, Alcala del Rio; shuts its gates against Varro, C. ii. 20
Itius Portus, Caesar embarks there for Britain, G. v. 5
It[=u]raea, a country of Palestine, Sacar
Jacet[=a]ni, or Lacet[=a]ni, a people of Spain, near the Pyrenean Mountains; revolt from Afranius and submit to Caesar, C. i. 60
Jadert[=i]ni, a people so called from their capital Jadera, a city of Illyricum, Zara
Juba, king of Numidia, strongly attached to Pompey, C. ii. 25; advances with a large army to the relief of Utica, 36; detaches a part of his troops to sustain Sabura, 40; defeats Cario, ii. 42; his cruelty, ii. 44
J[=u]ra, a mountain in Gallia Belgica, which separated the Sequani from the Helvetians, most of which is now called Mount St. Claude. The name appears to be derived from the Celtic, jou-rag, which signifies the "domain of God;" the boundary of the Helvetians towards the Sequani, G. i. 2
Labi[=e]nus, one of Caesar's lieutenants, is attacked in his camp, G. v. 58, vi. 6; his stratagem, G. vii. 60; battle with the Gauls, G. vii. 59; is solicited by Caesar's enemies to join their party, G. viii. 52; built the town of Cingulum, C. i. 15; swears to follow Pompey, C. iii. 13; his dispute with Valerius about a peace, C. iii. 19; his cruelty towards Caesar's followers, C. iii. 71; flatters Pompey, C. iii. 87
Lacus B[)e]n[=a]cus, Lago di Guardo, situated in the north of Italy, between Verona, Brescia, and Trent
Lacus Lem[)a]nus, the lake upon which Geneva stands, formed by the River Rhone, between Switzerland to the north, and Savoy to the south, commonly called the Lake of Geneva, G. i. 2, 8
Larin[=a]tes, the people of Larinum, a city of Italy, Larino; C. i. 23
Larissa, the principal city of Thessaly, a province of Macedonia, on the river Peneo
L[)a]t[=i]ni, the inhabitants of Latium, an ancient part of Italy, whence the Latin tongue is so called
Lat[=o]br[)i]gi, a people of Gallia Belgica, between the Allobroges and Helvetii, in the country called Lausanne; abandon their country, G. i. 5; return, G. i. 28; their number, G. i. 29
Lemnos, an island in the Aegean Sea, now called Stalimane
Lemov[=i]ces, an ancient people of Gaul, le Limosin, G. vii. 4
Lemov[=i]ces Armorici, the people of St. Paul de Leon
Lenium, a town in Lusitania, unknown

Lent[)u]lus Marcellinus, the quaestor, one of Caesar's followers, C. iii. 62
Lentulus and Marcellus, the consuls, Caesar's enemies, G. viii. 50; leave Rome through fear of Caesar, C. i. 14
Lenunc[)u]li, fishing-boats, C. ii. 43
Lepontii, a people of the Alps, near the valley of Leventini, G. iv. 10
Leuci, a people of Gallia Belgica, where now Lorrain is, well skilled in darting. Their chief city is now called Toul, G. i. 40
Lev[)a]ci, a people of Brabant, not far from Louvain, whose chief town is now called Leew; dependants on the Nervii, G. v. 39
Lex, law of the Aedui respecting the election of magistrates, G. vii. 33
Lex, Julian law, C. ii. 14
Lex, the Pompeian law respecting bribery, C. iii. 1
Lex, two Caelian laws, C. iii. 20, 21
Lexovii, an ancient people of Gaul, Lisieux in Normandy, G. iii. 11, 17
Liberty of the Gauls, G. iii. 8; the desire of, G. v. 27; the sweetness of, G. iii. 10; the incitement to, G. vii. 76; C. i. 47
Libo, praefect of Pompey's fleet, C. iii. 5; converses with Caesar at Oricum, C. iii. 16; takes possession of the Island at Brundisium, C. iii. 23; threatens the partisans of Caesar, C. iii. 24; withdraws from Brundisium, ibid.
Liburni, an ancient people of Illyricum, inhabiting part of the present Croatia
Liger, or Ligeris, the Loire; one of the greatest and most celebrated rivers of France, said to receive one hundred and twelve rivers in its course; it rises in Velay, and falls into the Bay of Aquitain, below Nantz, G. iii. 5
Lig[)u]ria, a part of ancient Italy, extending from the Apennines to the Tuscan Sea, containing Ferrara, and the territories of Genoa
Limo, or Lim[=o]num, a city of ancient Gaul, Poitiers
Ling[)o]nes, a people of Gallia Belgica, inhabiting in and about Langres, in Champagne, G. i. 26, 40
Liscus, one of the Aedui, accuses Dumnorix to Caesar, G. i. 16, 17
Lissus, an ancient city of Macedonia, Alessio
Litavicus, one of the Aedui, G. vii. 37; his treachery and flight, G. vii. 38
Lucani, an ancient people of Italy, inhabiting the country now called Basilicate
Luceria, an ancient city of Italy, Lucera
Lucretius Vespillo, one of Pompey's followers, C. iii. 7
Lucterius or Laterius, one of the Cadurci, vii. 5, 7
Lusit[=a]nia, Portugal, a kingdom on the west of Spain, formerly a part of it

Lusitanians, light-armed troops, C. i. 48
Lutetia, Paris, an ancient and famous city, now the capital of all France, on the river Seine
Lygii, an ancient people of Upper Germany, who inhabited the country now called Silesia, and on the borders of Poland
M[)a]c[)e]d[=o]nia, a large country, of great antiquity and fame, containing several provinces, now under the Turks
Macedonian cavalry among Pompey's troops, C. iii. 4
Mae[=o]tis Palus, a vast lake in the north part of Scythia, now called Marbianco, or Mare della Tana. It is about six hundred miles in compass, and the river Tanais disembogues itself into it
Maget[)o]br[)i]a, or Amagetobria, a city of Gaul, near which Ariovistus defeated the combined forces of the Gauls. It is supposed to correspond to the modern Moigte de Broie, near the village of Pontailler
Mandub[)i]i, an ancient people of Gaul, l'Anxois, in Burgundy; their famine and misery, G. vii. 78
Mandubratius, a Briton, G. v. 20
Marcellus, Caesar's enemy, G. viii 53
Marcius Crispus, is sent for a protection to the inhabitants of Thabena
Marcomanni, a nation of the Suevi, whom Cluverius places between the
Rhine, the Danube and the Neckar; who settled, however, under Maroboduus, in Bohemia and Moravia. The name Marcomanni signifies
border-men. Germans, G. i. 51
Marruc[=i]ni, an ancient people of Italy, inhabiting the country now called Abruzzo, C. i. 23; ii. 34
Mars, G. vi. 17
Marsi, an ancient people of Italy inhabiting the country now called Ducato de Marsi, C. ii. 27
Massilia, Marseilles, a large and flourishing city of Provence, in France, on the Mediterranean, said to be very ancient, and, according to some, built by the Phoenicians, but as Justin will have it, by the Phocaeans, in the time of Tarquinius, king of Rome
Massilienses, the inhabitants of Marseilles, C. i. 34-36
Matisco, an ancient city of Gaul, Mascon, G. vii. 90
Matr[)o]na, a river in Gaul, the Marne, G. i. 1
Mauritania, Barbary, an extensive region of Africa, divided into M. Caesariensis, Tingitana, and Sitofensis
Mediomatr[=i]ces, a people of Lorrain, on the Moselle, about the city of Mentz, G. iv. 10
Mediterranean Sea, the first discovered sea in the world, still very famous, and much frequented, which breaks in from the Atlantic

Ocean, between Spain and Africa, by the straits of Gibraltar, or Hercules' Pillar, the ne plus ultra of the ancients
Meldae, according to some the people of Meaux; but more probably corrupted from Belgae
Melodunum, an ancient city of Gaul, upon the Seine, above Paris, Melun, G. vii. 58, 60
Menapii, an ancient people of Gallia Belgica, who inhabited on both sides of the Rhine. Some take them for the inhabitants of Cleves, and others of Antwerp, Ghent, etc., G. ii. 4; iii. 9
Menedemus, C. iii. 34
Mercurius, G. v. 17
Mes[)o]p[)o]t[=a]mia, a large country in the middle of Asia, between the
Tigris and the Euphrates, Diarbeck
Mess[=a]na, an ancient and celebrated city of Sicily, still known by the name of Messina, C. iii. 101
M[)e]taurus, a river of Umbria, now called Metoro, in the duchy of Urbino
Metios[=e]dum, an ancient city of Gaul, on the Seine, below Paris, Corbeil, G. vii. 61
Metr[)o]p[)o]lis, a city of Thessaly, between Pharsalus and Gomphi, C. iii. 11
Milo, C. iii. 21
Minerva, G. vi. 12
Minutius Rufus, C. iii. 7
Mitylene, a city of Lesbos, Metelin
Moesia, a country of Europe, and a province of the ancient Illyricum, bordering on Pannonia, divided into the Upper, containing Bosnia and Servia, and the Lower, called Bulgaria
Mona, in Caesar, the Isle of Man; in Ptolemy, Anglesey, G. v. 13
Mor[)i]ni, an ancient people of the Low Countries, who probably inhabited on the present coast of Bologne, on the confines of Picardy and Artois, because Caesar observes that from their country was the nearest passage to Britain, G. ii. 4
Moritasgus, G. v. 54
Mosa, the Maess, or Meuse, a large river of Gallia Belgica, which falls into the German Ocean below the Briel, G. iv. 10
Mosella, the Moselle, a river which, running through Lorrain, passes by Triers and falls unto the Rhine at Coblentz, famous for the vines growing in the neighbourhood of it
Mysia, a country of Asia Minor, not far from the Hellespont, divided Into Major and Minor
Nabathaei, an ancient people of Arabia, uncertain

Nann[=e]tes, an ancient people of Gaul, inhabiting the country about Nantes, G. iii. 9
Nantu[=a]tes, an ancient people of the north part of Savoy, whose country is now called Le Chablais, G. iii. 1
Narbo, Narbonne, an ancient Roman city in Languedoc, in France, said to be built a hundred and thirty-eight years before the birth of Christ, G. iii. 20
Narisci, the ancient people of the country now called Nortgow, in Germany, the capital of which is the famous city of Nuremburg
Nasua, the brother of Cimberius, and commander of the hundred cantons of the Suevi, who encamped on the banks of the Rhine with the intention of crossing that river, G. i. 37
Naupactus, an ancient and considerable city of Aetolia, now called Lepanto, C. iii. 35
Nem[=e]tes, a people of ancient Germany, about the city of Spire, on the
Rhine, G. i. 51
Nemetocenna, a town of Belgium, not known for certain; according to some, Arras, G. viii, 47
Neocaesarea, the capital of Ponts, on the river Licus, now called Tocat
Nervii, an ancient people of Gallia Belgica, thought to have dwelt in the now diocese of Cambray. They attacked Caesar on his march, and fought until they were almost annihilated, G. ii. 17
Nessus, or Nestus, a river is Thrace, Nesto Nicaea, a city of Bithynia, now called Isnick, famous for the first general council, anno 324, against Arianism
Nit[=o]br[)i]ges, an ancient people of Gaul, whose territory lay on either side of the Garonne, and corresponded to the modern Agennois, in the department of Lot-et-Garonne. Their capital was Agrimum, now Agen, G. vii. 7, 31, 46, 75
Noreia, a city on the borders of Illyricum, in the province of Styria, near the modern village of Newmarket, about nine German miles from Aquileia, G. i. 5
N[=o]r[)i]cae Alpes, that part of the Alps which were in, or bordering upon, Noricum
N[=o]r[)i]cum, anciently a large country, and now comprehending a great part of Austria, Styria, Carinthia, part of Tyrol, Bavaria, etc., and divided into Noricum Mediterraneum and Ripense. It was first conquered by the Romans under Tiberius, in the reign of Augustus, and was celebrated for its mineral treasures, especially iron
N[)o]v[)i][)o]d[=u]num Belgarum, an ancient city of Belgic Gaul, now called Noyon
N[)o]v[)i][)o]d[=u]num Bitur[)i]gum, Neuvy, or Neufvy, G. vii. 12

N[)o]v[)i][)o]d[=u]num Aeduorum, Nevers, G. vii. 55
N[)o]v[)i][)o]d[=u]num Suessionum, Soissons, al. Noyon, G. ii. 12
N[)o]v[)i]om[=a]gum, Spire, an ancient city of Germany, in the now upper circle of the Rhine, and on that river
Numantia, a celebrated city of ancient Spain, famous for a gallant resistance against the Romans, in a siege of fourteen years; Almasan
Numeius, G. i. 7
Num[)i]dae, the inhabitants of, G. ii. 7
Numid[)i]a, an ancient and celebrated kingdom of Africa, bordering on Mauritania; Algiers, Tunis, Tripoli, etc.
N[=y]mphaeum, a promontory of Illyricum, exposed to the south wind, and distant about three miles from Lissus, Alessio, C. iii. 26
Oc[)e]llum, a town situated among the Cottian Alps, Usseau in Piedmont,
G. i. 10
Octavius, C. iii. 9
Octod[=u]rus, a town belonging to the Veragrians, among the Pennine Alps, now Martigny in the Valois, G. iii. 1 Octog[=e]sa, a city of Hispania Tarraconensis, Mequinenza, C. i. 61
Ollovico, G. vii. 31
Orch[)o]m[)e]nus, a town in Boeotia, Orcomeno, C. iii. 5 5
Orcynia, the name given by Greek writers to the Hercynian forest
Orget[=o]rix, G. i. 2, 3
Or[)i]cum, a town in Epirus, Orco, or Orcha, C. iii. 11, 12
Osc[=e]nses, the people of Osca, a town in Hispania Tarraconensis, now Huescar, C. i. 60
Os[=i]sm[)i]i, an ancient people of Gaul, one of the Gentes Armoricae. Their country occupied part of Neodron Brittany; capital Vorganium, afterwards Osismii, and now Korbez. In this territory also stood Brivatas Portus, now Brest, G. i. 34
Otacilii, C. iii. 28
Padua, the Po, the largest river in Italy, which rises in Piedmont, and dividing Lombardy into two parts, falls into the Adriatic Sea, by many mouths; south of Venice
Paem[=a]ni, an ancient people of Gallia Belgica; according to some, those of Luxemburg; according to others, the people of Pemont, near the Black Forest, in part of the modern Lugen, G. ii. 4
P[)a]laeste, a town in Epirus, near Oricurn
Pann[=o]n[)i]a, a very large country in the ancient division of Europe, divided into the Upper and Lower, and comprehended betwixt Illyricum, the Danube, and the mountains Cethi

P[)a]ris[)i]i, an ancient people of Gaul, inhabiting the country now called the Isle of France. Their capital was Lutetia, afterwards Parisii, now Paris, G. vi. 3
P[=a]rth[)i]a, a country in Asia, lying between Media, Caramania, and the Hyreanian Sea
Parthians at war with Rome, C. iii. 31
P[=a]rth[=i]ni, a people of Macedonia; their chief city taken by storm, C. iii. 41
P[=e]l[=i]gni, a people of Italy in Abruzzo, C. i. 15
P[)e]l[)o]ponn[=e]sus, the Morea, a famous, large, and fruitful peninsula of Greece, now belonging to the Venetians
P[=e]l[=u]s[)i]um, an ancient and celebrated city of Egypt, Belbais; Pompey goes to it, C. iii. 103; taken by Mithridates
P[=e]rg[)a]mus, an ancient and famous city of Mysia, Pergamo
Per[)i]nthus, a city of Thrace, about a day's journey west of Constantinople, now in a decaying condition, and called Heraclea
P[=e]rs[)i]a, one of the largest, most ancient and celebrated kingdoms of Asia
P[=e]tra, an ancient city of Macedonia, uncertain
Petreius, one of Pompey's lieutenants, C. i. 38
P[=e]tr[)o]g[)o]r[)i]i, a country in Gaul, east of the mouth of the Garumna; their chief city was Vesuna, afterwards Petrocorii, now Perigueux, the capital of Perigord
Pe[=u]c[=i]ni, the inhabitants of the islands of Peuce, in one of the mouths of the Danube
Ph[=a]rs[=a]l[)i]a, a part of Thessaly, famous for the battle between Caesar and Pompey, which decided the fate of the Roman commonwealth
Pharus, an isle facing the port of Alexandria in ancient Egypt; Farion
Phasis, a large river in Colchis, now called Fasso, which flows into the Euxine Sea
Ph[)i]lippi, a city of Macedonia, on the confines of Thrace, Filippo
Ph[)i]l[=i]pp[)o]p[)o]lis, a city of Thrace, near the river Hebrus, Filippopoli
Phr[)y]g[)i]a, two countries in Asia Minor, one called Major, the other Minor
P[=i]c[=e]num, an ancient district of Italy, lying eastward of Umbria; the March of Ancona; according to others, Piscara
P[=i]cti, Picts, an ancient barbarous northern people, who by inter-marriages became, in course of time, one nation with the Scots; but are originally supposed to have come out of Denmark or Scythia, to the Isles of Orkney, and from thence into Scotland

P[=i]ct[)o]nes, an ancient people of Gaul, along the southern bank of the Liger, or Loire. Their capital was Limonum, afterwards Pictones, now Paitross, in the department de la Vienne, G. iii. 11
Pir[=u]stae, an ancient people of Dalmatia, Illyricum, on the confines of Pannonia. They are the same as the Pyraci of Pliny (H. N. iii. 22), G. v. i
P[)i]saurum, a city of Umbria in Italy, Pisaro
Piso, an Aquitanian, slain, G. iv. 12
Placentia, an ancient city of Gallia Cisalpina, near the Po, now the metropolis of the duchy of Piacenza, which name it also bears
Pleum[)o]si, an ancient people of Gallia Belgica, subject to the Nervians, and inhabiting near Tournay
Pompey, at first friendly to Caesar, G. vi. 1; subsequently estranged, G. viii. 53; could not bear an equal his authority, power, and influence, C. i. 61; sends ambassadors to Caesar, C. i. 8, 10; always received great respect from Caesar, C. i. 8; Caesar desires to bring him to an engagement, C. iii. 66; his unfortunate flight, C. iii. 15, 94, 102; his death, C. iii. 6, 7.
Pomponius, C. iii. 101
Pontus Eux[=i]nus, the Euxine, or Black Sea, from the Aegean along the Hellespont, to the Maeotic Lake, between Europe and Asia
Posth[)u]m[)i][=a]na Castra, an ancient town in Hispania Baetica, now called Castro el Rio
Pothinus, king Ptolemy's tutor, C. iii. 108; his death, C. iii. 112
Praeciani, an ancient people of Gaul, Precius; they surrendered to the Romans, G. iii. 27
Provincia Rom[=a]na, or Romanorum, one of the southern provinces of France, the first the Romans conquered and brought into the form of a province, whence it obtained its name; which it still in some degree retains, being called at this day Provence. It extended from the Pyrenees to the Alps, along the coast. Provence is only part of the ancient Provincia, which in its full extent included the departments of Pyr['e]n['e]es-Orientales, l'Arri[`e]ge, Aude[**Note: misprint "Ande" in the original], Haute Garonne, Tarn, Herault, Gard, Vaucluse, Bouches-du- Rh[^o]ne, Var, Basses-Alpes, Hautes-Alpes, La Dr[^o]me, l'Is[`e]re, l'Ain
Prusa, or Prusas, Bursa, a city of Bithynia, at the foot of Olympus, built by Hannibal
Ptolemaeius, Caesar interferes between him and Cleopatra, C. iii. 107; his father's will, C. iii. 108; Caesar takes the royal youth into his power, C. iii. 109
Pt[)o]l[)e]m[=a]is, an ancient city of Africa, St. Jean d'Acre

Publius Attius Varus, one of Pompey's generals, C. ii. 23 Pyrenaei Montes, the Pyrenees, or Pyrenean mountains, one of the largest chains of mountains in Europe, which divide Spain from France, running from east to west eighty-five leagues in length. The name is derived from the Celtic Pyren or Pyrn, a high mountain, hence also Brenner, in the Tyrol Ravenna, a very ancient city of Italy, near the coast of the Adriatic Gulf, which still retains its ancient name. In the decline of the Roman empire, it was sometimes the seat of the emperors of the West; as it was likewise of the Visi-Gothic kingdom, C. i. 5
Raur[=a]ci, a people of ancient Germany, near the Helvetii, who inhabited near where Basle in Switzerland now is; they unite with the Helvetii, and leave home, G. i. 5, 29
Rebilus, one of Caesar's lieutenants, a man of great military experience, C. ii. 34
Remi, the people of Rheims, a very ancient, fine, and populous city of France, in the province of Champagne, on the river Vesle; surrender to Caesar, G. ii. 3; their influence and power with Caesar, G. v. 54; vi. 64; they fall into an ambuscade of the Bellovaci, G. viii. 12
Rh[-e][)d]ones, an ancient people of Gaul inhabiting about Rennes, in Bretagne; they surrender to the Romans, G. ii. 34
Rhaetia, the country of the Grisons, on the Alps, near the Hercynian Forest
Rhenus, the Rhine, a large and famous river in Germany, which it formerly divided from Gaul. It springs out of the Rhaetian Alps, in the western borders of Switzerland, and the northern of the Grisons, from two springs which unite near Coire, and falls into the Meuse and the German Ocean, by two mouths, whence Virgil calls it Rhenus bicornis. It passes through Lacus Brigantinus, or the Lake of Constance, and Lacus Acronius or the Lake of Zell, and then continues its westerly direction to Basle (Basiliae). It then bends northward, and separates Germany from France, and further down Germany from Belgium. At Schenk the Rhine sends off its left-hand branch, the Vahalis (Waal), by a western course to join the Mosa or Meuse. The Rhine then flows on a few miles, and again separates into two branches—the one to the right called the Flevo, or Felvus, or Flevum—now the Yssel, and the other called the Helium, now the Leek. The latter joins the Mosa above Rotterdam. The Yssel was first connected with the Rhine by the canal of Drusus. It passed through the small lake of Flevo before reaching the sea which became expanded into what is now called the Zuyder Zee by increase of water through the Yssel from the Rhine. The whole course of the Rhine is nine hundred miles, of which six hundred and thirty are navigable from Basle to the sea.—G. iv. 10, 16, 17; vi. 9, etc.; description of it, G. iv. 10

Rh[)o]d[)a]nus, the Rhone, one of the most celebrated rivers of France, which rises from a double spring in Mont de la Fourche, a part of the Alps, on the borders of Switzerland, near the springs of the Rhine. It passes through the Lacus Lemanus, Lake of Geneva, and flows with a swift and rapid current in a southern direction into the Sinus Gallicus, or Gulf of Lyons. Its whole course is about four hundred miles
Rhod[)o]pe, a famous mountain of Thrace, now called Valiza
Rh[)o]dus, Rhodes, a celebrated island in the Mediterranean, upon the coast of Asia Minor, over against Caria
Rhynd[)a]gus, a river of Mysia in Asia, which falls into the Propontis
R[)o]ma, Rome, once the seat of the Roman empire, and the capital of the then known world, now the immediate capital of Camagna di Roma only, on the river Tiber, and the papal seat; generally supposed to have been built by Romulus, in the first year of the seventh Olympiad, B.C. 753
Roscillus and Aegus, brothers belonging to the Allobroges, revolt from Caesar to Pompey, C. iii. 59
Roxol[-a]ni, a people of Scythia Europaea, bordering upon the Alani; their country, anciently called Roxolonia, is now Red Russia
R[)u]t[-e]ni, an ancient people of Gaul, to the north-west of the Volcae Arecomici, occupying the district now called Le Rauergne. Their capital was Segodunum, afterwards Ruteni, now Rhodes, G. i. 45; vii. 7, etc.
S[=a]bis, the Sambre, a river of the Low Countries, which rises in Picardy, and falls into the Meuse at Namur, G. ii. 16, 18; vi. 33
Sabura, general of king Juba, C. ii. 38; his stratagem against Curio, C. ii. 40; his death, C. ii. 95
Sadales, the son of king Cotys, brings forces to Pompey, C. iii. 4
Salassii, an ancient city of Piedmont, whose chief town was where now Aosta is situate
Salluvii, Sallyes, a people of Gallia Narbonensis, about where Aix now is
Sal[=o]na, an ancient city of Dalmatia, and a Roman colony; the place where Dioclesian was born, and whither he retreated, after he had resigned the imperial dignity
S[=a]lsus, a river of Hispania Baetica, Rio Salado, or Guadajos
S[)a]m[)a]r[:o]br[=i]va, Amiens, an ancient city of Gallia Belgica, enlarged and beautified by the emperor Antoninus Pius, now Amicus, the chief city of Picardy, on the river Somme; assembly of the, Gauls held there, G. v. 24
S[=a]nt[)o]nes, the ancient inhabitants of Guienne, or Xantoigne, G. i. 10

S[=a]rd[)i]n[)i]a, a large island in the Mediterranean, which in the time of the Romans had forty-two cities, it now belongs to the Duke of Savoy, with the title of king
S[=a]rm[=a]t[)i]a, a very large northern country, divided into Sarmatia Asiatica, containing Tartary, Petigora, Circassia, and the country of the Morduitae; and Sarmatia Europaea, containing Russia, part ofPoland, Prussia, and Lithuania
Savus, the Save, a large river which rises in Upper Carniola, and falls into the Danube at Belgrade
Scaeva, one of Caesar's centurions, displays remarkable valour, C. iii. 5 3; his shield is pierced in two hundred and thirty places
Sc[=a]ldis, the Scheld, a noted river in the Low Countries, which rises in Picardy, and washing several of the principal cities of Flanders and Brabant in its course, falls into the German Ocean by two mouths, one retaining its own name, and the other called the Honte. Its whole course does not exceed a hundred and twenty miles. G. vi. 33
Scandinav[)i]a, anciently a vast northern peninsula, containing what is yet called Schonen, anciently Scania, belonging to Denmark; and part of Sweden, Norway, and Lapland
Scipio, his opinion of Pompey and Caesar, C. i. 1, 21; his flight, C. iii. 37
S[)e]d[=u]l[)i]us, general of the Lemovices; his death, G. vii. 38
S[=e]d[=u]ni, a people of Gaul, to the south-east of the Lake of Geneva, occupying the upper part of the Valais. Their chief town was Civitus Sedunorum, now Sion, G. iii. i
S[=e]d[=u]s[)i]i, an ancient people of Germany, on the borders of Suabia, G. i. 51
S[=e]gni, an ancient German nation, neighbours of the Condrusi, Zulpich
S[=e]g[=o]nt[)i][=a]ci, a people of ancient Britain, inhabiting about Holshot, in Hampshire, G. v. 21
Segovia, a city of Hispania Baetica, Sagovia la Menos
S[)e]g[=u]s[)i][=a]ni, a people of Gallia Celtica, about where Lionois Forest is now situate
Sen[)o]nes, an ancient nation of the Celtae, inhabiting the country about the Senonois, in Gaul
Sequ[)a]na, the Seine, one of the principal rivers of France, which rising in the duchy of Burgundy, not far from a town of the same name, and running through Paris, and by Rouen, forms at Candebec a great arm of the sea
Sequ[)a]ni, an ancient people of Gallia Belgica, inhabiting the country now called the Franche Comt['e], or the Upper Burgundy; they bring the Germans into Gaul, G. vi. 12; lose the chief power, ibid.

Servilius the consul, C. iii. 21
S[=e]s[=u]v[)i]i, an ancient people of Gaul, inhabiting about Seez; they surrender to the Romans, G. ii. 34
Sextus Bibaculus, sick in the camp, G. vi. 38; fights bravely against the enemy, ibid.
Sextus Caesar, C. ii. 20
Sextus, Quintilius Varus, qaestor, C. i. 23; C. ii. 28
Sib[=u]z[=a]tes, an ancient people of Gaul, inhabiting the country around the Adour; they surrender to the Romans, G. iii. 27
Sicil[)i]a, Sicily, a large island in the Tyrrhene Sea, at the south-west point of Italy, formerly called the storehouse of the Roman empire, it was the first province the Romans possessed out of Italy, C. i. 30
S[)i]c[)o]ris, a river in Catalonia, the Segre
S[)i]g[)a]mbri, or S[)i]c[)a]mbri, an ancient people of Lower Germany, between the Maese and the Rhine, where Cuelderland is; though by some placed on the banks of the Maine, G. iv. 18
Silicensis, a river of Hispania Baetica, Rio de las Algamidas. Others think it a corruption from Singuli
Sinuessa, a city of Campania, not far from the Save, an ancient Roman colony, now in a ruinous condition; Rocca di Mondragon['e]
Soldurii, G. iii. 22
S[)o]t[)i][=a]tes, or Sontiates, an ancient people of Gaul, inhabiting the country about Aire; conquered by Caesar Aquillus, G. iii. 20, 21
Sp[=a]rta, a city of Peloponnesus, now called Mucithra, said to be as ancient as the days of the patriarch Jacob
Spolet[)i]um, Spoleto, a city of great antiquity, of Umbria, in Italy, the capital of a duchy of the same name, on the river Tesino, where are yet some stately ruins of ancient Roman and Gothic edifices
Statius Marcus, one of Caesar's lieutenants, C. iii. i 5
S[)u][=e]ss[)i][=o]nes, an ancient people of Gaul, les Soissanois; a kindred tribe with the Remi, G. ii. 3; surrender to Caesar, G. iii. 13
Su[=e]vi, an ancient, great, and warlike people of Germany, who possessed the greatest part of it, from the Rhine to the Elbe, but afterwards removed from the northern parts, and settled about the Danube; and some marched into Spain, where they established a kingdom, the greatest nation in Germany, G. i. 37, 51, 54; hold a levy against the Romans, G. iv. 19; the Germans say that not even the gods are a match for them, G. iii. 7; the Ubii pay them tribute, G. iv. 4
S[=u]lmo, an ancient city of Italy, Sulmona; its inhabitants declare in favour of Caesar, C. i. 18
Sulpicius, one of Caesar's lieutenants, stationed among the Aedui, C. i. 74

Supplications decreed in favour of Caesar on several occasions, G. ii. 15; ibid. 35; iv. 38
Suras, one of the Aeduan nobles, taken prisoner, G. viii. 45
Sylla, though a most merciless tyrant, left to the tribunes the right of giving protection, C. i. 5, 73
Syrac[=u]sae, Saragusa, once one of the noblest cities of Sicily, said to have been built by Archias, a Corinthian, about seven hundred years before Christ. The Romans besieged and took it during the second Punic war, on which occasion the great Archimedes was killed
S[=y]rtes, the Deserts of Barbary; also two dangerous sandy gulfs in the Mediterranean, upon the coast of Barbary, in Africa, called the one Syrtis Magna, now the Gulf of Sidra; the other Syrtis Parva, now the Gulf of Capes
T[)a]m[)e]sis, the Thames, a celebrated and well-known river of Great Britain; Caesar crosses it, G. v. 18
Tan[)a]is, the Don, a very large river in Scythia, dividing Asia from Europe. It rises in the province of Resan, in Russia, and flowing through Crim-Tartary, runs into the Maeotic Lake, near a city of the same name, now in ruins
T[=a]rb[=e]lli, a people of ancient Gaul, near the Pyrenees, inhabiting about Ays and Bayonne, in the country of Labourd; they surrender to Crassus, G. iii. 27
Tarcundarius Castor, assists Pompey with three hundred cavalry, C. iii. 4
Tarr[)a]c[=i]na, an ancient city of Italy, which still retains the same name
T[=a]rr[)a]co, Tarragona, a city of Spain, which in ancient time gave name to that part of it called Hispania Tarraconensis; by some said to be built by the Scipios, though others say before the Roman conquest, and that they only enlarged it. It stands on the mouth of the river Tulcis, now el Fracoli, with a small haven on the Mediterranean; its inhabitants desert to Caesar, C. i. 21, 60
Tar[=u]s[=a]tes, an ancient people of Gaul, uncertain; according to some, le Teursan; they surrender to the Romans, G. iii. 13, 23, 27
Tasg[=e]t[)i]us, chief of the Carnutes, slain by his countrymen, G. v. 25
Taur[=o]is, a fortress of the inhabitants of Massilia
Taurus, an island in the Adriatic Sea, unknown
Taurus Mons, the largest mountain in all Asia, extending from the Indian to the Aegean Seas, called by different names in different countries, viz., Imaus, Caucasus, Caspius, Cerausius, and in Scripture, Ar[)a]rat. Herbert says it is fifty English miles over, and 1500 long
Taximagulus, one of the four kings or princes that reigned over Kent, G. v. 22

Tect[)o]s[)a]ges, a branch of the Volcae, G. vi. 24
Tegea, a city of Africa, unknown
Tenchth[)e]ri, a people of ancient Germany, bordering on the Rhine, near Overyssel; they and the Usip[)e]tes arrive at the banks of the Rhine, iv. 4; cross that river by a stratagem, ibid.; are defeated with great slaughter, ibid. 15
Tergeste, a Roman colony, its inhabitants in the north of Italy cut off by an incursion, G. viii. 24
Terni, an ancient Roman colony, on the river Nare, twelve miles from Spol[=e]tum
Teutomatus, king of the Nitobriges, G. vii. 31
Teut[)o]nes, or Teutoni, an ancient people bordering on the Cimbri, the common ancient name for all the Germans, whence they yet call themselves Teutsche, and their country Teutschland; they are repelled from the territories of the Belgae, G. ii. 4
Thebae, Thebes, a city of Boeotia, in Greece, said to have been built by Cadmus, destroyed by Alexander the Great, but rebuilt, and now known by the name of Stives; occupied by Kalenus, C. iii. 55
Therm[)o]pylae, a famous pass on the great mountain Oeta, leading into
Phocis, in Achaia, now called Bocca di Lupa
Thessaly, a country of Greece, formerly a great part of Macedonia, now called Janna; in conjunction with Aetolia, sends ambassadors to Caesar, C. iii. 34; reduced by Caesar, ibid. 81
Thessalon[=i]ca, a chief city of Macedonia, now called Salonichi
Thracia, a large country of Europe, eastward from Macedonia, commonly called Romania, bounded by the Euxine and Aegean Seas
Th[=u]r[=i]i, or T[=u]r[=i]i, an ancient people of Italy, Torre Brodogneto
Tigur[=i]nus Pagus, one of the four districts into which the Helvetii were divided according to Caesar, the ancient inhabitants of the canton of Zurich in Switzerland, cut to pieces by Caesar, G. i. 12
Titus Ampius attempts sacrilege, but is prevented, C. iii. 105
Tol[=o]sa, Thoulouse, a city of Aquitaine, of great antiquity, the capital of Languedoc, on the Garonne
Toxandri, an ancient people of the Low Countries, about Breda, and Gertruydenburgh; but according to some, of the diocese of Liege
Tralles, an ancient city of Lydia in, Asia Minor, Chara, C. iii. 105
Trebonius, one of Caesar's lieutenants, C. i. 36; torn down from the tribunal, C. iii. 21; shows remarkable industry in repairing the works, C. ii. 14; and humanity, C. iii. 20
Trev[)i]ri, the people of Treves, or Triers, a very ancient city of Lower Germany, on the Moselle, said to have been built by Trebetas, the

brother of Ninus. It was made a Roman colony in the time of Augustus, and became afterwards the most famous city of Gallia Belgica. It was for some time the seat of the western empire, but it is now only the seat of the ecclesiastical elector named from it, G. i. 37; surpass the rest of the Gauls in cavalry, G. ii. 24; solicit the Germans to assist them against the Romans, G. v. 2, 55; their bravery, G. viii. 25; their defeat, G. vi. 8, vii. 63
Tr[)i]b[)o]ci, or Tr[)i]b[)o]ces, a people of ancient Germany, inhabiting the country of Alsace, G. i. 51
Tribunes of the soldiers and centurions desert to Caesar, C. i. 5
Tribunes (of the people) flee to Caesar, C. i. 5
Trin[)o]bantes, a people of ancient Britain, inhabitants of the counties of Middlesex and Hertfordshire, G. v. 20
Troja, Troy, a city of Phrygia, in Asia Minor, near Mount Ida, destroyed by the Greeks, after a ten years' siege
Tubero is prevented by Attius Varus from landing on the African coast, G. i. 31
Tulingi, an ancient people of Germany, who inhabited about where now Stulingen in Switzerland is; border on the Helvetii, G. i. 5
Tungri, an ancient people inhabiting about where Tongres, in Liege, now is
Tur[=o]nes, an ancient people of Gaul, inhabiting about Tours
Tusc[)i], or Hetrusci, the inhabitants of Tuscany, a very large and considerable region of Italy, anciently called Tyrrh[=e]nia, and Etruria
Ubii, an ancient people of Lower Germany, who inhabited about where Cologne and the duchy of Juliers now are. They seek protection from the Romans against the Suevi, G. iv. 3; tributary to the Suevi,ibid.; declare in favour of Caesar, G. iv. 9, 14
Ulcilles Hirrus, one of Pompey's officers, C. i. 15
Ulla, or Ulia, a town in Hispania Baetica, in regard to whose situation geographers are not agreed; some making it Monte Major, others Vaena, others Vilia
Umbria, a large country of Italy, on both sides of the Apennines
Unelli, an ancient people of Gaul, uncertain, G. ii. 34
Urbigenus, one of the cantons of the Helvetii, G. i. 27
Usip[)e]tes, an ancient people of Germany, who frequently changed their habitation
Usita, a town unknown
Uxellod[=u]num, a town in Gaul, whose situation is not known; according to some, Ussoldun besieged and stormed, G. viii. 32
Vah[)a]lis, the Waal, the middle branch of the Rhine, which, passing by Nim[)e]guen, falls into the Meuse, above Gorcum, G. iv. 10

Valerius Flaccus, one of Caesar's lieutenants, C. i. 30; his death, C. iii. 5 3
Val[=e]t[)i][)a]cus, the brother of Cotus, G. vii. 32
Vangi[)o]nes, an ancient people of Germany, about the city of Worms, G. i. 51
V[=a]r[=e]nus, a centurion, his bravery, G. v. 44
Varro, one of Pompey's lieutenants, C. i. 38; his feelings towards Caesar, C. ii. 17; his cohorts driven out by the inhabitants of Carmona, C. ii. 19; his surrender, C. ii. 20
V[=a]rus, the Var, a river of Italy, that flows into the Mediterranean Sea, C. i. 87
Varus, one of Pompey's lieutenants, is afraid to oppose Juba. C. ii. 44; his flight, C. ii. 34
Vatinius, one of Caesar's followers, C. iii. 100
V[)e]launi, an ancient people of Gaul, inhabiting about Velai
Vellaunod[=u]num, a town in Gaul, about which geographers are much divided; some making it Auxerre, others Chasteau Landon, others Villeneuve in Lorraine, others Veron. It surrenders, G. vii. 11
Velocasses, an ancient people of Normandy, about Rouen, G. ii. 4
V[)e]n[)e]ti, this name was anciently given as well to the Venetians as to the people of Vannes, in Bretagne, in Gaul, for which last it stands in Caesar. They were powerful by sea, G. iii. 1; their senate is put to death by Caesar, G. iii. 16; they are completely defeated, ibid. 15; and surrender, ibid. 16
Veragri, a people of Gallia Lugdunensls, whose chief town was Aguanum, now St. Maurice, G. iii. 1
Verb[)i]g[)e]nus, or Urb[)i]g[)e]nus Pagus, a nation or canton of the Helvetians, inhabiting the country in the neighbourhood of Orbe
Vercelli Campi, the Plains of Vercellae, famous for a victory the Romans obtained there over the Cimbri. The city of that name is in Piedmont on the river Sesia, on the borders of the duchy of Milan
Vercingetorix, the son of Celtillus, receives the title of king from his followers, G. vii. 4; his plans, G. vii. 8; is accused of treachery, G. vii. 20; his acts, G. vii. 8; surrenders to Caesar, G. vii. 82
Vergasillaunus, the Arvernian, one of the Gallic leaders, G. vii. 76; taken prisoner, G. vii. 88
Vergobr[)e]tus, the name given to the chief magistrate among the Aedui,
G. i. 16
V[)e]r[)u]doct[)i]us, one of the Helvetian embassy who request permission from Caesar to pass through the province, G. i. 7
Veromand[)u]i, a people of Gallia Belgica, whose country, now a part of

Picardy, is still called Vermandois
Ver[=o]na, a city of Lombardy, the capital of a province of the same name, on the river Adige, said to have been built by the Gauls two hundred and eighty-two years before Christ. It has yet several remains of antiquity
Vertico, one of the Nervii. He was in Cicero's camp when it was attacked by the Eburones, and prevailed on a slave to carry a letter to Caesar communicating that information, G. v. 49
Vertiscus, general of the Remi, G. viii. 12
Vesontio, Besan[,c]on, the capital of the Sequani, now the chief city of Burgundy, G. i. 38
Vett[=o]nes, a people of Spain, inhabiting the province of Estremadura, C. i. 38
Vibo, a town in Italy, not far from the Sicilian Straits, Bibona
Vibullius Rufus, one of Pompey's followers, C. i. 15
Vienna, a city of Narbonese Gaul, Vienne in Dauphiny, G. vii. 9
Vindel[)i]ci, an ancient people of Germany, inhabitants of the country of Vindelicia, otherwise called Raetia secunda
Viridomarus, a nobleman among the Aedui, G. vii. 38
Viridorix, king of the Unelli, G. iii. 17
Vist[)u]la, the Weichsel, a famous river of Poland, which rises in the Carpathian mountains, in Upper Silesia, and falls into the Baltic, not far from Dantzic, by three mouths
Visurgis, the Weser, a river of Lower Germany, which rises in Franconia, and, among other places of note, passing by Bremen, falls into the German Ocean, not far from the mouth of the Elbe, between that and the Ems
V[)o]c[=a]tes, a people of Gaul, on the confines of the Lapurdenses, G. iii. 23
Vocis, the king of the Norici, G. i. 58
V[)o]contii, an ancient people of Gaul, inhabiting about Die, in Dauphiny, and Vaison in the county of Venisse
Vog[)e]sus Mons, the mountain of Vauge in Lorrain, or, according to others, de Faucilles, G. iv. 10
Volcae Arecom[)i]ci, and Tectosages, an ancient people of Gaul, inhabiting the Upper and Lower Languedoc
Volcae, a powerful Gallic tribe, divided into two branches, the Tectosages and Arecomici, G. vii. 7
Volcatius Tullus, one of Caesar's partisans, C. iii. 52

Printed in Great
Britain
by Amazon